X

SOCIAL RESEARCH

SOCIAL RESEARCH

Issues, Methods and Process

Tim May

OPEN UNIVERSITY PRESS
Buckingham • Philadelphia

Open University Press
Celtic Court
22 Ballmoor
Buckingham
MK18 1XW

and
1900 Frost Road, Suite 101
Bristol, PA 19007, USA

First Published 1993
Reprinted 1993

A catalogue record of this book is available from the British Library

ISBN 0 335 19054 5 (pb)

Library of Congress Cataloging-in-Publication Data
May, Tim, 1957–
    Social research: issues, methods, and process/Tim May.
        p.   cm.
    Includes bibliographical references and index.
    ISBN 0-335-19054-5 (pbk.)
    1. Social sciences–Research.   2. Social sciences–Research–
    Methodology.   3. Sociology–Research.   4. Sociology–Methodology.
    I. Title.
    H62.M325   1993
    300'.72–dc20   92-43089   CIP

Typeset by Vision Typesetting, Manchester
Printed in Great Britain by St Edmundsbury Press Ltd, Bury St Edmunds, Suffolk

Contents

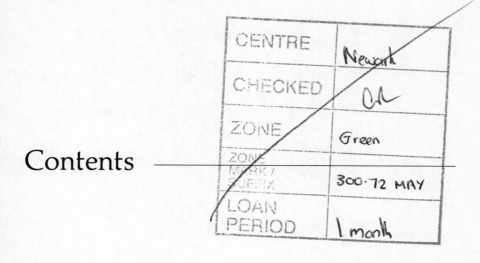

Acknowledgements ———————————

This book evolved from the writing of supported-self study courses in social research and social policy. With the social research course, the idea was to further a philosophy which was supportive of students and gave them practical experience of research, while not committing the common error of separating social and political theory and data production. Therefore, I would like to thank Louise Ackers with whom I worked in the earlier stages. I also wish to thank Lyn Bryant. Lyn remains supportive and encouraging in the competitive and unsupportive environment which all too often characterizes academia.

Thanks to Mel, Pete, Kate and Tam for giving me the breaks from writing and to Malcolm for reading a part of this work in such a short time, and to Dick Hobbs for injecting sanity into a mad world! Also, to David and Sue for allowing me to celebrate the end of an intensive period in which this book was produced.

My love and gratitude to Dee who, at the time of writing this book, provided me with the space to write while, at the same time, enjoying a break from her demanding work. Lastly, my thanks to the staff of Open University Press, in particular, Pat Lee, John Skelton, Jacinta Evans, Carolyn Medd and Christine Firth.

Introduction

Research methods are a central part of the social sciences, an important part of undergraduate curricula and a means through which the intellectual development of social sciences is enhanced. Indeed, the status of 'science' is often justified by alluding to the technical aspects of research methods, while the very term 'science' carries with it ideas of important and aloof studies which are accessible only to those who have undergone a lengthy training process in understanding its inner workings. Yet there are also those within these subjects who would prefer to be 'theorists' rather than 'researchers'. The latter concentrate on the process of research, while the former might see a virtue in being apart from the world they seek to understand, hence the term 'armchair theorizing'.

There is some merit in both of the above views, for innovative thinking and a meticulous attention to the detail of data gathering characterize the practice of social research. These differences, however, frequently lead to disputes over the aims of research and the methods which it should employ. For this reason, in the first three chapters, there is an examination of the ways in which we gain our knowledge of the social world, the relationship between theory and research, and the place of values and ethics in research practice. While these issues are complicated, they are also fundamental to research methods, for in separating issues and methods, readers can be left with the impression that they simply have to learn various techniques in order to undertake research.

This separation perpetuates the idea that theory, ethics, values and methods of social research are distinct topics and that researchers, despite living and participating in society, are somehow distinct from the social world which they study. This distance between them and the subjects of their study permits a particular idea of value-freedom to be maintained. As will become evident in Part I, this position is open to considerable debate, for our very membership of a society, it may be argued, is a necessary condition for understanding the social world of which we are a part, as well as being a fact of life from which we cannot escape. Further, in having an understanding of these debates and the applicability of different methods of research, improved research and more inquiring and confident researchers will result.

The aim of the book

This creates the starting-point for the philosophy underlying this book: issues and methods in research cannot be separated and that we, as researchers, will produce a more systematic understanding of the social world by being aware of these debates, their implications for research and our place within them. At the same time, this book is intended for those not familiar with the practices and issues within social research. They are therefore presented in a way that does not assume a great deal of prior knowledge on the part of the reader.

The book is divided into two parts: Part I examines the issues and Part II discusses the methods used in research. Because the aim is to produce a text for those relatively new to social research, there is a limit to which the connections between Parts I and II can be developed. Both sides of a debate are presented and parallels are drawn between Part II and the earlier discussion. All too often, however, reading can be a passive exercise in which we, as the readers, act as the recipients of the text, but do not engage with it by criticizing, analysing and cross-referencing the materials covered (May 1992). To help in this process, I have written questions at the end of each chapter which are intended to assist you in reflecting upon its contents.

An overview of Part I

Part I introduces the debates involved in and around the research process. This part of the book is based on the belief that values, prejudices and prior beliefs affect the way we all think about an event, person or subject. An awareness and consideration of how these relate to the research process can therefore sharpen and focus our decisions and choices in research work.

Towards this end, Chapter 1 covers the different perspectives which exist on social research by examining their arguments and intellectual foundations. To use a building analogy, if we do not understand the foundations of our work, then we are likely to end up with a shaky structure! Terms such as 'realist', 'empiricist', 'idealist', 'positivist', 'subjective' and 'objective' require clarification in order to consider the implications of these for research practice. Towards this end, Chapter 1 also introduces the reader to the wide-ranging criticisms that have been made of methodology from a feminist viewpoint.

Chapter 2 develops the points raised above by examining the relationship between social theory and research and Chapter 3 discusses the place of values and ethics in social research. These topics are often thought to present such intractable problems for the researcher that they take a 'backstage position' in the research process. The development of theory, however, is a necessary part of the intellectual development of social research, while ethics are a fundamental component of the idea of a 'discipline' and the confidence which people have in the actions of its members. The place of values in social research is also central and an understanding of the nature and effect of values a necessary part of its practice. As I hope will become evident, to ignore these issues does not mean that they are no longer an influence, for they routinely inform and affect research practice.

An overview of Part II

Chapter 4 begins the second part of the book by considering the main sources of official statistics that researchers use, followed by an account of their strengths and weaknesses. By tracing the issues which surround the production of crime statistics, the questions regarding their place in contemporary social research and, more generally, the use of other official statistics, can be considered.

Chapters 5–8 examine the process and methods of analyses involved in the major techniques used in social research. These cover questionnaire design, interviewing, participant observation and documentary research. In order to provide for ease of comparison between these different methods, each of the chapters follows a similar structure. First, the chapter begins with a discussion of the place of the method in social research which makes links with the discussions in Part I. Second, there is an examination of the actual process of undertaking research using the method, and third, the techniques of data analysis for each method are discussed. My intention at this point is to enable you to consider the different ways of approaching your data and to direct you to specific sources for further investigation of the topic. Therefore, should you decide to utilize the method for your own research, you will be aware not only of the ways in which the data are collected, but also of the methods employed for its analysis. Finally, each of these chapters ends with a critique of the method. By comparing this last section in each of the four chapters, together with the other sections and the issues covered in Part I, the advantages and disadvantages of each method can be assessed.

Chapter 9 is an introduction to comparative research. While the idea of comparison has long been used in social sciences, a growth in information technology and institutions such as the European Community has led to an increase in funding for comparative research. As such, there are important developments taking place in this field. Awareness of both the potential and problems involved in these developments and the methods of comparative research is therefore becoming an increasing part of the social researcher's knowledge base.

Within the text, references are used to other works on social research. The bibliography is therefore a resource intended for you to use in exploring themes and topics beyond the levels covered in this book. Research is not only an exciting and fundamental part of the practice and future of the social sciences, but also an important component in understanding and explaining human relations. It only remains for me to say that I hope this book achieves a greater understanding of the methods and issues involved in social research.

PART I

ISSUES IN
SOCIAL RESEARCH

1

Perspectives on research

The aim of this chapter is to introduce perspectives which assist in understanding the aims and practice of social research. These perspectives do not determine the nature of research itself, for there is a constant interaction between ideas about the social world and the data collected on it. Nevertheless, a discussion of the main debates between these schools of thought, together with the key terms used, will enable a consideration of their arguments and the assumptions which each make about the social world. These may then be linked with the discussions in Part II on the actual practice of research methods.

Schools of thought in social research

A science is often thought of as being a coherent body of thought about a topic over which there is a broad consensus among its practitioners. However, the actual practice of science shows that there are not only different perspectives on a given phenomenon, but also alternative methods of gathering information and of analysing the resultant data. While these differences do affect the natural sciences, they are a central part of the history and practice of social sciences.

Differences of perspective appear to many to be problematic. After all, if there is no consensus within a discipline then surely that is because its methods and theories simply don't work? However, perhaps we should challenge the idea that science is an all-embracing explanation of the social or natural world beyond our criticism. Instead, why do we not see the methods and theories of science as the outcome of disciplines which are contested because there are political and value considerations which affect our lives and are therefore a central part of their practice? These are not within the power of science to alter, nor in any democracy should they be. Their role in society would then be to understand and explain social phenomena, to focus attention on particular issues and to challenge conventionally held beliefs about the social and natural worlds:

> Scientific work depends upon a mixture of boldly innovative thought and
> the careful marshalling of evidence to support or disconfirm hypotheses and
> theories. Information and insights accumulated through scientific study and
> debate are always to some degree *tentative* – open to being revised, or even
> completely discarded, in the light or new evidence or arguments.
>
> (Giddens 1989: 21)

In the social sciences, theories which challenge our understanding of the social
world and the systematic gathering of data are a central part of its practice.
However, while this characterization might appear attractive, the disputes
within social science are more complicated (and more exciting) than any single
definition could encompass: for example, what constitutes a 'science', the nature
of its methods and the types of data which it should collect are open to dispute.
In order to see how this situation arises, an excursion into the main ideas and
debates within social science is required, before moving on (in Chapter 2) to
examine the relationship between social theory and research.

Objectivity

The Introduction noted that objectivity, along with generalization and
explanation, were considered as fundamental characteristics of a science. To
many researchers, debates around these questions are considered peripheral to
their activities. However, if we are to hold to the view that social science
research offers us knowledge about the social world which is not necessarily
available by other means, then we are making some privileged claims about our
work. Research then becomes more than the simple replication of our opinions
and prejudices: it either substantiates, refutes, organizes or generates our
theories and produces evidence which may challenge not only our own beliefs,
but also those of society in general.

It is at this point that the debate over objectivity in the social sciences enters.
It is often assumed that if our values do not enter into our research, it is
objective and above criticism. After all, many people accept what scientists say
is the 'truth'. On the other hand, the subject matter of the social sciences is social
life itself. People are obviously a part of that and the question is now raised that
as social researchers and as members of a society, is it possible or desirable for us
to suspend our sense of belonging? Different perspectives have provided
answers to these questions.

Positivism

We may argue that people react to their environment much as molecules which
become 'excited' when heat is applied to a liquid. Clearly, science does not have
then to ask the molecules what they think. So is it necessary that we, as social
scientists, ask people? We may, of course, be interested in people's opinions in

terms of their reactions to events that affect their lives, but only in so far as they are reacting and we wish to explain and predict their behaviour accordingly. However, don't we all believe that we possess something called free-will? That is we can, to some extent, control our own destinies rather than have it controlled, like the molecules, by a change in our environment. In other words that we can 'act on', as well as behave in 'reaction to', our social environments. Some social science experiments do take the form of altering the environment and seeing how people react to it. Is social life really like that? Surely experiments in a laboratory are artificial and do not reflect the complications, decisions and contradictions involved in social life?

If we believe ourselves to be the product of our environment – created by it – then to some extent we are the mirror image of it. It defines our nature, or our being. We do not have to refer directly to the people themselves because we can predict how they will behave. Simply expressed, this is the position of two schools of thought in social research: behaviourism and positivism. For a positivist, the social scientist must study social phenomena

> in the same state of mind as the physicist, chemist or physiologist when he probes into a still unexplored region of the scientific domain.
> (Durkheim 1964: xiv)

Objectivity is defined by positivism as being the same as that of natural science and social life may be explained in the same way as natural phenomena. We can characterize this tradition in the same terms as the aims of natural science: the prediction of the behaviour of phenomena; explanation of the behaviour of phenomena and the pursuit of objectivity, which is defined as the researcher's 'detachment' from the phenomena under investigation. The results of research using this method of investigation are then said to produce a set of 'true', precise and wide-ranging 'laws' (known as covering laws) of human behaviour. In fulfilling these aims, we would then be able to generalize from our observations on social phenomena to make statements about the behaviour of the population as a whole. In this process, positivism explains human behaviour in terms of cause and effect (in our example above, heat is the cause and the effect is the molecules becoming excited as the liquid increases in temperature). 'Data' must then be collected on the social environment and people's reactions to it. Given this attention to the detail of data collection by researchers, positivism shares similar ideas to another perspective on the research process: empiricism.

Empiricism

If the aim of positivism is to collect and assemble data on the social world from which we can generalize and explain human behaviour through the use of our theories, then it shares with empiricism the belief that there are 'facts' which we can gather on the social world, *independently* of how people interpret them. As researchers, we simply need to refine our instruments of data collection in order that they are neutral recording instruments as the ruler might measure distance, or the clock measure time.

The fundamental difference between empiricism and positivism is in the realm of theory. As will be developed in Chapter 2, data within positivism is theory-driven and designed to test the accuracy of the theory. Empiricism, on the other hand, is a method of research which lacks, or more usually has not referred explicitly to, the theory guiding its data collection procedures:

> 'empiricism' refers to a conception of social research involving the production of accurate data – meticulous, precise, generalisable – in which the data themselves constitute an end for the research. It is summed up by the catchphrase 'the facts speak for themselves'.
>
> (Bulmer 1982b: 31)

At this stage, it is important not to confuse the words empirical and empiricism. The word empirical refers to the collection of data on the social world to test or generate the propositions of social science, while, as Bulmer's quote indicates, the empiricist school of thought believes that the facts speak for themselves and require no explanation through theoretical propositions.

While there are differences between positivism and empiricism, the former does rely on the methods of the latter. They also both assert that there are facts about the social world which we can gather. Objectivity is then defined in terms of researchers' detachment from the social world, as well as the accuracy of their data collection instruments. Therefore, there is a world out there that we can record and we can analyse independently people's interpretations of it. This is termed the 'correspondence theory of reality' which, as we shall see below, is a highly disputed contention.

Realism

This tradition shares with positivism the aim of explanation; beyond that, the similarity ends. It enjoyed a particular boost in the social sciences with the publication of Russell Keat and John Urry's work (Keat and Urry 1975) and also of Roy Bhaskar's work (1975; 1989a; 1989b). However, it has a long history and is associated with the works of Karl Marx and Sigmund Freud. Marx, for example, constructed his typology (a method of classification) of capitalism on the basis that there are certain essential features which distinguish it from other economic and political systems. Within this economic system there exist 'central structural mechanisms' and the task of researchers is 'to organize one's concepts so as to grasp *its* essential features successfully' (Keat and Urry 1975: 112, original emphasis).

In referring to underlying structural mechanisms, an important argument within this perspective is being employed. If researchers simply content themselves with studying everyday social life, such as conversations and interactions between people, this will distract them from an investigation of the underlying mechanisms which make those possible in the first instance. The task of researchers within this tradition is to uncover the structures of social relations in order to understand why we then have the policies and practices that we do. Similarly, Sigmund Freud argued that our consciousness was determined by our subconsciousness. Thus people's neuroses are the visible manifestations of their sexual and aggressive desires that are repressed in their subconscious. Psychoanalytic theory then attempts to trace a line 'from certain adult or adolescent activities to certain infantile experiences' (Wollheim 1977: 156). While people may not be directly aware of these experiences, they still affect the way that they act.

Realism also argues that the knowledge people have of their social world affects their behaviour and, unlike the propositions of positivism and empiricism, the social world does not simply 'exist' independently of this knowledge. However, people's knowledge may be partial or incomplete. The task of social research is not simply to collect observations on the social world, but to explain these within theoretical frameworks which examine the underlying mechanisms which structure people's actions and prevent their choices from reaching fruition, for example, how schools function to reproduce a workforce for capitalism (Willis 1977).

The aim of examining and explaining underlying mechanisms cannot use the methods of empiricism as these simply reflect the everyday world, not the conditions which make it possible. Therefore, along with others in this tradition (Sayer 1992), Keat and Urry (1975) argue realism must utilize a different definition of science to positivism. In particular, a realist conception of social science would not necessarily assume that we can 'know' the world out there independently of the ways in which we describe it, as positivism would argue. For these reasons, there are those within this tradition who have built bridges between the idea that there is a world out there independent of our interpretation of it (empiricism and positivism) and the need for researchers to understand the process by which people interpret the world. Before discussing those who have attempted this, I shall first examine the perspectives which argue, contrary to positivism and empiricism, that there is no social world beyond people's perceptions and interpretations of it.

Subjectivity

Up to now, we have spoken of the ways in which our environment or its underlying structures – of which we are not necessarily aware – structure us, or create us as objects (positivism) or subjects and objects (realism). Perhaps you are not happy with the idea that you are created or formed in this way. We like to believe that we exercise free-will and make judgements which alter the courses of our lives. Positivism does not pay much attention to the detail of people's inner mental states. Realism, on the other hand, may refer to people's consciousness in so far as it reflects the conditions under which they live and their desires are frustrated.

When we refer to people's consciousness we are concerned with what takes place – in terms of thinking and acting – within each of us. These subjective states refer to our 'inner' world of experiences, rather than the world out there. To concentrate on subjectivity we focus on the *meanings* that people give to their environment, not the environment itself. Contrary to the contentions of positivists we, as researchers, cannot know this independently of people's interpretations of it. The only thing that we can know with certainty is how people interpret the world around them. Our central interest, as researchers, is now focused upon people's understandings and interpretations of their social environments.

Idealism

Some schools of thought emphasize our creation of the social world through the realm of ideas, rather than our being simply conditioned or created by it. They would argue that our actions are not governed by cause and effect, as in the case of molecules in a test tube, but by the rules which we use to interpret the world. As natural science deals with matter which is not 'conscious', researchers of this persuasion argue that its methods cannot deal with social life and should therefore be discarded from its study. To speak of cause (heating of molecules, for example) and effect (excitement of molecules) is not applicable to researching social life for people, unlike molecules, contemplate, interpret and act within their environments. For these reasons, the methods of the social sciences are fundamentally different from, but *not* inferior to, the natural sciences. It is the world of ideas in which we are interested as social researchers:

> 'human beings uniquely use complex systems of linguistic signs and cultural symbols to indicate to themselves and to others what they intend and mean to do. Such a viewpoint suggests that human activity is not behaviour (an adaption to material conditions), but an expression of meaning that humans give (via language) to their conduct.
> (Johnson, Dandeker and Ashworth 1990: 14)

Rules exist in social action through which we understand each other. Rules, of course, are often broken and also subject to different interpretations. For that reason, we cannot predict human behaviour. People are constantly engaged in the process of interpretation and it is this which we should seek to understand. In other words, researchers should concentrate upon *how* people produce social life. Social life cannot simply be observed (empiricism), it can be understood only as the result of examining people's selection and interpretation of events and actions. Understanding these processes and the rules which make them possible is the aim of research for schools of thought within this tradition. It is not explaining why people behave in certain ways by reference to their subconscious states or environmental conditions, but how people interpret the world and interact with each other. This process is known as *inter-subjectivity*. The idea of an external social 'reality' has now been abandoned because the meanings which we attach to the world are not static, nor universal, but always multiple and variable and constantly subject to modification and change.

In order to produce systematic studies of society, there are those within this tradition who argue that researchers need to employ 'hermeneutic principles'; hermeneutics refers to the theory and practice of interpretation. We are no longer proclaiming our 'disengagement' from our subject matter as a condition of science (positivism), but our 'commitment' and 'engagement' as a condition of understanding social life. As William Outhwaite puts it in a discussion of the German hermeneutic theorist Hans-George Gadamer: 'understanding is not a matter of trained, methodical, unprejudiced technique, but an encounter...a confrontation with something radically different from ourselves' (Outhwaite 1991: 24).

Our sense of belonging to a society and the techniques which we use for understanding are not now impediments to our studies. The procedures through which we understand and interpret our social world are now necessary conditions for us to undertake research. In the process we both utilize and challenge our understandings in doing social science research. Contrary to positivism and empiricism, the social researcher now stands at the centre of the research process as a requirement of understanding social life. The idea of science is now very different from positivism and empiricism:

> Hermeneutics was, then, determined to show that the generalising of the natural science model of knowledge to all spheres of knowledge was unacceptable.
>
> (Anderson, Hughes and Sharrock 1986: 65)

For these reasons, as will be noted in Part II, there is a tendency in this tradition of social thought to prefer methods of research such as participant observation and focused interviewing.

Building bridges

There are those who have attempted to synthesize some aspects of these major perspectives. One social theorist, in particular, has argued that our everyday actions are meaningful to us, but they also reproduce structures which both enable and constrain our actions (Giddens 1976; 1984). The insights of psychoanalysis and linguistics have also been employed to argue that while human actions are meaningful and variable, this does not mean that we cannot then agree on what is valid or 'true' about the social world. This bridge-building attempt fuses the twin aims of 'how' (understanding) and 'why' (explanation) in social research (Habermas 1984; 1987; 1988). There is also the school of 'poststructuralism' of which the French theorist Jacques Derrida is a part, as was Michel Foucault until his death in 1984. Foucault's thought, in particular, evolved in reaction to both the subjectivism of some social science perspectives and the naive empiricism imported from the natural sciences (Foucault 1977; 1980; Dreyfus and Rabinow 1982).

While an exposition of these ideas and their implications for research are well beyond the stated aims of this book, I have deliberately included them so you can refer directly to their works, or studies about their works (see Anderson, Hughes and Sharrock 1986). They demonstrate the ingenuity with which some theorists have attempted to tackle issues which are so central to social research.

The waters of the above perspectives are more muddy than as presented. For instance, a positivist such as Durkheim will not necessarily deny subjectivity nor would an idealist necessarily deny objectivity defined as 'detachment' from the social world. However, there is a fundamental difference between them which relates to the methods of social research: that is, social science is not the same as natural science and human actions, unlike the observed effects of molecules when heated, are meaningful and involve a process of interpretation of events by conscious actors. For this reason they must utilize different methods of investigation. However, this is not to say they are inferior as a result, simply different.

Feminist criticisms of research

All of the thinkers whom I have mentioned so far have been men. Does this matter? If these men have produced theories and research results which accurately enabled us to understand social relations, then it would remain a matter of concern if more women wished to become theorists and researchers, but were prevented from doing so because men, either intentionally or otherwise, stood in their way and occupied key positions in social research centres. On the other hand, if these theories and research results did not advance our understanding, but reflected a deep-rooted male bias which defined society and science in terms of male values, then not only would the aims of research be incomplete, but also its results would be a distorted representation of the social world. What we take to be science not only would reflect this state of affairs by collecting so-called facts on the social world (empiricism), but also could be perpetuating the subordination of women by providing a scientific cloak behind which an unequal status between men and women is justified.

These contentions form the starting-point of feminist criticisms of science. Perhaps the first point which should be made is that, like the social sciences in general, feminist perspectives are not a unified body of thought and it is more accurate to talk of 'feminisms' (Humm 1992). However, in the following discussions it should be borne in mind that they do share several beliefs. First, women and their fundamental contributions to social and cultural life have been marginalized and this is reflected in research practice. Second, the norms of science perpetuate and disguise the myth of the superiority of men over women and reflect a desire to control the social and natural worlds. Third, gender, as a significant social category, has been absent from our understandings and explanations of social phenomena in favour of categories such as social class. Clearly, these characterizations do not convey the depth and sophistication of arguments employed by different schools of feminism (see Tong 1989; Harding 1991). At the same time, the extensive and cogent criticisms which have been made by feminists of social science cannot be ignored. Therefore, in order to add to our understanding of social life in general and research methods in particular, it must occupy a centre-stage position in any discussion of research perspectives.

Challenging the scientific cloak

As noted in the first section of this chapter, the claims of objectivity, explanation and understanding are a central part of the social sciences. However, what if these claims are based on limited ideas? In order to illustrate how this occurs, a brief excursion into the dominant aspects of social thought is required.

Our notions of the roles, relations and forces within society are, according to feminist critiques, built upon unexamined assumptions about women which are then reproduced in our theories about society. When the roles of women are considered in social life, they are characterized as passive and emotional. Although this assumption has long been challenged by groups of women, their voices were lost by a selective reading of historical events (Spender 1982). In particular, there is the reference to something called 'human nature', that is a belief in the fundamental characteristics of people regardless of their history or social context. Social thinkers have provided many a justification for the belief that social roles are natural, rather than the product of social and political manipulation by men over women. An influential philosopher, John Locke (1632–1704), for example, believed people to be innately 'reasonable' (a view of human nature). At the same time, he also believed in a need for a 'social contract' so that order could be brought to what would otherwise be a chaotic social and political world.

From these positions of reasonableness and the need for a social contract he then took a 'leap' to argue that because of their reproductive capacity, women were 'emotional' and were also unable to provide for themselves so were 'naturally' dependent on men. As in contemporary society, property rights were crucial in Locke's ideas and due to women's natural dependence, he argued that they do not then possess such rights. Marriage was a contract they entered in order to produce sons who can then inherit property. The contract of marriage thus ensures that property rights are stable within society and men have sons in order to perpetuate their lineage.

As feminist scholars have noted (Sydie 1987) Locke equated 'rights' with the capacity to be reasonable which he then argued that women did not posses. This splitting of so-called natural differences, feminists argue, occurs through-out western thought and provides the foundation upon which we base our thinking and scientific practice. Buried within these assumptions are not scientific statements, but deep-rooted biases against women by male thinkers. The German philosopher Hegel (1770–1831), for instance, believed that women's position in the family, as subordinate to men, was the natural realm for their 'ethical disposition'. Similarly, Darwin (1809–82) believed he had found a scientific basis for traditional assumptions about the division of labour between the sexes. Again, we are led to believe that these are natural differences. If we believe them to be natural, then tampering with them would upset the 'natural order of social life'. However, this is precisely the point of contention. Feminists argue that women's position within society is not a natural phenomenon, but a social, political and economic product which is reflected and perpetuated by the bias of 'science' (Okin 1980; Lieven 1981).

According to feminist critiques, sociology, social policy and other social sciences have, like the natural sciences, perpetuated this myth (Dale and Foster 1986; Pascall 1986; Sydie 1987; Abbott and Wallace 1990). For instance, in the earlier studies on the family and work, before feminist research had some impact on dominant practices, women were 'wives', 'mothers' or 'housewives', but not people in their own right. The American sociologist Talcott Parsons (1902–79) believed that the major 'status' (an important concept in sociology and social policy) of an urban, adult woman was therefore that of a housewife. Her status in this domestic sphere was, in turn, determined by the status of the husband or, as is also commonly referred, head of household. The positivist Emile Durkheim, who so adhered to the idea of a natural science of society, did not in fact produce a scientific account of society, but a moralizing one hidden behind the guise of science. His views on the family were, according to what is probably the most authoritative study of his life and work, an 'alliance of sociological acumen with strict Victorian morality' (Lukes 1981: 533). The use of the term 'family' in social policy research is also criticized for being a 'unit of analysis in which women's particular interests are often submerged' (Pascall 1986: 4).

If our claims to theorize about social life simply function to disguise such moralizing, then they will be distortions of the social world which we seek to understand. In the separation of the 'public' from 'private' social worlds men have become the people of action in the public realm, while women are subordinated to the private realm of the family and their status determined accordingly. For feminists, perspectives on social life have either reflected this political phenomenon or attempted to justify it as a natural state of affairs.

Our understanding of social life is thereby limited by this silencing of women's voices and the perpetuation of particular and narrow ideas of science. Social research often focuses selectively in the public realm: it is men who paint pictures; men who think about the world; men who make money and men who shape our destiny. If the contribution of women is acknowledged, it is in terms of being the 'power behind the throne'; 'the boss in the house' or what has been described as 'drawing-room manipulation'. In research on the world of work, for example, we operate according to definitions which remain unchallenged:

> Workplaces are generally thought of as strictly demarcated from the home and family life. Similarly, we think of workers as people who leave home in the morning to travel to work and who work a certain number of hours... These conceptions of work and workers would seem to be an accurate characterization of some kinds of paid work. However, they are not very satisfactory as a characterization of women's paid work.
>
> (Beechey 1986: 77–8)

Theories of the social world and practices of research are *androcentric*. What we call science is not based upon universal criteria which are value-free, but upon male norms and, in particular, the mythical separation of reason (men) and emotion (women):

> From an androcentric perspective women are seen as passive objects rather than subjects in history, as acted upon rather than actors; androcentricity prevents us from understanding that both males and females are always acted upon as well as acting, although often in very different ways. Two extreme forms of androcentricity are gynopia (female invisibility) and misogyny (hatred of women).
>
> (Eichler 1988: 5)

Reason and emotion

Men are assumed to be reasonable and women emotional. Yet definitions of words are interpreted by individuals or groups in certain ways and their political translation takes subtle forms. The nature of this is rendered highly problematic by the fact that women are excluded from scientific practices by virtue of men saying they are incapable of 'reason'. As Lloyd puts it: 'our ideas of Reason have historically incorporated an exclusion of the feminine, and... femininity itself has been partly constituted through such processes of exclusion' (quoted in Whitford 1988: 110). From this idea we then base science upon reason and reason is based upon truth. Feminists, on the other hand, argue that you cannot separate, nor should you, reason and emotion. Therefore, the idea of disengagement or an aloof detachment by the researcher from the researched is criticized by feminist thought.

The critique of 'disengagement'

The idea that 'rigorous research' involves the separation of the researcher from the subject of their research simply reflects the idea that reason and emotion must be separated. Instead of seeing people in the research process as simply sources of data, feminists argue that research is a two-way process. This is known as 'dialogic retrospection', 'which is defined as an open and active exchange between the researcher and participant' (Humm 1989: 50). Frequently, however, textbooks speak of not becoming 'over involved' with participants. Over-identifying with the 'subject' of the research is said to prevent 'good' research. The researcher should be detached and hence objective. According to feminists, this is not only a mythical aim, but also an undesirable one which disguises the myriad of ways in which the researcher is affected by the context of the research or the people who are a part of it.

Biography

In much the same way as the ideas of disengagement and objectivity are challenged, so too is the idea that a researcher's biography is not important or relevant to the research process. Both the researcher and those people in the research carry with them a history, a sense of themselves and the importance of their experiences. However, personal experience is frequently devalued as being too subjective, while science is objective. There is much to be gained from exploring the lives and experiences of women in understanding society and correcting the silence which surrounds women's voices. As will be apparent in Part II, this is a fundamental aspect of research methods in, for example, interviewing and oral histories. Researchers should therefore be aware of the ways in which their own biography is a fundamental part of the research process. It is both the experiences of the researched *and* researchers which are important. Despite this, it is a subject in social research reserved for separate publications (Bell and Newby 1977; Bell and Roberts 1984; Roberts 1990; Hobbs and May 1993).

Feminist epistemologies

We now have the critique of disengagement, the critique of the absence of gender as a significant social category in social research and the critique of the nature and method through which science is constructed based upon a male perspective and limited ideas of what constitutes reason. These add up to a considerable indictment of the practice of science. The question now remains: what alternatives have feminists proposed which are of importance to us as researchers? This brings us round to questions of *epistemology* and *ontology*.

These are complex subjects, but for the purposes of our discussion, they refer to the ways in which we perceive and know our social world and the theory concerning what 'exists'. Therefore, without explicitly saying as much, we have examined the epistemologies and ontologies of positivism, empiricism, realism and idealism. Feminists, on the other hand, start with the above critiques of science and may be considered under three headings: feminist empiricism, feminist standpoint and feminist relativist epistemologies.

Standpoint feminism has developed in contrast to many of the dominant ways of viewing knowledge (Harstock 1987; Smith 1988). Its basis lies in taking the disadvantage of women's exclusion from the public realm by men and turning that into a research advantage. Because women are 'strangers' to the public realm and excluded from it, this provides them with a unique opportunity for undertaking research:

> The stranger brings to her research just the combination of nearness and remoteness, concern and indifference, that are central to maximizing objectivity. Moreover, the 'natives' tend to tell a stranger some kinds of things they would never tell each other; further, the stranger can see patterns of belief or behaviour that are hard for those immersed in the culture to detect.
>
> (Harding 1991: 124)

Therefore, a female researcher is able to operate from both an oppressed position as a woman and a privileged position as a scholar (Cook and Fonow 1990). A woman's biography and experiences, as a researcher, are central to the production of unbiased accounts of the social world. However, it is not experience itself which provides the basis of claims to objectivity by standpoint feminists. While experience is a fundamental starting-point, experiences themselves are reflections of the dominant social relationship of the subordination of women by men. Experience is a beginning point to research, but for standpoint feminists this must then be situated within the wider context of women's lives in general. However, male-science overrides experience and claims to know better. Thus, in order that the theorist does not then become the expert on people's lives, as is the usual hierarchical way in which science proceeds, any thinking about women's lives by the researcher must take place in a democratic and participatory way involving other women.

Two emphases within standpoint epistemology are apparent from this discussion. First, women's experiences are an excellent starting-point upon which to base research as they occupy a marginalized position within society and can therefore 'look in' as the stranger might to a new social scene. As Sandra Harding puts it, the aim

> is not so much one of the right to claim a label as it is of the prerequisites for producing less partial and distorted descriptions, explanations, and understandings.
>
> (Harding 1987b: 12)

Second, an emphasis on the scientific study of society whose aim is to place women's experiences within a wider theory of their location in society. For this reason, there are parallels between feminist standpoint epistemologies and realism (see Cain 1990). Although the idea of science is maintained, its norms have changed. It becomes a feminist stance and one which does not marginalize, but promotes the cause of women in general.

These two contentions form the starting-point for the differences between feminist standpoint and feminist relativist epistemologies. First, feminist relativists would reject the idea of any type of science for this would be just another way in which women's experiences are sequestrated by those who claim to be experts:

> the inconvenient fact that much human behaviour cannot be described, let alone understood, in unexplicated categorical terms is largely ignored, or rather 'resolved' by treating people's experiences as faulty versions of the theoretician's categories.
>
> (Stanley and Wise 1990: 24)

To treat people's experiences as 'faulty' is argued to be a dominant approach to theory. Second, they would also reject the view that knowledge or 'truth' about women's position in society is possible. Instead there are many versions of social reality, all of which are equally valid. Women's experiences are therefore a starting *and* finishing point for feminist relativist research:

> Women's lives, women's bodies, women's experiences, demonstrate that the social (and physical) world is complicated. 'Reality' is shown to be multi-dimensional and multi-faceted. But 'reality' is constructed as one reality, simple and unseamed. And thus the necessity to suppress, distort, use, oppress, women's differences.
>
> (Stanley and Wise 1983: 187–8)

To impose some theoretical idea on the social world conspires with this suppression of difference. Women's experiences and feelings are not limited in this perspective, but are valid in themselves. The means by which research is undertaken should then be made available for all to see as part of this process of validating experiences. However, are all experiences equally valid and not limited and/or biased? Is the opinion of the middle-class woman who says women are not oppressed, the same as the working-class woman who says they are? For some feminists, the answer to this question has been to accept the basis of science, but to move away from its male-centred perspective and place women at its centre.

Those feminists who fall under the category of feminist empiricism would 'see themselves as primarily following more rigorously the existing rules and principles of the sciences' (Harding 1991: 111). Margrit Eichler's (1988) work, for example, provides a series of technical steps that the researcher should avoid in order to produce research which does not fall into the four 'traps' of malestream research which are: androcentric practices; the over-generalization of research findings which are solely based on men's experiences; an absence of explanations for the social and economic influences of gender relations; and finally, the use of 'double standards', for example, in terms of language the use of 'man' and 'wife', when we should refer to 'man' and 'woman'. The aim is to produce less partial and more accurate accounts of social life. In other words, its criticism is focused not so much on the *foundations* of science, but upon its *practice*. For this reason, it has been criticized for replicating male norms of scientific inquiry which, according to other feminist epistemologies, should be both challenged and changed.

While there are, as with malestream research perspectives, a variety of points from which feminism approaches the issue of research we can, nevertheless, take the following lessons for research practice. As researchers, we should seek to avoid the age-old fallacy of a woman's reproductive capacity as being a hindrance to her participation in society. The important questions are first, how the fact of women's reproduction is manipulated in the organization of social life. Second, how women are marginalized in the public sphere. Third, a greater understanding of the fundamental contribution which women make to cultural, political and economic life. Fourth, the implications of feminist analysis for research in particular and social life in general. Fifth, a general challenging not only of androcentric thought, but also of heterosexist assumptions within our society. For these reasons

> feminism does not start from a detached and objective standpoint on knowledge of the relations between women and men. Even the most moderate advocates of women's rights must take the view that men have rights which are unjustly denied to women. This commitment does not mean that feminist knowledge is not valid knowledge, but it does entail asking what we mean by knowledge, and why some forms of knowledge are seen as more valid than others. Feminism implies a radical critique of reason, science and social theory which raises questions about how we know what we think we know.
>
> (Ramazanoglu 1990: 9)

Women, race and research

Feminisms, while correcting the class-based accounts of research, have faced similar criticisms as research in general, for its neglect of the issue of race. The ways in which sexual and racial stereotypes cut across each other has been documented by researchers (Ackers 1993). An exclusive concentration on gender and class within research, however, is to the detriment of differences which exist between women on ethnic and racial lines:

> The oppression of women knows no ethnic nor racial boundaries, true, but that does not mean it is identical within those differences. Nor do the

reservoirs of our ancient power know those boundaries. To deal with one without ever alluding to the other is to distort our commonality as well as our difference.

(Lorde 1992: 139)

Angela Davies (1981) documents the racism of the early women's movement with its assumptions concerning the intellectual inferiority of black men and women. Class-based accounts of society, on the other hand, have been criticized for being economically determinist and ignorant of the political dimensions of gender and race. In our research and, as far as is possible, within the limits of our power, we should be aware of these issues and address them. For instance, in her criticisms of the discipline of criminology, Marcia Rice (1990) notes that it has been both racist and sexist in a 'machocentric' frame of reference which she defines as

a discourse which is male-centred. It represents 'masculinity' as the primary defining characteristic and as qualitatively different from 'femininity', but it is more extreme than the normal usage of masculinity as aggression is central to it.

(Rice 1990: 68, n.1)

Not only does she consider that criminology is male-centred, but also she criticizes feminism for its ethnocentricity. As a result, she suggests the following ways of overcoming the limitations of this approach. First, researchers should avoid racist stereotypes and ethnocentric approaches to research for this is not only an inaccurate representation of the social world, but also ignores important differences between people's experiences. This would avoid what Fiona Williams (1989) calls the 'danger of homogenization' whereby the use of terms such as 'blacks' and 'women' which do not specify their composition, assumes such categories are universal and therefore does not allow for the diversity of people's histories, cultures and experiences. Second, there should be an increase in research which examines the ways in which 'gender roles and differential opportunity structures are affected by racism as well as sexism' (Rice 1990: 68). Third, an increase in comparative studies of the dimensions of race, class and gender would assist in our understanding of the operation of power and discrimination within society. Fourth, empirical studies, in order to enhance understanding, should be situated within a wider sphere of social, political and economic contexts. Finally, as with feminism in general, the experiences of those researched should not be separated from the researchers. An exchange based on consultation and participation should take place in which each learns from the other.

Summary

This chapter has provided an introductory tour of major perspectives in social research. We have moved from the idea that social science should reflect the aims and methods of natural science, through a critique of these methods as inapplicable to social research, to feminist criticisms of the foundations and aims of science as male-centred and hierarchical, finishing on a critique of research practice as ethnocentric and racist.

The debates themselves are complicated, but no less important for that. These perspectives do not simply dictate the nature of research, although the issues covered so far inform the nature of the research process and its aims. Research which is not only aware of these issues, but also acts accordingly, is more likely to produce an enhanced and systematic study of social life.

CHAPTER 1: QUESTIONS FOR YOUR REFLECTION

1   What is the difference between the terms empirical and empiricism?

2   How do positivism, realism and idealism differ in their ideas on social research, its aims and the role of the researcher?

3   What are the main criticisms that feminists have made of science in general and the practice of social research in particular?

4   As a social researcher, what issues might preoccupy your practice as a result of the issues raised in this chapter?

2

Social theory and
social research

In this chapter I wish to explore the relationship between theory and research. What exactly is the role of theory in social research? Is it a neutral medium through which we interpret our findings; should it be a critical endeavour which challenges our dominant ways of thinking about social phenomena; should the data we produce about the social world refute our theories or generate them? In the process, questions will be raised concerning the place of values in theory and research. For this reason, Chapter 3 then moves on to explore some of the issues raised in this chapter.

Exploring the relationship between social theory and social research

The idea of theory, or the ability to interpret and understand the findings of research within a conceptual framework which makes 'sense' of the data, is the mark of a discipline whose aim is the systematic study of particular phenomena. In our case, as social researchers, these phenomena are the dynamics, content and context of social relations. We aim, in terms of our own biographical and research training and experiences, together with the perspectives which guide our thinking, to explain and understand the social world. This requires the development and application of social theory.

Social theory is not something which can be separated from the process of social research. Theory informs our thinking which, in turn, assists us in making research decisions and sense of the world around us. Our experiences of doing research and its findings, in its turn, influences our theorizing; there is a constant relationship that exists between social research and social theory. The issue for us as researchers is not simply *what* we produce, but *how* we produce it. An understanding of the relationship between theory and research is part of this *reflexive* project which focuses not just upon our abilities to apply techniques of data collection, but to consider the nature and presuppositions of the research process in order that we can sharpen our insights into the practice and place of social research in contemporary society.

Theory and research: a symbiotic relationship

While social theory is taken to be a grand enterprise, the problems which preoccupy theorists are not so different from those which often occupy 'non-theorists':

> they are problems we all face in our everyday lives, problems of making sense of what happens to us and the people around us, the problems involved in making moral and political choices.
>
> (Craib quoted in Fennell, Phillipson and Evers 1988: 41)

What is different, and for our purposes as researchers, important, is the approach of theorists to these questions. Some float over our social landscapes as if they were unfettered by the problems of everyday life. This ability to transcend or abstract theories from everyday life allows us to have a perspective on our social universe which breaks free from our everyday actions with which we are, understandably, preoccupied. Such theories allow us to make links from our own specific fields of interest to those of other researchers, as well as locate our research findings within a general theory of the workings of society. On the other hand, while these theories may enable us to break-free from everyday thinking, their level of generality may be of little use to us in researching a particular area of social life. For this reason some have been disparaging of the inability of 'grand theorists' to grasp the social problems which are important to specific 'historical and structural contexts' (Mills 1959: 42). So abstracted are these theories from the dynamics of society, they are regarded as the 'philosophization of social theory' (Rex, in Mullan 1987: 19).

An alternative to such abstraction or generality is, in the words of one book on this subject, to ground social theories in our observations of everyday life (Glaser and Strauss 1967). As researchers, we should seek to render the attachment between theory and data as close as possible (unlike grand theory which is stated at such a general level we could not possibly match data to theory). Instead of descending upon the social world armed with a body of theoretical propositions about how and why social relations exist and work as they do, we should first observe those relations, collect data on them, and then proceed to generate our theoretical propositions.

Another option, of course, is to ignore the idea of theory altogether and presuppose, along with the empiricists, that the facts speak for themselves. Our aim would then to be to act as technicians, as opposed to scholars, and concentrate on techniques of research. This is exactly what often occurs in research practice. However, to choose this course of action does not mean our research is then more 'relevant', if by that we mean that it suits the ends of particular vested interests. It simply means that our presuppositions about social life remain more hidden, but still influence our research decisions and interpretations.

We are now back to the same issue – except at the different end of the spectrum from which we left grand theory. If we assume that we can neutrally observe the social world, we shall simply reproduce the assumptions and stereotypes of everyday actions and conversations which are buried within society. We need, therefore, to understand and acknowledge these influences in our own thinking and that of society in general. Facts, in other words, do not speak for themselves and theory 'is everywhere...intimately connected to issues of problem, method and substance' (Plummer 1990: 122). Thus, for social research to both intellectually develop and to be of use in understanding or explaining the social world, we need theory and theory needs research. There is, in the words of Martin Bulmer, a 'mutual interdependence' between the two (1986a: 208). The exact nature of this relationship requires some investigation.

The relationship between theory and research

In the process of research, we embark on empirical work and collect data which either initiates, refutes or organizes our theories which then enable us to understand or explain our observations. Bearing in mind the above references to 'grounded' and 'grand' theories, we may proceed to achieve this by using one of two routes. First, we might consider a general picture of social life and then research a particular aspect of it to test the strength of our theories. This is known as *deduction* where theorizing comes before research. Research then functions to produce empirical evidence to test or refute theories. On the other hand, we might examine a particular aspect of social life and derive our theories from the resultant data. This is known as *induction*. Research comes before theory and we seek to generate theoretical propositions on social life from our data. I shall now examine both induction and deduction and their relationship to theory.

Induction has a long history in the philosophy of science. It is based on the belief, as with empiricism, that we can proceed from a collection of facts concerning social life and then make links between these to arrive at our theories. The first point of consideration in this process refers to the relationship between theory and data in order to demonstrate that the 'facts' can speak for themselves and are distinct from the interpretation of researchers. An example will help to explain how this relates to social theory.

Consider the proposition, once maintained by the results of psephological research (Butler and Stokes 1969), that 'more manual workers vote labour than they do conservative'. This is an empirical generalization about the voting behaviour of a particular group within society. However, it is not a theory or explanation of the pattern of behaviour observed, but a statement of observation on voting behaviour collected by asking people, via surveys, about their voting intentions. However, for it to be explained (in other words, *why* manual workers vote Labour) we need a theory. This might take the form of explaining voting behaviour in terms of the different primary and secondary socialization process that manual workers undergo in comparison to non-manual workers. Alternatively, manual workers tended to vote Labour because they believed that party best represented their interests in maintaining material securities such as housing, employment prospects, etc. Now, while this connection between class position and voting behaviour has diminished since Butler and Stokes' research (see Dunleavy and Husbands 1985), this illustrates that we require a theory to interpret the findings of social research. As social researchers, our findings on the social world are devoid of meaning until situated within social theory.

The question remains, however, as to why researchers decide to collect such data in the first place? They might be representing particular interests who are funding the research, or are personally interested in this area and have access to resources to test ideas which they have on the relationship between class membership and voting behaviour. Whether the research is 'pure' or 'applied' in this sense, interests have guided our decisions *before* the research itself is conducted. It cannot be maintained that research is a neutral recording instrument. As a result, researchers should make their theories or hypotheses explicit and not hide behind the notion that facts can speak for themselves. This is not a situation from which researchers can escape for their interpretations are an inevitable part of the research process. An alternative to induction is to make the theories or hypotheses which guide our research explicit.

Deduction rejects the idea that we can produce research on the basis of initially rejecting theory. It seeks to fuse the empiricist idea that there are a set of rules of method by which we proceed as researchers, with the ideas of deductive reasoning which hold that if our hypothesis or ideas about social life are 'true', then they will be substantiated by the data which we produce. In order for this to take place, data collection is driven by our theoretical interests, not the other way round. Thus according to one famous exponent of this tradition: 'scientists try to express their theories in such a form that they can be tested, i.e., refuted (or else corroborated) by such experience' (Popper 1970: 654–5). A theory concerning social life must not only be based upon empirical evidence, but also be capable of being *falsified* by such evidence: '*it must be possible for an empirical scientific system to be refuted by experience*' (Popper 1959: 41, original emphasis).

The attraction with this system is that it acknowledges, unlike inductivism, that data is theory-driven. It also sustains social theory only in so far as it is corroborated by empirical evidence. Therefore, it proceeds on the same basis as the methods of natural scientific inquiry to enable the production of a 'science of society'. However, attractive as this sounds, we are still left with problems. First, if our empirical evidence falsifies a theory, is this a sufficient reason for rejecting it? We might simply assert that we have found a deviant or exceptional piece of evidence which does not falsify our theory as such. Second, there is a pragmatic point for us to consider as researchers. Until a new theory comes along to explain our research findings, we are unlikely to abandon existing theories which still assist us in understanding or explaining social life. Finally, deductivism is still, like inductivism, assuming that we can derive theories of the social world independent of our preconceptions or values due to its adherence to a natural scientific method of research.

The idea that we might derive our theories on the social world, independent of our preconceptions is thus highly problematic. Theorists, for instance, take-for-granted certain aspects of the social world which are not subjected to empirical falsification (the assumptions concerning the 'natural' roles of women in society for instance). As was noted in Chapter 1, we research a social world which people are already in the process of busily interpreting and acting within. To assume that we can separate these activities from scientific fact may be considered an impossibility.

In accepting this, our focus of attention is now transferred away from the procedures of generating or testing theories, to the influences which inform theorizing and research. This provides us with a starting-point for examining a seminal contribution on the way in which science has developed – as opposed to how it should develop according to the rules of deduction and induction.

Thomas Kuhn's work (1970) was a historical study of scientific progression. He argued that science does not progress according to the criteria of falsifying theories, as Popper would maintain. On the contrary, evidence which does not support theories is regarded as only a temporary problem to which future research is directed. In this way theories are not falsified, but become the subject of continuous research. It is this that Kuhn calls 'normal science':

> 'normal science' means research firmly based upon one or more past scientific achievements, achievements that some particular scientific community acknowledges for a time as supplying the foundation for its further practice.
>
> (quoted in Barnes 1991: 87)

Given that any deviant data serve as the basis for future research, the theory is never falsified because there will always be evidence which both supports and refutes it. Kuhn therefore refers to scientific *paradigms* as characterizing the practice of science. These paradigms do not, unlike deductivism and inductivism, provide rules which the methods of research must slavishly follow, but provide only examples

> of good practice ... And scientists must themselves determine how the model is to be used ... Thus, scientists doing normal science do not merely have to agree upon what should serve as the basis of their work; they also have to agree upon how it should serve that purpose in every particular case. They are obliged to employ a paradigm much as a judge employs an accepted judicial decision.
>
> (Barnes 1991: 88)

Science develops according to the culture that scientists inhabit and this, not the rules of deduction and induction, determines their practices and choices of theories. If an example of counter-evidence is found to falsify a theory, then it will be the competence of the individual researcher which is called into question, not the theory. Scientists do attempt to falsify theory as such: 'Instead, they attempt to extend and exploit it in a variety of ways' (Kuhn 1972: 91). However, unlike other commentators who see no logic to the practice of science (Feyerabend 1978), Kuhn views science as a conservative endeavour which is challenged only by what he calls 'scientific revolutions'. At this point, a new paradigm replaces the old. This does not result from mounting empirical evidence which refutes the old paradigm but, for example, is due to younger scientists entering the field and bringing with them a new set of ideas and problems upon which they too can research and make their names. Despite the change of personnel, the conclusions of the discipline would, once again, not reflect some 'objective reality' independent of the minds of scientists, but would depend on 'the scientist's theoretical preferences rather than the empirical evidence' (Papineau 1978: 36).

We have travelled from the problems of inductivism and its atheoretical stance, through deductivism with its concentration on rules to which no science can, or arguably should, live up to, to arrive at the idea of Kuhn's paradigms which are argued to reflect the actual practices of science. These debates prompt a continual reflection upon the relationship between theory and research and 'the academic mode of production' (Stanley 1990b) in which it all takes place. In the next section, I therefore wish to examine the ways in which different researchers and theorists have attempted to tackle the problems raised during the above discussions.

Situating social theory and research

There are several issues which Kuhn's concept of the practice of science raises for us as social researchers. In particular, the attempt to separate *what* we do, from *how* we do it, as considered by both inductivism and deductivism, is problematic. The ways in which we conduct research are inevitably affected by the social context in which it takes place and this raises several issues for social research. First, within our disciplines (as noted in Chapter 1) there are different ways of viewing how we gain knowledge of social phenomena in the first instance. Therefore, our disciplines are characterized not by one single paradigm, but by divisions with regards to the aims and methods of social research. These, however, do not simply reflect schisms within the disciplines themselves, but the subject matter with which we are concerned: social life itself is characterized by divisions and is not unified phenomena. Second, all sciences, not just social sciences, are directly influenced and affected by interests which exist 'externally' to the discipline: for example, the values and interests of sponsors of research or the ways of working within the discipline itself which exclude, for instance, the reception of feminist ideas.

At the same time, we are able, to some extent, to sever ourselves from particular interests at particular points in time. As a result, feminist critiques exist alongside, but not yet within, mainstream research practices. Third, paradigms are not closed systems of thought hermetically sealed off from one another and this gives us an advantage. There is a constant process in the practice of social science which enables us to compare one paradigm with another and to see the strengths and weaknesses of each. A process of clarification and mediation of theories within the practice of social research is then able to occur. As Anthony Giddens (1976), from whose discussions the above characterizations are drawn, notes:

> The process of learning a paradigm or language-game as the expression of a form of life is also a process of learning what a paradigm is not: that is to say, learning to mediate it with other, rejected, alternatives, by contrast to which the claims of the paradigm in question are clarified.
>
> (Giddens 1976: 144)

Social researchers do not then have to content themselves with one paradigm as Kuhn would suggest. Social sciences are dynamic disciplines within which, depending upon the disposition and power of the researcher, other paradigms can be considered. This enables an understanding and explanation of empirical inquiries and adds to the challenging of assumptions about social life as an important part of research practice. It is this 'openness' to engage in reflection upon which our basis as a discipline depends. A community of researchers should then be 'able, willing, and committed to engage in argumentation' (Bernstein 1976: 111).

Apart from this ability, there are also fundamental differences which exist between the natural and social sciences. First, we are constantly dealing with social phenomena which people have already endowed with meaning before we arrive on the social scenes with our notebooks, questionnaires or interview schedules. Our work, therefore, involves the interpretation of social settings, events or processes by taking account of the meanings which people have already given to those settings or processes. Our own understanding, once again, becomes a precondition of our research. Second, the results and practices of social research also feed back into social life. People, unlike molecules, engage in the interpretation of its findings and are co-participants in its process.

Given this 'feedback' of research into social life, researchers have to make connections between the language which is used in social theory and the methods of interpretation which people already use in attributing meaning to their social environment. Social theory, in other words, must take account of people's everyday understandings. Anthony Giddens refers to this process as the 'double hermeneutic' (1976; 1984). This acknowledges that there is a constant slippage between the language which we use as researchers to understand and explain social life and the meanings which people already employ to get on with the business of everyday life. Given this relationship, the question is now raised as to whether we can have a theory of social life which does not take full account of people's experiences and understandings in everyday life. In order to assist in seeing the importance of this process for the relationship between theory and research, I wish to examine the ingenious ways in which social theorists have attempted to address this question.

We have already seen (in Chapter 1) how standpoint feminism regarded people's experiences as a starting but not finishing point for research. Theory was then required to situate the experiences of women within the wider context of women's position in society as a whole. The production of knowledge is then regarded as a social activity. If a certain type of knowledge predominates in a society, this is not necessarily because it is scientific, but due to the power that certain groups have to define what is right or wrong, or true and false. Theorizing about this state of affairs must then take place within a democratic and participatory situation, otherwise it will become, like the practice of science itself, another way of regarding people's experiences as faulty. The production of theory and research then become 'critical projects' which go hand in hand in challenging oppression in society — whether on gender, race, class or other lines. This brings us round to a discussion of the relationship between critical theory and an understanding of everyday life.

Critical theory has a long tradition in the work of the Frankfurt School with the works of Adorno, Horkheimer and Marcuse who were influenced by Marx and Freud. It does not assume, unlike positivism, that the differences between facts and values can be sustained. It is also in opposition to the idea that the world cannot be changed. The interests of the researcher towards this end are not then bracketed by a concentration on 'fact-gathering' or neutrality, nor the development of hypotheses to be tested. Instead

> A critical social theory frames its research program and its conceptual framework with an eye to the aims and activities of those oppositional social movements with which it has a partisan, though not uncritical, identification. The questions it asks and the models it designs are informed by that identification and interest . . . if struggles contesting the subordination of women figured among the most significant of a given age, then a critical theory for that time would aim, among other things, to shed light on the character and bases of such subordination.
>
> (Fraser 1989: 113)

Critical theory therefore approaches the question of the relationship between people's everyday meanings and the generation of social theory by not assuming that there is a truth that we can reach as researchers by simply concentrating on techniques of social research (as with positivism and empiricism). Further, it would not regard research results feeding back into social life as a 'problem' for researchers. On the contrary, in the works of Karl Marx, the adequacy of social theory was not its ability to discover social facts, but its value 'in informing actions, and in particular, political actions' (Johnson, Dandeker and Ashworth 1984: 144). The Italian social theorist Antonio Gramsci produced a social theory which was 'designed primarily to analyze capitalist relations in order to point out the strategic lessons for the socialist movement' (Hall 1988: 57). In the works of the contemporary German critical theorist Jürgen Habermas (1971; 1973), theory is considered by its ability to diagnose the ills of society and form part of the process of political action for their remedy.

Habermas is critical of the separation of so-called facts from people's experiences. The potential for change then exists in the creation of what he calls 'ideal-speech situations' (Habermas 1984; 1987). In such situations, people would discuss matters in a rational way, free from the constraints and power relations which impose weights upon them in society, and reach a consensus about the social world. Research based on critical theory would then be measured by its ability to reveal the relations of domination which exist in society:

> At the heart of critical social research is the idea that knowledge is structured by existing sets of social relations. The aim of a critical methodology is to provide knowledge which engages the prevailing social structures. These social structures are seen by critical social researchers, in one way or another, as oppressive structures.
>
> (Harvey 1990: 2)

Aspects of critical theory has been considerably modified in recent years with the advent of postmodernism and poststructuralism (Laclau and Mouffe 1985; Heller and Fehér 1988; Fraser 1989; Agger 1991). Despite this, critical theory might be argued to be claiming to know the 'wishes and struggles of the age' regardless of whether people are conscious of this or not. Its theories would not then represent the everyday understandings which people have of their social environments and we would still be left with a gap between social theory and people's interpretations of social life. Perhaps, therefore, we should abandon the idea of attempting to invent a theory which aims to transcend or supplant people's everyday understandings?

We now turn to the 'interpretative paradigm' of social theory and social research and an underlying drift away from realism, towards idealism. This was most clearly represented by the works of the German theorist Max Weber (1949) for whom subjective meanings used by people in social interaction are a starting point for the objective analysis of society. However, a gap still remains between everyday subjective meanings and the use of objective theories to explain the social world. Thus, while influenced by Weber, some theorists have argued that the theoretical constructs of research should simply reflect the same everyday constructs which people use to interpret social life. In this way, there would not be a gap between social theory and the data generated on social relations. The topic of investigation for researchers would then be the common-sense methods that people use in making sense of their social environments.

This was the argument of the social theorist Alfred Schutz and his criteria for the 'postulate of adequacy' of a social theory. This simply means that our theoretical constructs of the social world must be compatible 'with the constructs of everyday life' (Schutz 1979: 35). Our research would then focus on people's subjective experiences and, in the words of Stanley and Wise (1990), not treat these as 'faulty' in terms of the theoreticians' categories. The focus would be on how people 'make up' the social world by sharing meanings and how they 'get on' with each other (inter-subjectivity). However, we are not then able according to Schutz, in contrast to Weber, to theorize beyond this world of common-sense understandings about social life. In other words, the gap is closed by regarding any attempt to explain the social world beyond people's everyday understandings as unfounded.

Unlike critical theory, which emphasizes the way in which we are constrained by society, this method of theorizing examines how we create the social world through an inter-subjective process. We could take this even further to make a link between data and social theory in two ways. First, we should not even presuppose, as Schutz does, that there are shared meanings in the social world through which people interact with each other. Second, we should cease to try and uncover meanings behind appearances and instead take those appearances at face value. As a result, all social interactions should be treated as skilled performances by people and, it is argued, our presuppositions about social life would then be open to full scrutiny. We do not, therefore, seek to find 'motives' behind people's actions. Our topic of inquiry is the way in which people view society and render it comprehensible to each other using a 'documentary method of interpretation' (Garfinkel 1967). Common sense itself is a topic of research. We then assume very little about social life and dispel the idea that we can have access to an objective social world beyond people's interpretations of it. Our theories are now assumed to be fully grounded in people's everyday understandings.

This particular form of closing the gap between theory and data has, its exponents would argue, a very different aim in mind to conventional research and theorizing (Sharrock and Watson 1988). Despite this, we are back to the same issue raised by critical theory and, in particular, the work of Antonio Gramsci (1971). Gramsci argued that common sense resulted from the operation of political and economic power within society. If we study the operation of common sense then we are studying the product of these relations. Critical theorists, on the other hand, would argue that we should be interested in the process through which they are constituted so they might be challenged and changed. For this reason, Schutz's and Garfinkel's forms of theorizing are criticized as being conservative and empiricist.

Another way of characterizing the differences between the above approaches is that between micro and macro theory. Micro theory is more concerned with understanding face-to-face interactions between people in everyday life whereas macro theory is concerned with the behaviour of collections of people and the analysis of social systems or structures. How these two strands of theory might be synthesized has been addressed by researchers and theorists (see Knorr-Cetina and Cicourel 1981; Fielding 1988). There are also those who have advocated middle-range theories (Merton 1957) which should situate themselves between grand theory and empiricism. Research would then be left with a series of testable hypotheses on particular aspects of people's behaviours . Once again, however, underlying this is the notion that there are facts independent of theory.

In examining the relationship between social theory and social research, we have moved from critical theory to an interest in the practical usage of common sense. In an innovative way, rather than try to seek knowledge about society through theory and research, some researchers have examined, historically, how knowledge in society is produced and intimately connected with social power. We do not then seek to find a truth about society simply beyond people's conceptions of it, or simply in people's everyday practices, but how truth is formed in a relationship between knowledge and power in social practices (see Foucault 1980; Barrett 1991). This has been applied to areas such as the operation of punishment and discipline within society (Foucault 1977) and the social construction of 'madness' (Foucault 1971).

Summary

The basis of theory has been examined in several ways: first, in terms of its needing to be based solely in fact (inductivism); second, by its being subject to empirical falsification (deductivism); third, by its reflecting the dominant trends of the discipline – based not on rules of method, but the preferences of its scientists (Kuhn's paradigms); fourth, by its ability to diagnose and inform change (critical theory), and finally, by being grounded in the same constructs as people use in interpeting their social environment in everyday life (Schutz and Garfinkel).

Each of the above has been subjected to examination in terms of its relationship to research. While these are complicated discussions, the distinction between social fact and social values is often maintained by theorists. It is commonly thought that if values enter the research process, this renders its findings void. However, it has also been argued that values should enter our theories as a condition of research which is capable of critically evaluating how knowledge is produced and why some groups, more than others, are able to perpetuate their beliefs within society. The adequacy of such a theory focuses not only on the ability to understand and explain social life, but also the potential to change it.

How does this leave us as researchers? We are left, it seems, with an ambiguity over the question of the relationship between theoretical construction, empirical work and values. The practice of science is not simply a choice between facts and theory as there is, in the words of one commentator on methodology, 'no longer a reliable difference between theory construction and empirical work' (Baldamus 1984: 292). Further, social life itself is complicated and not amenable to understanding by the use of a single paradigm. These should not deter us. On the contrary, it provides food for conceptual thought. Instead of seeing this as a problem, perhaps we should be subjecting our own values and practices and those of others, to critical scrutiny? How values enter the research process and affect the product of research now becomes part of our focus. We are also acknowledging that social researchers are

> *always* the medium through which research occurs; there is not method or technique for doing research other than through the medium of the researcher.
>
> (Stanley and Wise 1983: 157)

To understand how this occurs and its effect on the research process requires, as noted at the beginning, a reflexivity on the part of researchers or, to express it another way, a consideration of the practice of research and our place within it. This is assisted by the constant interaction that exists between different interpretations of social life and the data which we collect on it. It also requires a further understanding of the issues involved in research practice: in particular, the relationship between values, ethics and social research. It is to these subjects that I now turn.

CHAPTER 2: QUESTIONS FOR YOUR REFLECTION

1   Define what is meant by the terms deduction and induction.

2   What are the aims of critical theory and how are these justified by critical researchers?

3   Alfred Schutz called for the 'postulate of adequacy of a social theory'. What did he mean by this and what are the problems associated with it?

4   Is the production of a social theory devoid of social values a possible and/or desirable aim?

3

Values and ethics in the research process

The approach adopted in this book is to stimulate a 'problem consciousness' − not in the belief that there are easy answers, but to be aware of the assumptions and limitations of social research, as well as its strengths. In this chapter I shall therefore examine the nature of value judgements, how values enter the research process and the different perspectives which exist on their influence in the production of social data. In the second section, the place of ethics in social research will be considered which, given the values and interests which often guide the research process, can be an important part of maintaining the integrity and honesty of social research practice.

Values and social research

Without doubt, an enormous amount of energy has been devoted to the relationship between science and values. The purpose of this section, however, is not to review this literature but to assist in the process of reflecting on research practice in three ways. First, by understanding the nature of value judgements; second, by considering the ways in which values enter the research process; and finally, by examining ideas which exist on the relationship between values and research.

What are value judgements?

In our everyday conversations and judgements, we make statements of two kinds: *positive* and *normative*. One idea of science prides itself on the ability to separate statements of what does happen (positive) and statements of what scientists would like to happen (normative):

> Positive statements are about what is, was or will be; they assert alleged facts
> about the universe in which we live. Normative statements are about what

ought to be. They depend on judgements about what is good or bad, and they are thus inextricably bound up with our philosophical, cultural and religious positions.

(Lipsky 1982: 5)

According to such a distinction science should strive to make judgements free from contamination by values. While this appears to clearly separate questions about 'what are' the facts from 'what ought to be' the facts, this is rendered doubtful by the constant interaction between ideas within society and the ideas within science. For instance, some religious groups in the nineteenth century believed that the world was only a few thousand years old. Subsequent advances in the science of geology demonstrated that some rocks were a million years old and others considerably older. In the face of such findings these religious groups had several choices: to deny the validity of the scientific findings; to modify their religious beliefs accordingly; or perhaps even to hold on to both belief and evidence at the same time. A 'positive' scientific finding had apparently countered a religiously held belief. On the other hand, positive scientific findings can be accommodated within belief systems. The 'Big Bang' theory of the origin of the universe, for instance, can be incorporated by arguing that God was responsible for that initial occurrence.

Just these two examples demonstrate that the social or natural world is not as clear cut as a strict separation between fact and value, or positive and normative statements, would suggest. On the contrary, there is a constant interaction between scientific practice and societal beliefs which affects research practice. Scientists, for example, debate among themselves the concept and effects of global warming and the relationship between the amount of sugar a person consumes and the health of that person's teeth – to say nothing of the origins of the universe! In the social sciences, we have seen that we deal with phenomena which people are already busily interpreting and endowing with meanings and values which makes our task as researchers a different one. In accomplishing our aims, we therefore need to ask 'what exactly are value judgements?'

To answer this question I shall use some examples (from Emmett 1981). In the first example, two people are asked to say which is the longer of two sticks by looking at and touching them (using their senses). We can then measure them with instruments to apparently solve any debate over which is the longer. This is said to be a matter of fact. However, is it as simple as that? Say the sticks were made of metal. At one temperature one stick may be longer than another (they have different coefficients of linear expansion). Which can we then say is the longer stick? Similarly, I place one stick in water and the other on a table. Which is then the longer? If I ask someone to tell me by looking at the sticks, then the way in which the light is reflected back to the person's eyes will be distorted by the medium. Which stick is the longer now depends on their temperature, their coefficients of expansion, the accuracy of the measuring instruments and the conditions under which they are observed. We might then be able to say which is the longer by adding these 'clauses' to our conclusions.

In another example, someone asks you which of two runners is the 'better'. As a researcher who seeks clarification before accepting definitions as self-evident, you ask what the questioner means by 'better'. Such questions take the form of 'it depends what you mean by X'. You may know that runner A is better than runner B over 400 metres, but runner B is better than runner A over 1,500 metres. So you need clarification before you can answer because you are being asked to make a *comparative assessment* between the runners. There is not a 'correct' answer, because each is faster than the other at certain distances. Your answer will depend on which you prefer and why?

Finally, I have a chair and ask two people to sit in it and express an opinion on its comfort. One person says it is comfortable; the other says it is the most uncomfortable chair she has ever sat in. These people are expressing an opinion which they hold about the comfort of a chair. It is not a matter of fact capable of being verified, but a matter of personal taste. In between so-called matters of fact and matters of taste, we have a whole realm of judgements – simply called value judgements with which we, as social researchers, are constantly dealing. We make such judgements when we rate one thing against another, for example, lecturers rating one essay as better than another.

Many people find the idea of value judgements uncomfortable – why can't they be factual? It might simply be replied that values are a fundamental part of the human condition and we should pose the question in a different way and therefore seek a different answer. We should not seek the impossible – the elimination of value judgements – but ask the more important question: what type of values are the judgements based upon and how do these affect the judgements?

Value judgements are dependent on beliefs and experiences in everyday life. They also concern what we would like our experience to be. This may arise from a bad experience in circumstances which we thought would be more pleasant. For instance, we attend a political meeting and find that everyone is not as friendly as we hoped they would be. We went with an expectation which was not met by our experiences. However, we come away with an idea about how that meeting should run perhaps along more co-operative lines. Thus, we do not seek to eliminate values as they inform the very reasons for which we and others attended in the first place. Nevertheless, we might seek to change the values which guided the way in which the meeting was conducted. We would then need to understand the ways in which values entered this process.

Values in the research process

The majority of social research in Britain is sponsored by governments, or other organizations or agencies with a vested interest in the results. This is not to suggest that this necessarily invalidates the conclusions because the work is 'interested' as opposed to 'disinterested' (often assumed to be a characteristic of scientific activity). However, it is important to be aware of the issues which surround the production of a piece of work and the place and influence of values within it. As a matter of routine the following questions can be asked of any piece of research: who funded the research? With what intention in mind? How was it conducted? What were the problems associated with its design and execution and how were the results interpreted and used? This enables an understanding of the context in which research takes place and the influences upon it, as well as countering the tendency to see the production and design of research as a technical issue uncontaminated by political and ethical questions. All research, implicitly or explicitly, contains issues of this sort. This is not to render the research invalid but, on the contrary, to recognize such issues heightens our awareness of the research process itself. Thus, Table 1 illustrates the stages in the research process and is followed by a discussion on the place of values within each one.

Table 1   Values in the research process

(1) THE DESIGN AND AIM OF RESEARCH
(2) THE ACTUAL COLLECTION OF DATA
(3) THE INTERPRETATION OF THE FINDINGS
(4) THE USE MADE OF THE RESEARCH FINDINGS

As we are all aware, different groups within society have different interests and frequently behave in ways to further those interests. An ability to define a problem or issue according to values will, in its turn, affect all stages of the research process but, in the first instance, its design and aim.

Consider this definition of social policy research as the

> *process of conducting research on, or analysis of, a fundamental social problem in order to provide policymakers with pragmatic, action-orientated recommendations for alleviating the problem.*
>
> (Majchrzak 1984: 12, original emphasis)

In such instances, social researchers should be cautious in accepting that a problem exists for which there must be a solution. How a problem is defined will depend on several factors, all of which either influence values, or enable some groups' values to predominate over others. Three factors, in particular, are significant: culture, history and social power. First, different cultures have different values. Because the values of different groups vary, what may often be a problem to one group is not a problem to another. Monogamous marriage is a value which has found its way into law in this country. However, the idea that this is the only acceptable form of two people living together is challenged not only by other cultures, but also by groups within our own society. The Lele tribe of East Africa practise polyandry (one women may marry two or more men), while in Britain the phenomenon of heterosexism is increasingly challenged by lesbian and gay groups who wish to possess positive rights to live in a way which society accepts as legitimate, not 'deviant'. Thus, values not only between but also within societies differ, and research cannot assume that societies are characterized by something called 'value-consensus' or agreement over social practices.

Second, history changes and with it the way we perceive social problems. As history changes, so attitudes towards events and groups can change. What is considered wrong or deviant at one point in time can be considered normal at another time: for example, the suffragette movement was considered subversive in the earlier part of the twentieth century. While attitudes to women's liberation still, in the main, range from support to suspicion and hostility, it is clear that women's rights have altered to some extent – particularly in the case of voting rights. As a result, social research needs to be aware of the changing conditions which define social problems.

Finally, social power is not evenly distributed between groups. The definition that there exists a problem will often depend on the relative power that the people who define the social problem have over those who are defined: for instance, those with access to the media may possess more power in the construction of social problems than those with limited access. Given these factors rather than simply accepting the definition, it is equally valid to examine the process through which a phenomenon became defined as a problem. In this way, the accepted truth that there exists a problem is abandoned in favour of researching how it became constructed as one. This is a subtle but profound difference in research technique where social values themselves may be researched.

The call for 'relevant' research is frequently heard, despite the considerable ambiguity over what this actually means (Eldridge 1986). Yet, even if researchers are given a free rein to design research in any way they decide, or to undertake a research project into any social area they wish, this does not mean that it is immune from values. Feminists argue that androcentric values of male researchers tend to affect all aspects of their research practice from design, through data collection to interpretation and application. Similarly, a racist attitude can affect the way in which research is conducted, while social researchers are often heterosexist in their methods and interpretation, believing and perpetuating, for example, that a 'normal' family is one man and one women who are married and have two children. In this instance, normality is a value term which is used to refer to the statistically most regular pattern of family life in Britain. While this is open to doubt (Abbott and Wallace 1990: 83–4), the use of such a term assumes that people living together who do not meet this criteria are 'deviant' or 'abnormal'. In addition, as we shall see in Part II, there are a number of ways in which data are collected by social scientists. Each is said to have its strengths and weaknesses. The decision as to which method to use may be based upon the researcher's own value judgements. Further, within the data collection process itself, there are a number of ethical and political decisions to be made. Researchers may wish to concentrate on one group of people rather than another, reflecting their own bias towards that group. More instrumentally, they may concentrate on one group because it is easier to study that group (a frequent criticism of social research is its concentration on less powerful groups; as such we know little about 'elite' groups who possess the power to prevent research being conducted upon themselves).

The anticipation of the needs of a sponsor throughout the research process can also lead to the selection of data and the interpretation of those aspects of the research findings which 'prove' the sponsors' prejudices. This is a problem of *selectivity*. In being selective, a number of interesting findings can be dismissed which could aid understanding and explanation. In addition, researchers may not only anticipate the needs of the sponsors, but also interpret what they consider 'society at large' believes. Thus a researcher who is examining crime statistics may feel that society is concerned about football hooliganism given all the media attention and police resources which have been devoted to this issue. However, in the process of undertaking their investigations they discover that a large percentage of violence takes place against women in domestic situations. Evidence of this type would clearly question the values of not only the researcher, but also society in general.

In research design, data collection and interpretation the researcher will, depending on the circumstances, influence the conduct of the research. This is not necessarily a disadvantage, bearing in mind the arguments of standpoint feminists that women's experiences are fundamental for the production of less distorted knowledge. It does mean that from the first stage (the design and aim of the research), through the second stage, to the third stage (interpretation of findings) researchers must be aware of the place of values in the research process. What is more difficult to control and account for are the wider influences of values and how they affect research. This becomes a particular problem when the results reach a wider audience (the use made of research findings).

At this point, political circumstances can take over regardless of the good will or intentions of the researcher. The research results may then be used for purposes for which they were not intended (known as the 'unintended consequences' of social action). For instance, during the Vietnam War, social scientists asked the people in rural areas of Indo-China questions which were designed to elicit or discover their moral and political allegiances. Despite the researchers being told that it was for scientific purposes, the information was allegedly used by the military to select bombing targets (Barnes 1979: 17). This brings us round to the section on ethics and a discussion of means and ends in social research. Before this, however, I wish to finish this part of the chapter by examining perspectives on the relationship between values and research.

The connection between values and research

For those who adhere to the idea of 'value neutrality' throughout the research process, there are insurmountable problems in mounting a defence for this position. Most scientists would not, if asked, attempt to maintain this in the face of overwhelming arguments to the contrary. However, there are those who would adhere to the values of science and objectivity.

Ernest Nagel (1961) was aware of the arguments that social science cannot be value-free, but critics failed to take account of different types of value judgements. He therefore made a distinction between *characterizing* and *appraising* value judgements (Nagel 1961: 492–5). When scientists make a characterizing value judgement they are expressing an estimate of the degree to which something is present, such as dissent among prisoners in Scottish jails or a population's attitude to pollution and global warming. On the other hand, appraising value judgements express approval or disapproval of some moral or social ideal: multilateralists expressing disapproval of the views of unilateralists.

In drawing this distinction, Nagel notes how the two are often indistinguishable. We make statements which contain both characterizing and appraising value judgements. Nevertheless, he argues that their separation is a practical task and not an insoluble one. If we succeed in separating the two, then we are left with characterizing judgements as a routine part of both the social and natural sciences. The possibility of a value-free social science (in terms of appraising judgements) is therefore a technical matter, not a theoretical impossibility.

Max Weber (1949), unlike Nagel, argued that the subject matter of the social sciences is fundamentally different from the natural sciences. In trying to understand people, we are obviously dealing with specifically human characteristics and these include 'meaning' and also phenomena such as 'spirituality'. However, despite our goal being an understanding of the subjective meaning that people attribute to their world, Weber does share Nagel's belief that social science can be objective. It is, he argued, logically impossible for the social sciences to establish in a scientific manner the truth of ideals which people believe in: the normative or 'what ought to be' statements. Social science can then allow us to determine the suitability of a given range of means for the attainment of a specified end. In other words, if people desire a particular goal, then social science can assist them in finding the best way to achieve that goal. Social science cannot, however, tell people that they should accept a given end as a value, or tell people what they ought to believe in. In this way, the role of the social scientist is to demonstrate the pros and cons of different means and perhaps the social, economic and political costs involved, but not tell people what they should desire as ends:

> Science today is a 'vocation' organized in special disciplines in the service of self-clarification and knowledge of interrelated facts. It is not the gift of grace

of seers and prophets dispensing sacred values and revelations, nor does it partake of the contemplation of sages and philosophers about the meaning of the universe.

(Weber, in Gerth and Mills 1948: 152)

Why does Weber believe this? Quite simply, values are a matter of faith and not of scientific knowledge. As social scientists we may be sufficiently committed to choose a particular area of study and so make a value judgement, yet from this point on, our work can be objective. Thus, values enter into research only in the problem selection stage. In a similar vein, in his discussion of social theory and social policy, Robert Pinker (1971) argues that social theory should be based upon what the members of society actually believe, not what the theorist tells them they ought to believe. Beyond this, the researcher may seek 'to inform or change public opinion, and to help create consciousness of problems where this consciousness is absent' (Pinker 1971: 131). The overt nature of the role of values in social research is therefore recognized in this formulation, but values must not determine the final product: 'the first function of scientific theory is . . . to help us distinguish correct from incorrect knowledge' (Pinker 1971: 130).

Weber, Nagel and Pinker all share, to one extent or another, a belief in the possibility of fact-gathering, while recognizing the crucial role which values play in the research process (even objectivity is a value position). What is at issue is the place, role and type of values in social research. According to critics of these positions, social research is not a neutral medium for generating information on social realities (Gouldner 1962). It is

> an activity recognized by many as not just unveiling the facts but as constructing them, and the researcher plays a major role in this. Thus enters the question of values in research activities as well, and a fuller discussion of what is good — that is, what values should guide the researcher in her studies and interventions — is required.
>
> (Ravn 1991: 112)

Once we accept that values not only enter the process of research, but also inform it at all points, then it can be argued that the above accounts of Weber, Nagel and Pinker are based on a certain version of objectivity that feminists and critical theorists have rejected. Values do not simply affect *some* aspects of research, but *all* aspects. Furthermore, the idea of objectivity as detachment was criticized in Chapter 1 as being based upon a limited idea of science through its separation of reason and emotion. Instead of the attempt to separate the researcher from the researched, there are those who then argue for the taking of sides in the research process (Becker 1967). Others, influenced by feminist-based research, argue for 'dialogic retrospection',

> which is defined as an open and active exchange between the researcher and participant in a partnership of co-research.
>
> (Humm 1989: 50)

This formulation of active partnership is said to recognize that values, feelings and experiences are a routine part of the research process. In order to address this issue, rather than attempt to distinguish correct from incorrect knowledge (Pinker) or subjective realities from objective analysis (Weber), research must be a co-operative endeavour in which the researchers and participants share information and experiences. 'Correct' knowledge does not then come from detachment based on a limited concept of reason, as we saw in Chapter 1. Further, to reject the relationship between research and objectivity as 'detachment' is not to reject the claim that research produces accurate knowledge. Those thinkers who argue for value-freedom, in whatever form, are viewed as inheriting a mythical distinction between reason and emotion so characteristic of the scientific claims which feminists seek to debunk. The consequences are that the researcher is expected to perform a role which no individual could possible live up to

> We must present our research in such a way that we strip 'ourselves' from descriptions, or describe our involvements in particular kinds of ways – as somehow 'removed' rather than full-blown members of the events and processes we describe.
>
> (Stanley and Wise 1983: 155)

In this criticism, values, experiences and commitment now become a fundamental part of the research process (see Roseneil 1993). Most feminist researchers do not seek their elimination, but their understanding; they do not seek to detach themselves from research, but instead seek to understand their place and experiences within social research as a central part of its process and product. This focus places the researcher and her experiences at the centre of research which also enables a greater understanding of the social world:

> In my research diary (which was hard to distinguish from a personal diary since I was concerned to record my experiences and interactions within the prison, rather than so called 'objective observations'), I noted a number of points which were relevant to the influence of (my) gender, age and race.
>
> (Gelsthorpe 1990: 95)

Feminist goals of personal commitment, experience and the improvement of women's position within society and the goals of a rational science, detached from the social world, are argued to be incompatible and impossible to sustain (Ramazanoglu 1992). Research which is explicitly and consistently feminist in orientation is often conducted for the purposes of overcoming women's oppression. Values then explicitly inform the design, process and product of social research.

To separate the means of doing research, from its end, as Weber suggests, could not be sustained by any such commitment as feminist or critical research. Research which assumes 'facts' can be collected on the social world simply reflects and perpetuates unequal power relations which already exist in society. Weber's position would then preclude the researcher from making any analysis and critique of the ends which a society, organization or group pursues. Richard Titmuss, who placed values such as social justice at the forefront of his work on social policy, recognized this:

> There is no escape from values in welfare systems ... Not only is 'policy' all about values but those who discuss problems of policy have their own values (some would call them prejudices). But, whatever they are called, it is obvious that the social sciences – and particularly economics and sociology – are not, nor can ever be, 'value-free'.
>
> (Titmuss 1974: 132)

The above view does not lead to an 'anything goes' view of research. Certain standards are still needed in the conduct of research, particularly if the idea of a 'discipline' is to be maintained. The researcher, whatever their perspective on values and research, is still faced with choices about what is right or wrong in the conduct of her or his research. For this reason, ethics are part of research practice.

Ethics and their relation to social research

Continuing with the theme of reflexivity in the research process, this section is divided into two parts. The first part asks the question 'what are ethics'? The second section then looks at the actual place of ethics in social research by considering the relationship between means and ends and the main ethical issues raised by the process of research.

What are ethics?

How may we define the term ethics? To the layperson

> the word 'ethics' often suggests a set of standards by which a particular group or community decides to regulate its behaviour – to distinguish what is legitimate or acceptable in pursuit of their aims from what is not. Hence we talk of 'business ethics' or 'medical ethics'.
>
> (Flew 1984: 112)

In so far as researchers critically reflect upon their own views or those of others, or consider the justification for their actions in comparison to others, they then enter the realm of philosophical ethics. Such considerations are known as '2nd Order' questions: they are questions 'about things', rather than simply taking them at face value.

A definition of ethical problems as they apply to social research is given by John Barnes (1979). He defines ethical decisions in research as those which arise when we try to decide between one course of action and another not in terms of expediency or efficiency but by reference to standards of what is morally right or wrong.

(Barnes 1979: 16)

Barnes is making a distinction here and basing ethical decisions upon *principles* rather than *expediency*. This is an important point. Ethical decisions are not being defined in terms of what is advantageous to the researcher or the project which they are working on. They are concerned with what is right or just, in the interests of not only the project, its sponsors or workers, but also others who are the participants in the research.

At the same time, the particular interests that govern a research project can influence those decisions which take place within it. Knowledge is not simply a politically neutral product as would be maintained by positivism and empiricism. Ethical decisions will therefore depend upon the values of the researchers and their communities and will inform the negotiations which take place between the researcher, sponsors, research participants and those who control access to the information which the researcher seeks ('gatekeepers'). The amount of control the researcher can exercise over the research process will also influence the exercise of ethical decisions themselves. For these reasons, the relationship between ethics and social research is a complicated one. While the development of a code of ethics for social research is a laudable aim, many argue that it must also recognize these factors which so influence the conduct of research. Warwick and Pettigrew (1983) attempt just such a set of guidelines, but still note that there are

sources of ethical difficulties beyond the confines of social science itself – the sponsors of research and the mass media of communication. Repeatedly, our discussion has shown how these influences contribute to ethical problems in policy research.

(Warwick and Pettigrew 1983: 368)

Given such a state of affairs, there are two ways in which approaches to ethics and social research have proceeded. These two approaches may not accurately reflect all ethical decisions which are made, but they are useful 'heuristic' devices (which, in this case, means helping to study or discover). These two approaches are known as *deontology* and *consequentialism*.

Deontological approaches to morality are often associated with the work of Immanuel Kant (1724–1804). Quite simply, ethical judgements in social research would, from this point of view, follow a set of principles which guide the conduct of research itself. Research ethics take on a universal form and are intended to be followed regardless of the place and circumstances in which the researcher finds themselves. One such doctrine is that of 'informed consent':

Social research inquiries involving human subjects should be based as far as practicable on their freely given informed consent. Even where participation by subjects is required by law, social researchers should try to ensure that this participation is as informed as possible.

('Draft Principles for Social Research Association Code of Ethics',
November 1982)

On the other hand, consequentialism is not so concerned with following a set of inviolate rules, but with the situation in which researchers find themselves and with the consequences of their acts. According to this view, a set of doctrinal rules for the conduct of social research does not take account of the context of social research and would result in undue restriction on the researcher's activities and creativity. In this sense, to lie may be justified if it prevents harm or offence to a person. The dilemmas that the researcher encounters are then believed to be not so different from those which we all face in everyday life:

> The only difference is normally one of degree. That is, in 'research' settings most social scientists rarely have very intimate friends. If we had intimates in the settings, we would not be likely to think of the settings as a 'research' one. Since they are not intimates, we are under less social obligations to keep secrets about them. And we can normally deal with almost all our problems of privacy by maintaining the anonymity of the people we write about.
>
> (Douglas 1979: 29)

That said, Douglas does not rule out those who believe in professional ethics, simply those who believe that ethical rules of research must be applied rigorously in all settings. In particular, he notes that the development of professional ethics provides something of a safeguard against the encroachment on freedom of speech and research (Douglas 1979: 32).

A rigid and inflexible set of ethical rules for social research (deontology) could well leave us with an undesirable consequence:

> the only safe way to avoid violating principles of professional ethics is to refrain from doing social research altogether.
>
> (Bronfenbreener, quoted in Barnes 1979, 'preface')

On the other hand, a loose and flexible system of 'anything goes' ethics can so easily open the research door to the unscrupulous. As a result, there are those who feel that both sides have their merits and weaknesses (Plummer 1990: 141). If research is to be viewed as a credible endeavour, then perhaps the relations which are established with all those party to the research must utilize some ethical basis which provides guidelines for, but not simply constraints on, the researcher?

With the huge growth in information technology and the routine invasions of people's privacy, it becomes more likely that people may refuse to co-operate with research. The formulation of ethical guidelines would then enable the researcher to continually reflect on the expectations which they make of people and their relationships with those party to the research. This could be argued, as

Douglas suggests, not only to help prevent social research simply becoming a mouthpiece of powerful vested interests, but also to assist in maintaining public co-operation and trust in social research (Bulmer 1979b).

Ethics and social research

In comparing ethical issues in social and natural sciences, John Barnes (1979) notes that ethical issues in the natural sciences relate more to the application than the gathering of information. However, there are pressure groups who are bringing to the public's attention the use of animals for experimentation and the ethical issues surrounding nuclear energy and genetic engineering. This difference, therefore, as Barnes has speculated (1979: 17), is now less apparent.

I have deliberately raised the question of ethics and natural science research. When reading about ethics in social sciences, there is a tendency to believe that ethical issues are often not important in the conducting of natural science as opposed to social science research. In addition, the use of the term 'science' often carries with it a justification of using various means of collecting information in terms of the pursuit of 'truth'. There are also those for whom the end may be justified in terms of the furtherance of a political cause or the heightening of a particular issue in the public conscience. This relationship between the means and ends of research has thus provided the focus for much heated debate in the social sciences.

Max Weber refers to the 'ethic of ultimate ends'. Under the banner of scientific inquiry in the search of truth, some would argue that it is possible to justify their actions. However, whatever the merit of their ends,

> From no ethics in the world can it be concluded when and to what extent the ethically good purpose 'justifies' the ethically dangerous means and ramifications.
>
> (Weber, in Gerth and Mills 1947: 121)

The means, in other words, cannot justify the ends. Yet in our current climate research is highly dependent on government and large agency funding. These bodies have a vested interest in the conduct and findings of research. They may even impose their own conditions or, perhaps more commonly, their political expectations govern the ethical decisions which can be made during the research: for example, research on poorer sections of the community for the purposes of determining their 'eligibility' for state support. Should such information be gathered at any cost to the dignity of the individuals concerned, in order to try and save the government of the day money? If the government of the day justify their actions by reference to democracy and the 'wishes of the majority' would this be satisfactory? The researchers would then have to ask themselves a number of questions to justify being part of such a project.

First, if we are talking about a majority wish, this would work in a 'direct democracy' where all people have a channel of communication to all political decisions made in their interest. This is clearly not the case in any country which claims to be a democracy. Second, even if the majority 'willed' it, as one of the greatest advocates of democracy (Alexis de Tocqueville) was only too aware, the exercise of the 'tyranny of the majority' may predominate. Minority rights can then become ignored and we do not have to look deep into history to see the disastrous consequences of such a course of action. Third, the researchers would also ask themselves what autonomy from the sponsors they would have in the project in order to exercise some discretion in the design, collection and analysis of data.

Of course, if researchers ignored the ends for which their research is intended, they could still provide the means for dubious ends. Claims of ignorance or lack of control may be justified in some instances, but 'collusion' can still occur whether the researchers intended it or not. For Weber, however, social science could provide only the means, but not tell people the ends to which it should then be put. Researchers may even advise on which is the best means to pursue given ends, but again may not comment, as a social scientist, on the ends themselves. This is problematic. Critical theorists, for example, would challenge the values which govern the ends to which research is put. They might argue that the means themselves inherit the ends and may further oppression. In other words, Weber's idea of social science fails to see that the means can affect the ends.

The relationship between means and ends in research is a problematic one to which there are no simple answers. It is further clouded by the widespread practice of temporary employment contracts for social researchers who are not then in a position to challenge dubious practices for fear of a bad reference or non-renewal of their contracts.

We are now left with the question: 'should the production of knowledge be pursued at any cost?' If so, we can then justify our means in terms of our ends. There is no simple answer to this question. Once research reaches the public domain, as Warwick and Pettigrew (1983) noted, the control that the researcher can exercise over it changes. With a growth in information technology and the use to which research findings can be put, in the face of mass communication researchers find their power limited over the way in which that knowledge is then used. However, researchers can still make tactical decisions in the process of research which have ethical consequences. In the balance between people's privacy and the generation of knowledge, one of the classic debates centred around a research project undertaken by Laud Humphreys (1970).

Humphreys conducted his doctoral dissertation as a covert participant observer (conducted without the knowledge of those being observed) of a number of homosexual acts in what were known as 'tearooms' (public rest-rooms). He became a familiar part of the social scene, assisted by his pastoral experiences in a part of Chicago known as 'queen parish', by making the 'rounds of ten gay bars then operating in the metropolitan area' and by attending 'private gatherings and the annual ball' (Humphreys 1970: 25). He was then able to adopt the role of 'watch-queen', whose function was to act as a look-out, but who was also recognized as deriving pleasure from watching homosexual encounters. In this role, which he calls the 'sociologist as voyeur', Humphreys was able to record the events he witnessed.

During this time he made a note of 134 licence plate numbers of the cars belonging to the men. By pretending to be a market researcher and making use of friendly contacts in the police force, he collected their names and addresses. Approximately one year later, after changing his appearance and now being employed on a social health survey of men, he sought the permission of the project director to add 100 of those original names to the health survey in order to collect further data on the participants. Most of the men in his study were married and not members of the gay community – considering themselves neither bisexual or homosexual. He then called on them under the guise of the health survey, to conduct further research. Their names were kept in a safe deposit box, no identification appeared on the questionnaire and the interview cards themselves were destroyed after completion of the schedule (Humphreys 1970: 42).

The reactions to the publication of his study were variable. As Humphreys notes in a postscript to the book: 'several have suggested to me that I should have avoided this research subject altogether' (1970: 168). He was accused of deceit, the invasion of privacy and increasing the likelihood of the sample's detection by the police force. One account suggest that some faculty members at Washington University were so outraged 'that they demanded (unsuccessfully) that Humphreys' doctoral degree be revoked' (Kimmel 1988: 23). On the other hand:

> The research was applauded by members of the gay community and some social scientists for shedding light on a little-known segment of our society, and for dispelling stereotypes and myths.
>
> (Kimmel 1988: 23)

In this sense, the means justified the end. He brought into the public domain an understanding of an issue which American society had done so much to repress. To his critics, however, the means can never justify the ends:

> Social research involving deception and manipulation ultimately helps produce a society of cynics, liars and manipulators, and undermines the trust which is essential to a just social order.
>
> (Warwick 1982: 58)

To those who have used such methods, they may be justified according to the nature of the research materials which they produce. Rosenhan's (1982) research, which involved eight sane people gaining admission as 'pseudo-patients' to mental hospitals following their display of certain 'symptoms', may be argued to have gained information on the process of psychiatric diagnosis not available by other means. From this, it became apparent that, despite the 'science' of psychiatry: 'we cannot distinguish the sane from the insane in psychiatric hospitals' (Rosenhan 1982: 36). As he notes, this was a general criticism of the psychiatric system and not aimed at the individuals who treated these pseudopatients. Indeed, he notes that these staff were committed and cared for their patients (Rosenhan 1982: 37). This research therefore constituted

> a striking example of how knowledge as enlightenment may be obtained by the benign use of deception and where the use of deception on obtaining information increases rather than decreases its credibility.
>
> (Barnes 1979: 125)

Similarly, Nigel Fielding's reflection on his work on the National Front (Fielding 1981) saw him in the role as interpreter between the inner workings of this organization and society in general. His hope is that the end result assisted people outside of the organization to 'understand its appeal' and that in a more political vein, this enabled the National Front's opponents 'to persuade those susceptible to membership that the answers to our problems do not lie in racist politics' (Fielding 1982: 104).

The relationship between means and ends in social research and the ethical decisions, power and disposition of the researchers themselves, are clearly difficult issues. Any debate tends to focus upon the use of covert participant observation because it seems, so clearly, to raise the central issues of knowledge production and its relationship to privacy. Yet in an information society where so many data are routinely stored on individuals (Poster 1990), invasion of privacy is becoming a routine aspect of our lives. This does not give licence to social research to conduct itself without due consideration to privacy. It does, however, widen the scope of ethics and social research to incorporate surveys (Bulmer 1979a). It also focuses our attention on the relationship between the production of research and the use to which it is then put.

Summary

From our discussions on values and ethics, it is evident that the idea of research free from values is problematic. Social research takes place within a context in which many of its rules of procedures are taken for granted. These 'background assumptions' (Gouldner 1971), upon which research decisions and analysis are based, should be open to scrutiny, otherwise social research can so easily reflect the prejudices of society in general, or a research community in particular. At the same time, it is worth remembering that social life, while illuminated by social research, does not ultimately depend upon it. Decisions are constantly made which directly affect our lives and which are not based upon systematic research. As one commentator puts it: 'Life cannot wait for social research to catch up with it' (Shipman 1988: 67).

As feminist and radical critics have pointed out, simply 'knowing about' the issues of values and ethics is not a sufficient basis upon which to conduct research; they also need to form part of research practice. Values and the researcher's experiences are not then something to be bracketed away as if ashamed by their entry into the process. On the contrary, many now argue that an examination of the basis of these values and their relationship to decisions and stages in research is required for the foundations of good social research. The aim is not their elimination, for this is impossible. Instead, these criticisms acknowledge that research takes place within a context where certain interests and values often predominate to the exclusion of others. 'Objective' research is not then achieved by uncritically accepting these as self-evident: this is more likely to result in the perpetuation of discriminatory practices within society. At the same time, social researchers may have to acknowledge that their individual power may be limited in acting on this state of affairs. Despite their best efforts, they cannot guarantee to control the use to which research might be put, nor to exercise full control over the process. The development and application of research ethics is required in order to maintain public confidence in its exercise, while a democratic and open society will provide greater safeguards against the misuse of social research.

CHAPTER 3: QUESTIONS FOR YOUR REFLECTION

1   What is the difference between positive and normative statements?

2   Define value judgements; in what ways do values enter into social research?

3   How is an understanding of values important for research practice and is their presence an advantage or disadvantage in the production of research?

4   You have been given £15,000 by your Local Authority to conduct research into the characteristics of people on income support in your area. At the same time, you are also told that a 'black economy' thrives in the area and to remember this 'fact' when designing and analysing your research. What value and ethical dilemmas do you face in conducting this research?

PART II

METHODS OF
SOCIAL RESEARCH

4

Official statistics as a research source

Available information on the demographic characteristics of the population, their opinions and life styles is considerable. The sheer volume of material which is collected on a routine basis by the government and its agencies provides a rich source of data for the social researcher to analyse. In the first section of this chapter, I shall therefore examine the common types of official statistics that researchers can utilize. However, there is a temptation to use such data bases without due consideration to their weaknesses, as well as strengths. Official statistics, for example, often employ unexamined assumptions about social life which, if researchers are not cautious, they can inherit and reproduce in their studies. They are not simply 'social facts', but also social and political constructions which may be based upon the interests of those who commissioned the research in the first instance. Before using such statistics, the researcher therefore needs to understand how they were constructed. In order to assist in this process, the second section of this chapter will examine the construction of crime statistics. The third section will then outline various schools of thought on the use of official statistics for social research.

Sources of official statistics

The term 'official statistics' is normally used to refer to data collected by the state and its agencies. In 1837 the General Register Office was established, with registration of deaths placed on the political agenda. During the 1840s regular statistical reports began on subjects such as births, deaths and crimes. In contemporary times, official statistics cover the economy, crime, employment, education and health – to name but a few. This heading would also include the ten-year Census of the population, which began in 1801 with government concerns over the growth of the population exceeding its available resources; the Family Expenditure Survey, which began in the 1950s for constructing the

Retail Price Index as a cost of living indicator, but is also now used, for example, as an estimate for the number of people living in poverty (see McGregor and Borooah 1992). There are also the General Household Survey (GHS) and British Social Attitudes Survey (BSAS). The former began in the 1960s and the latter in 1983, both with the intention of being used for secondary analysis (see Kent 1981; Dale, Arber and Procter 1988), defined as

> any further analysis of an existing data set which present interpretations, conclusion of knowledge additional to, or different from, those presented in the first report on the inquiry as a whole and its main results.
> (Hakim 1982: 1)

Official statistics, such as the BSAS and GHS, represent an extensive source of data on changing attitudes to particular social issues and the composition and incomes of households which is available for analysis by social researchers. However, while the General Household Survey represents a rich data set, the topics included 'are those accepted as of significance to officialdom' (Dale, Arber and Procter 1988: 18). For this reason, as we shall see in the third section of this chapter, there is a debate over the use of such surveys.

This is not an exhaustive list of the sources of official statistics available to us as social researchers. However, it gives an idea of the enormous volume of data which is produced or sponsored by the state, government and its agencies. To these we could add what are referred to as 'ad hoc' or 'one-off' surveys conducted by the Office of Population Censuses and Surveys (OPCS). Dale, Arber and Procter (1988) note, for example, such studies as 'Smoking Attitudes and Behaviour', the 1984 Women and Employment Survey (WES) and the Family Formation Survey. These studies

> usually relate to a specific topic that is of current policy interest. They are commissioned not just for the purposes of providing background data but also with the aim of increasing understanding within the area of concern.
> (Dale, Arber and Procter 1988: 9)

Such statistics enable researchers to understand the dynamics of society – perhaps along race, class, age and gender lines – as well as charting trends within society (hence the term for one of the most detailed government statistical publications, 'Social Trends'). Such information also provides government and social policy formulators with data upon which to base their decisions and the means with which to forecast and evaluate the impact of new social policy provisions. In short, enormous amounts of information are collected, stored and used about individuals as part of society. This information is also used by market researchers who, for commercial reasons, are interested in the tastes, habits and opinions of the population.

Both the production of official statistics and secondary analysis performed on them is not an unproblematic enterprise. It is at this point that the different theoretical schools of thought and their approaches to research become apparent. Each of these considers the use of official statistics in a different way. It is therefore helpful to frame this discussion by using an example. For this purpose, I have chosen crime statistics. In so doing, the reader should be aware that these are commonly criticized for their limitations and some of the discussion may not be directly applicable to other types. However, this example demonstrates that the process through which official statistics are produced has a considerable effect on the final product. As we shall see in the third section, there are those who believe the product is useful for social research and those who reject their utility and consider only the process of their construction.

The social construction of crime statistics

Criminal Statistics are published for England and Wales each year. They provide policy-makers with an indication of the types of crimes being committed and the extent to which crime is increasing or decreasing according to the implementation and impact of criminal justice policies.

It is not uncommon for us to read in the newspapers of a 'new crime wave'. This contributes to a fear of crime which alters the habits of society's vulnerable groups: for example, elderly people locking their doors, not going out at night and avoiding certain areas. Researchers have also shown that women's fear of crime, in particular, is real enough and should not be dismissed as simply 'false' (Stanko 1990). At the same time, can we be sure that these statistics provide an accurate picture of the extent and nature of crime in this country? If not, then the decisions of policy-makers and media presentation of crime, based upon this information, will be limited and in some instances entirely wrong. In order to understand this question, we need to examine the way in which an act becomes officially defined as criminal.

To have confidence in using official statistics on crime, we must be sure that they fulfil the criteria of both *validity* and *reliability*:

> Research is valid when the conclusions are true. It is reliable when the findings are repeatable. Reliability and validity are requirements for both the design and the measurement of research. At the level of research design, we examine the conclusions and ask whether they are true and repeatable. At the level of measurement, we examine the scores of observations and ask whether they are accurate and repeatable.
>
> (Kidder 1981: 7)

The following conditions must therefore hold to sustain the validity and reliability of official statistics on crime. First, a similar incident or act of breaking the law must be categorized in the same way by those responsible for compiling the crime statistics. We must assume, therefore, that there is little room for the discretion of personnel to enter in recording such information and if such discretion should enter, it is exercised in exactly the same way to produce the same classification or, in Kidder's terms, observational score. If this is not the case, then similar incidents will be categorized in different ways. Second, our statistics must be mutually exclusive so that two different occurrences cannot be categorized in the same way. If two different incidents can be categorized in the same way, then our statistics cannot be reliable, that is accurate and repeatable. Third, it also follows that the categorization of criminal acts must be exhaustive: that is all criminal acts committed are categorized under a particular heading and included in the official statistics. For instance, all burglaries committed on a daily basis are recorded by the police. To consider how official statistics on crime measure up to these criteria, I shall examine the process through which a criminal act becomes a crime statistic.

Early on in this process is the act becoming defined as criminal. At this point, there are two important aspects to bear in mind. First, for an act to be 'criminal' it must be defined as such by the criminal law (and we make a distinction between criminal and civil law). Second, someone, apart from the perpetrator, must know that a criminal act took place, otherwise, quite simply, it will not be detected except in cases of self-confession, or the perpetrator is caught for another act and asks for others to be 'taken into consideration' (TICs). Even at this early stage, we face two immediate issues in the compilation of crime statistics: the *definition* of an act as criminal and the *detection* of that act by the police and members of the public.

While the idea of 'definition' may seem non-problematic, it is important to remember that what is criminal in one society may not be in another. As with the discussion on social problems in Chapter 3, the idea of what is criminal changes in societies with history, culture and the power that particular groups have to frame social definitions. In other words, the idea of a 'criminal' is not a static definition, but changes with time: it is a *diachronic* not *synchronic* concept.

The issue of detection is also problematic. The decision to report a crime by a member of the public will depend on the place where it is perpetrated, the identity of the perpetrator and whether it is thought to be an appropriate matter for the police (Mayhew, Elliott and Dowds 1989). We are often faced in the media with the spectre of the 'anonymous attacker' on our streets. Of course, this occurs. However, it is not necessarily the public arena where women, for instance, are most threatened:

> While initial concerns about sexual danger focused on the malevolence of faceless men, familiar and familial men in women's lives — intimates, acquaintances, authorities and service providers, pose the greatest threat to women's physical and sexual safety.
>
> (Stanko 1990: 175)

Therefore, will a woman who is the victim of domestic violence perpetrated by her husband or partner necessarily report it to the police? Studies have shown that women tend to conceal such experiences from the police and social researchers (Stanko 1990). The detection of the crime of domestic violence then also depends upon the possibility of the victim reporting it without fear of repercussion – physical, emotional or material. In addition, it also depends upon police practices and their willingness to see such an incident as a legitimate part of their duties. As Jill Radford (1990) concludes from her research on violence against women:

> routine harassment and assault, such as being followed, flashed at or verbally abused are such regular experiences for women and so readily dismissed as 'trivial' or discounted on the grounds that 'nothing actually happened' that few women even consider them as worth reporting to the police. Yet, it is clear from the accounts we heard that these attacks are as much a form of terrorism as those acknowledged by the patriarchy as 'criminal'.
>
> (Radford 1990: 35)

Although very different in form, crimes at work are often not reported for fear of losing jobs, or companies not wishing to attract adverse publicity or simply that there is a lack of confidence in the capabilities of official agencies to tackle the crime effectively (Croall 1992). For these reasons, crime statistics reflect so-called street crimes which are visible, rather than white-collar and domestic crimes which are difficult to detect and take place within the conventional working environment or domestic spheres.

Matters of detection, definition and police practices have now affected the production of crime statistics. In turning our attention to these issues, we have examined the initial process through which a crime statistic is produced. The compilation of official statistics on crime are now dependent upon two criteria which directly influence their validity and reliability. First, a set of *discretionary procedures*, for example, the decision of individuals to report an incident to the police and the decision of police officers to record an incident and take the matter seriously. Second, *institutional practices*, which would include the policies of the police force and the government in tackling certain offences. In practice, these two are very difficult to separate or may be inseparable. Thus, what a police officer decides to do will depend not only on the circumstances of the incident, but also on the organizational policies which they are instructed to follow and the culture of the police organization itself.

We are beginning to see that 'criminal facts' do not simply speak for themselves, but may tell us more about organizational practices and power relations within society. If an incident occurs where the police are faced with a case of violence in the home and their organizational or discretionary definitions of domestic violence are not capable of categorizing this, we cannot then say it did not happen! In addition, even if the police do act in such circumstances, the courts may then categorize such incidents as 'trivial' in comparison to other crimes – despite the severity of the offence (Edwards 1990). Quite simply, if such a crime is not defined in a way which enters the statistics then, officially at least, it did not occur! For these reasons, official statistics on crime are criticized by researchers for revealing little about violence against women in particular (Kelly and Radford 1987) and more generally, for their sexist nature (Oakley and Oakley 1979).

Officially, the procedure and ideas through which an act becomes a crime statistic looks like the stages shown in Table 2.

Table 2   The stages in the process of compiling official statistics – the official version

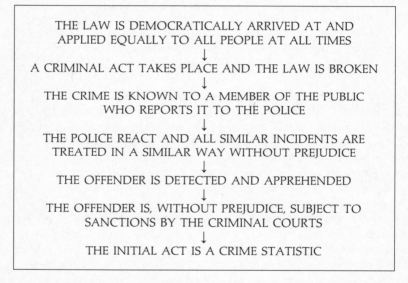

THE LAW IS DEMOCRATICALLY ARRIVED AT AND
APPLIED EQUALLY TO ALL PEOPLE AT ALL TIMES
↓
A CRIMINAL ACT TAKES PLACE AND THE LAW IS BROKEN
↓
THE CRIME IS KNOWN TO A MEMBER OF THE PUBLIC
WHO REPORTS IT TO THE POLICE
↓
THE POLICE REACT AND ALL SIMILAR INCIDENTS ARE
TREATED IN A SIMILAR WAY WITHOUT PREJUDICE
↓
THE OFFENDER IS DETECTED AND APPREHENDED
↓
THE OFFENDER IS, WITHOUT PREJUDICE, SUBJECT TO
SANCTIONS BY THE CRIMINAL COURTS
↓
THE INITIAL ACT IS A CRIME STATISTIC

If we move away from the formal definition in Table 2 to one which reflects the situation we have described so far, we end up not with 'facts' about crime, but the result of a series of decisions and practices which do not produce either a valid or reliable outcome. The diagram then becomes more like Table 3.

It appears that we cannot assume that the law applies equally to all incidents as this depends upon the initial detection of the act and the way in which the matter is dealt with by the police. Holding aside the question as to whether the law is biased in the first instance, it was noted that this will depend on whether the incident is reported and what action is taken as a result. From surveys conducted by interviewing a random sample of the general public, estimates show that only 36 per cent, or just under four out of every ten crimes committed on a daily basis are reported to the police (Hough and Mayhew 1983; Mayhew, Elliott and Dowds 1989). Thus, according to these

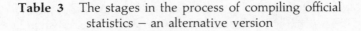

Table 3   The stages in the process of compiling official
statistics — an alternative version

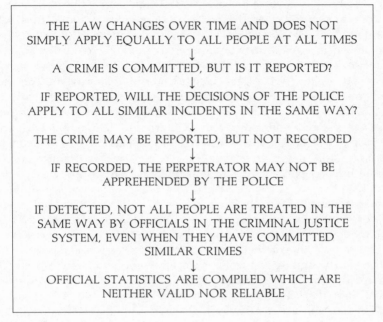

THE LAW CHANGES OVER TIME AND DOES NOT
SIMPLY APPLY EQUALLY TO ALL PEOPLE AT ALL TIMES
↓
A CRIME IS COMMITTED, BUT IS IT REPORTED?
↓
IF REPORTED, WILL THE DECISIONS OF THE POLICE
APPLY TO ALL SIMILAR INCIDENTS IN THE SAME WAY?
↓
THE CRIME MAY BE REPORTED, BUT NOT RECORDED
↓
IF RECORDED, THE PERPETRATOR MAY NOT BE
APPREHENDED BY THE POLICE
↓
IF DETECTED, NOT ALL PEOPLE ARE TREATED IN THE
SAME WAY BY OFFICIALS IN THE CRIMINAL JUSTICE
SYSTEM, EVEN WHEN THEY HAVE COMMITTED
SIMILAR CRIMES
↓
OFFICIAL STATISTICS ARE COMPILED WHICH ARE
NEITHER VALID NOR RELIABLE

estimates, six in every ten crimes committed never even reach the attention of
the police as gatekeepers of official crime statistics.

The key points in the alternative process as constructed in Table 3 are
interpretation and *discretion*. Between the construction of the law, someone
breaking that law and being sanctioned for the original act, there stands the
interpretation of the victim, police and other officials in the criminal justice
system. Will all officials act in a similar way so that we can say that they are both
valid (a true picture) and reliable (always recorded in the same way)? If different
people record the same incident in different ways and people are treated
differently for the same crime, then how can the statistics be valid? As we have
seen, the decision to report a crime in the first instance, the decision to pursue a
particular case and how its outcome will be determined are not neutral products
applying to all people at all times. As a final illustration for the purposes of
clarifying these issues, I shall illustrate this alternative scenario by considering
the link between crime statistics and race.

Afro-Caribbean groups form, approximately, 1.2 per cent of the total
population. In the prison population as a whole, they form nearly 10 per cent
(Home Office 1991). In other words, many more people from this group end up
in jails in comparison with their percentage in the general population. An
immediate conclusion from these official statistics seems to indicate that black

people are more criminal than white people. After all, the statistics certainly seem to demonstrate this because of the number of black people in prison. However, let us look at the criminal justice process to see if this is an 'objective' indicator of criminality, or the result of discretionary and discriminatory decisions.

We start again with the decision to report a crime. The police are reliant upon the general population to report crimes to them. Yet evidence shows that if an assailant is thought to be black, white people are more likely to report an offence to the police than if the same offence were committed by a white person (Carr-Hill and Drew 1988). Further, when it comes to the police detecting crime themselves, research conducted at two London police stations found that young black males, aged 16 to 24, were ten times more likely to be stopped by the police under stop and search powers (Willis 1983). Further, even if arrested for the same offence, white juveniles are significantly more likely to receive a caution than their black counterparts (Crow 1987). If then processed through the criminal courts, black people are also liable to be dealt with in a different way by the courts (Shallice and Gordon 1990). In addition, even when they have committed the same offence, evidence also suggests that black people are sent to prison more often than their white counterparts (Voakes and Fowler 1989).

What exactly is going on here? Is it a neutral process of reporting, detecting and processing criminals regardless of their race, or a discriminatory system? Research into the actual process of criminal justice appears to show that statistics which link race and crime are not neutral, but the product of a series of discriminatory decisions. It is for these reasons that so many black people end up in prisons. The creation of racial stereotypes within the criminal justice system has an indirect impact on attitudes and actions which, in turn, construct the crime statistics.

We have seen that criminal statistics do not simply reflect the number and type of incidents of crime committed. From the decision to report a crime, through the police decision to pursue an investigation, to the courts' decision to sanction an offender – if they are caught – a number of different practices leads to a variable outcome. For these reasons, we should treat official statistics on crime with considerable caution. Nevertheless, as we shall see in the next section, there still exists a debate on the use of official statistics for social research.

Official statistics: the debates

We have considered the means by which one of the most contentious of official statistics are compiled. However, in order to enable the reader to consider the issues surrounding their use, it is important to bear in mind two points. First, what *type* of official statistics are we talking about? Second, what is the *aim* of the research which is either compiling or examining these statistics? The type of official statistics will vary not only in their accuracy – statistics of birth rates compared, for example, with crime statistics – but also the way in which they are compiled. Thus, these considerations will affect our judgements about their use for analysis. Further, what are the statistics being used for? You may wish to examine statistics on crime as an indicator of the incidence of drug-taking. On the other hand, perhaps the police are concentrating on drug-taking and while this will mean an increase in the statistics, you decide not to examine the accuracy of the statistics themselves, but use them as an indicator of police practices. The aim of this project would be very different from one wishing to 'objectively' discover the incidence of drug-use in the population. Having made these points, attention will now be turned to the debate between schools of thought on official statistics.

There are, broadly, three schools of thought on official statistics. First, the *realist* school of thought, second, the *institutionalist* school of thought, and finally, the *radical* school of thought. What do these three terms mean? The realists (not to be confused with the school of thought covered in Chapter 1) consider official statistics to be objective indicators of the phenomena to which they refer. As a result, they draw their inspiration from positivism. The institutionalists, on the other hand, reject the idea that official statistics are objective. Instead, they consider official statistics neither valid nor reliable. For the institutionalists, official statistics tell us more about an organization's behaviour or the discretionary actions of individuals. In the above example on drug use, the institutionalists would argue that drug statistics which are compiled by the police tell us more about that organization's priorities than they do about the amount of drugs which the population are taking at any one time. This is why people refer to the 'iceberg phenomenon' when it comes to crime statistics: all we ever see is the tip of the iceberg and most crime is out of sight and undetected. This school of thought therefore parallels idealism as discussed in Chapter 1.

Finally, there is the radical perspective. While agreeing with the institutionalist that such statistics represent an organization's priorities or are the product of discretionary practices, they would locate these within a wider theory of the dynamics and structure of society. For instance, the government compiles social statistics on the health and income of the nation in order to regulate the population (Foucault 1980; Squires 1990). Alternatively, the police concentrate on and process more working-class crime because this group are relatively less powerful and their crimes more visible compared to middle-class groups (Hall et al 1978). What does this mean in practice? Let us take the example of child abuse.

Who are the people who sexually abuse children? The way such people are typified to us are through the newspapers, television and other agencies who have ready access to the media. So what is our *typical* offender? They hang around in old raincoats near children's playgrounds and school playing fields; they are isolated individuals who are inadequate in some way, but whose inadequacies constitute a danger to children. The police, in their turn, police public areas, not the private homes of individuals (the feminist criticism of the public/private dichotomy). They seek those individuals who may fit this stereotype and act on it by using grounds of 'reasonable suspicion'. Some individuals are apprehended who reflect the stereotype and are then added to the statistics. It appears that the 'truth' of the stereotype is established. However, as one writer on child abuse has noted:

> Whilst the popular press readily endorses the view that the child-molester is society's most hated criminal who deserves and receives the full rigour of the law, the reality is far less straightforward. The closer to home the abuse, the more ambivalent the legal and indeed the popular response, and the more the inadequacies of the criminal process become apparent.
>
> (Viinikka 1989: 132)

The compilation of such statistics is then said to reflect the notion of an ideal family and that 'every man's home is his castle'. The more private and invisible from agents of policing (including social services), the less the chance of detection of child abuse. Indeed, evidence suggests that such abuse is far more widespread than the statistics would have us believe (Driver 1989). Most child abuse takes place in families and is often not detected. It may not be the stranger in the old raincoat at the local park who constitutes a danger to children: the abuser is often a close relative, friend or acquaintance of the family. It is argued by critics of official statistics that they help to generate such myths by reflecting power relations and ideologies within society — in this case the 'familial' ideology of the harmonious and secure institution of the family. Of course, this is not to suggest that an abuser may not be a 'stranger', simply that official definitions distort the idea of those who are mostly responsible for this offence.

You will have noticed that I earlier quoted a statistic saying that under four out of ten crimes committed are reported to the police. If the official statistics are so inadequate, how did I know this? In 1981, 1983 and 1987 (Hough and Mayhew 1983; 1985; Mayhew, Elliott and Dowds 1989) the Home Office undertook a random survey of 11,000 people in England and Wales (5,000 in Scotland). By asking people questions about their experiences of crime, a picture was formed of the number of crimes committed in England and Wales, but which were not reported to the police for various reasons. The realist would argue that the problems in official statistics on crime can be adequately compensated by using such data as generated by the Home Office. It is not, therefore, a problem of power or discretion in the formulation of official statistics, but one of technical competence. We simply need to employ more accurate methods in order to account, objectively, for certain patterns of behaviour in society.

The above noted British Crime Survey (BCS) still has its limitations. For instance, if we go back to our example and consider domestic violence: if a woman is interviewed with a male partner present, will she admit to being a victim of domestic violence when the perpetrator is perhaps sitting next to her? On the other hand, it is argued to correct for weaknesses in official police statistics. It also allows researchers to note that over 98 per cent of car thefts are reported to the police (Hough and Mayhew 1985). They could then use official records upon which to base a sample of people to interview, bearing in mind this high rate of reporting (May 1986). However, if researchers wished to conduct a study on the incidence of burglary, they would omit 60 per cent of burglaries that take place in England and Wales if they simply relied upon police statistics (Mayhew, Elliott and Dowds 1989). Thus, realists would argue that official statistics do have their uses.

While those who contributed to the radical volume edited by Irvine, Miles and Evans (1979) regard official statistics as in need of 'demolition' and 'demystification', institutionalists concentrate on the social practices through which they are constructed. Studies adopting this perspective include Max Atkinson's (1978) on the social organization of suicide; Aaron Cicourel's (1976) work on juvenile justice and Gilbert Smith's (1977) work on the exercise of professional discretion in Scottish Children's Panels. Atkinson's work is particularly interesting because it also charts his change of research focus from the influence of Durkheim's (1952) positivistic approach on the subject of suicide, to a research focus influenced by the work of Garfinkel (1967).

This approach abandons the idea that suicide statistics represent facts about a certain type of behaviour (the realist position). Additionally, they are not simply regarded as indicative of wider power relations and structures in society (the radical position). Instead, they examine statistics as an 'accomplishment'. In Atkinson's study, he focuses on the methods by which coroners formulate judgements and categorize deaths as suicide. This is said not to assume that there is a 'shared definition' which coroners operate upon which, as noted in the discussion on the validity and reliability of crime statistics, is problematic. As soon as the idea that officials who make such judgements do not simply share definitions is abandoned, the aim of the research changes:

> The idea that there are or may be many different definitions and different types of definitions of suicide leads immediately to a bewilderingly complex situation from the point of view of doing empirical research into the subject.
> (Atkinson 1978: 87)

Instead of assuming that coroners use one definition, he investigated the factors which surrounded the circumstances of the death and led coroners to judge it as suicide: for example, suicide notes, previous threats of suicide, the mode, location and circumstances of the death and the biography of the deceased. The idea of a shared definition was abandoned in favour of an examination of the methods that coroners used in categorizing sudden death. Thus, we have now moved away from facts, to the process of their construction. In the words of John Heritage, the focus moves to

> what counts as 'reasonable fact' in a casual conversation, in a courtroom, a scientific laboratory, a news interview, a police interrogation, a medical consultation or a social security office? What is the nature of the social organization within which these facts find support? To what vicissitudes, exigencies and considerations are the formulation of these facts responsive?
>
> (Heritage 1984: 178)

An examination of the process, not the product, is the institutionalist approach to official statistics. Therefore, the methods that officials who are responsible for their compilation employ, become the topics of research and theorizing. Unlike the radical approach, the analysis does not fit within a more general theory of social and political organization: for example, a Marxist approach to the processing of the working classes by the criminal justice system as symptomatic of wider capitalist relations (Taylor, Walton and Young 1973).

Summary

Increasingly, social research is dominated by the government and its agencies (Bulmer 1986b). While social researchers do enjoy some latitude in the design and execution of such research, there has been increasing concern over the government's control of official information. The production of accurate information was questioned during 1989 by, among others, the former head of the Government Statistical Service and president of the Royal Statistical Society. In particular, the effect is to render such statistics increasingly invalid for the purposes of social policy research:

> in the absence of official enquiries and accurate statistics, it is difficult to judge the severity of the hardship caused to the poorer members of society by the social policies of the 1980s. Yet this is a crucial issue in judging the success of those policies.
>
> (Jones 1992: 204)

In contrast, Martin Bulmer (1984c) notes that while official statistics are problematic, they are still useful for research purposes. Contrary to the critics, he argues that official statistics produce interesting findings on contemporary society which, despite their shortcomings, have been used by radical and realist researchers alike, including Karl Marx. He also notes that the conceptual issues facing those who compile official statistics are not dissimilar to those faced by social researchers in general and while there may be differences in theoretical orientation between the two, they still provide useful empirical data. Finally, he notes, statisticians go to considerable lengths to reduce error:

British data derived from birth and death registration, for instance, is probably among the highest-quality data currently available.

(Bulmer 1984c: 140)

According to Bulmer, if researchers are aware of how these errors occur, they can then correct for shortfalls. Indeed, while there is much concern regarding their accuracy and political manipulation, researchers at the Unemployment Unit based in London still calculate the unemployment rate based on pre-1982 definitions in order to allow for accurate comparisons (the definition of unemployment has been altered over twenty times since 1980). This enables them to consider how successful government policies have been in reducing unemployment, rather than the government's success in altering the statistics. In addition, statisticians have used official data to show how they are systematically biased in one way or another (Bhat, Carr-Hill and Ohri 1988).

Of course, it is still possible to 'lie with statistics' (Huff 1981). Due to their susceptibility to such manipulation, the debate continues. The realist looks for more accurate techniques for generating such information; the radical criticizes and uses such information as indicative of wider power inequalities in society and the institutionalists concentrate on the process of their production for this is the only meaningful focus of inquiry.

Yet it may also be noted that official statistics do not simply exist independently of the actions of those who compile them. To return to Giddens' idea of the 'double hermeneutic' discussed in Chapter 2, they also feed back into everyday practices. Coroners, for example, construct the crime statistics, but they may well be guided by the ideas of social scientists on the causes of suicide: 'it would not be at all unusual to find a coroner who had read Durkheim' (Giddens 1990: 42). In this reflexive project, it is not simply the process (the institutionalists) or the product (the realists) which is part of the research focus, but the process affects the product and vice versa. While official statistics are formulated by the actions of individuals within organizational settings and by governmental policies, they also generate a view of the world which feeds back into those practices. A circle is then formed, rather than the straight line of examining process, or of uncritically using the final product.

As described in the first section of this chapter, official statistics are mainly based upon the use of surveys which are a common method of social research. As a main aim of this book is to examine the place and use of particular methods and the process through which they are constructed and then analysed, Chapter 5 is devoted to the use and design of questionnaires.

CHAPTER 4: QUESTIONS FOR YOUR REFLECTION

1   Consider the types of official statistics which are generated by the state and its agencies. What do you think they are used for?

2   In what ways are criminal statistics both similar to and different from other forms of official statistics?

3   Having considered the above arguments on the use and production of official statistics, would you consider yourself a realist, institutionalist, radical or none of these?

4   What is your opinion on the future use of social research by the government and its place in the production of official statistics?

5

The use and design of questionnaires

The image of a person standing in a crowded shopping centre with a clipboard, stopping people, asking them questions and then ticking boxes, is a common one. While this is usually market-based research, the use of questionnaires is also a central part of social research as they provide a rapid and relatively inexpensive way of discovering the characteristics and beliefs of the population at large. Towards these ends, the design of questionnaires is pivotal, for the quality of the data produced depends upon their design. Once designed and administered, the questionnaire then has to be analysed: this needs to be considered during the design stage. The second and third sections of this chapter therefore consider the design and analysis of questionnaires. The chapter is concluded by a discussion of the criticisms of the 'survey method'.

The place of questionnaires in social research

The purpose of questionnaires is to measure some characteristics or opinion of its respondents. Depending upon its aims, the procedures it adopts and the number of people who are interviewed, generalization can then take place from the sample of people interviewed to the population as a whole. A survey may therefore be defined as

> A method of gathering information from a number of individuals, a 'sample', in order to learn something about the larger population from which the sample is drawn. Thus, a sample of voters is surveyed in advance of an election to determine how the public perceived the candidates and the issues. A manufacturer makes a survey of the potential market before introducing a new product.
>
> (Ferber et al 1980: 3)

In order to justify this procedure, the sample is based upon statistical probability theory. By employing such techniques, researchers are able to ascertain the extent to which the sample they have interviewed is representative of the wider population.

There are parallels between the ideas which underlie questionnaires and positivism, in particular, the idea of causality. Moving away from the example of molecules in a test tube as discussed in Chapter 1, the aim of the questionnaire would be to examine how, for example, the possession of certain characteristics (age, sex, race, class etc) or reactions to particular conditions cause changes in attitudes and behaviour. Thus, take the statement 'students are absent from classes when it rains':

> This can be made into a causal theory, by stating the processes or mechanisms whereby rain causes students to miss classes: some decide not to come because they do not want to get wet; the rain makes traffic bad so others are late; some of them do not wake up on time when the sun is not shining, and so on.
>
> (Hage and Meeker 1988: 35)

Similarly, it is commonly believed that as people become older, they become more conservative in their outlook. In this instance, a questionnaire would be devised which measured a 'conservative orientation' to life and to what extent such attitudes were caused by the different ages of the respondents.

The parallels with positivism are also evident in the use of theoretical ideas which find their outlet in the survey questions. If the results of replies to the questions confirm the theory, then confidence in its explanatory potential is enhanced. On the other hand, if the results do not support the theory, then it is subject to falsification. There is also an empiricist preoccupation in the attention to details of measurement of attitudes and population characteristics. Further, a concern over the possibility of the researchers' values entering the research, it is argued, may be checked through the means of *replicability*:

> Replication can provide a means of checking the extent to which findings are applicable to other contexts. In addition, it is often seen as a means of checking the biases of the investigator.
>
> (Bryman 1988a: 37)

Another researcher could then employ the same questionnaire with a comparable sample to check upon its possible biases. In order to achieve this aim and that of accurate measurement, attention is turned to the concept of *standardization*.

Standardization refers to the conditions under which a questionnaire is administered and this covers the whole process of exactly specifying the questions to be asked, the manner of asking them, how the replies are to be scored etc. A standardized interview is one that has been constructed in this rigorous way, has been tried out, and is ready for use in the population to be studied.

(McMiller and Wilson 1984)

The theory is that if all respondents are asked the same questions in the same manner and if they express a difference in opinion in reply to those questions, these variations result from a 'true' difference of opinion, rather than as a result of how the question was asked or the context of the interview. Thus questionnaires concentrate upon the replies of respondents within a *structured* interviewing situation (see also Chapter 6). Their responses and characteristics are then quantified and aggregated with others in the survey sample, in order to examine patterns or relationships between them by employing the techniques of statistical analysis.

The place of the questionnaire in social research is characterized by several themes. First, the construction of questions which reflect theoretical propositions. Second, analysis through the means of employing statistical techniques often imported directly from natural sciences. Third, an ability to generalize from a sample of the population, to the population as a whole. Fourth, causality as an explanation of human behaviour: for example, the variation of a person's conservative orientation to social life with their increasing age (age causes an increase in conservative outlook). Fifth, the discovery of 'objective' indices of population characteristics and beliefs through the means of a meticulous attention to the detail of accurate measurement facilitated by standardization. Sixth, the ability to replicate the findings of questionnaires to check for bias, and finally, a focus on the replies of individual respondents. However, although individuals are interviewed in isolation from others, the focus of research may not be individuals *per se*, but more the statistical profiles or patterns of attitudes and characteristics of a given population. To draw conclusions about the exact attitudes of a particular individual within a sample, from methods which are designed to uncover the 'patterns' of attitudes among the sample may not, therefore, be a legitimate exercise. This is sometimes referred to as the *ecological fallacy*.

Having established the basis and aims of questionnaires in social research, I now turn to the types of surveys which are used and the different methods of sampling for determining the questionnaire population.

Survey types

Steven Ackroyd and John Hughes (1983) characterize surveys under four headings: factual, attitudinal, social psychological and explanatory. First, factual surveys were one of the earliest types to be used systematically in this country. They aimed to gain information from individuals concerning their material situation rather than attitudes or opinions as such. The cost of these surveys is an important consideration: to interview everyone in a population would be prohibitively expensive. For this reason, the 'Census' takes place only once every ten years and is not a sample, but a total *enumeration* of the population.

The second type of survey moved away from an interest in the material conditions of the population, towards the use of surveys for gaining data on attitudes: for example, what people think about life in general and events in particular. This constituted a shift away from the so-called 'hard data' basis of factual surveys. The idea of public opinion is perhaps the key to this type of survey. For countries with democratic aspirations, it is important that they gauge the beliefs of their citizens. Often a policy is justified by 'what the public demands'. However, how do we know what the public demands? Attitude surveys can fulfil the function of providing this information.

Political opinion polls also fall into this category. These attempt to *predict* how people will vote. Therefore, there is an assumed correspondence between what people say they will do and what they will actually do. (Will someone who says she is going to vote Liberal Democrat actually do so on the day?) On *average*, the polls are said to be fairly accurate. This does not suggest that one individual poll is correct, but that if you calculate the average results of all the polls, they will predict the outcome. However, the opinion polls did not predict the outcome of the 1992 General Election and, at the time of writing, pollsters are still pondering on the reasons for this. Similarly, attempts at accurate measurement of opinions do not address the argument that the polls themselves do not simply reflect, but also structure public opinion (Marsh 1979).

The results of using attitude surveys began to develop other interests among researchers, in particular, the relationship between attitudes and behaviour. In this sense, both the social psychological and explanatory surveys are more theoretically orientated. The measurement of attitudes became the subject of many an academic paper. The question is exactly how do you measure attitudes? Attention is also focused on the relationship between attitudes and behaviour: quite simply, does the possession of a certain attitude necessarily mean a person will then behave in a particular way? However, this change in focus was not so much an interest in attitudes themselves, but in attitudes as one characteristic of the 'personality' of an individual. By building up a profile of personality types – using attitude questions among other techniques – it is believed possible to explain a person's behaviour. These developments within social psychology also led to a movement away from an interest in general statistical profiles of the population – as in factual and attitude surveys – to a concern with small group behaviour.

To some extent all surveys are explanatory. They ask questions about, say, voting behaviour and seek to explain how people's attitudes or intentions are linked to their background or other *explanatory variable*. However, explanatory surveys are specifically designed to test hypotheses which are derived from theories: for example, Durkheim's (1952) idea that suicide is inversely related to social integration. To achieve this, there is an extensive use of statistical procedures.

Changes have taken place in the post-war period towards more 'subjective' indicators in questionnaires: for example, the scale of people's responses to particular consumer goods and the amount of market research now conducted is enormous. These use methods of explanation which locate people within particular groups and see if there are any similarities within groups along such dimensions as class, gender, type of housing, etc. The 'target groups' for a particular advertising campaign or a survey of 'market viability' can then be ascertained using such methods.

Sampling the population

The first question is why use sampling in the first place? Why not ask the whole population? The answer lies in sampling being a compromise between technical efficiency and time and resources. Sampling

> Provides a mechanism whereby we can make an estimate of a population characteristic and get, based on probability theory, a numerical measure of how good that estimate is.
>
> (Sprent 1988: 188)

Moser and Kalton (1983) list several advantages to this method. First, in contrast to a complete enumeration of the population, the data are cheaper to collect by this method. Second, it requires fewer people to collect and analyse the data. Third, it saves time as a sample is quicker to analyse and process. Fourth, it often permits a higher level of accuracy as the sample size allows a check on the accuracy of the design and administration of the questionnaire, while a small number of interviewing staff permits the researcher to train the interviewers and check on their accuracy in conducting interviews. Finally, 'fewer cases make it possible to collect and deal with more elaborate information from each' (Moser and Kalton 1983: 57).

For the purpose of sampling validity, it is necessary to use a method of randomly selecting a sample in order to make generalizations to the population at large. Two points require clarification at this stage:

> when we sample it is not necessarily people who are being sampled. We can just as legitimately sample other units of analysis such as organizations, schools, local authorities and so on. Second, by 'population' is meant a discrete group of units of analysis and not just populations in the conventional sense.
>
> (Bryman and Cramer 1990: 98)

Thus 'units of analysis' do not simple mean people, but could include firms of lawyers, particular types of businesses, etc, and the population could be those businesses themselves or the people within them.

Of those methods which employ this idea, *simple random sampling* is the easiest to understand: each element (be they a person or household, for example) in the population must have an equal chance of being selected for the sample. For this purpose, a *sampling frame* is used. This might be a list of employees in a factory or, if we are interested in households, the electoral register. Alternatively, if you wanted a sample of 2,000 households, you could take all 2,000, giving each a number, put them all in a hat and randomly draw out the number you wished to interview. However, not only is this a tedious method, but also the precision of this is dependent upon how accurate the sampling frame is in the first place. The electoral register, for example, omits certain groups in the populations as well those who have not registered, or who have just moved in or out of the district. Additionally, your final sample may live miles apart, increasing the cost of your research.

As strict simple random sampling is not usually a practical method upon which to base research, there are other methods used. These must fulfil two criteria. First, the researcher or interviewers must have no choice in whom they interview, and second, there is a systematic procedure involved in the selection of the units of analysis which must be random.

Systematic sampling takes place when the researcher knows the number in the population and then makes a decision to select every *n*th case. How is this done? The total number in the population is divided by the required sample size. The result of this calculation gives you the *sampling interval*. If the interval is five (for example, there are 1,000 people in the population and a sample size of 200 is required) then you randomly select one of the first five and so on, up to a sample of 200 people. The starting-point must itself be random which is assisted by using what is known as a table of random numbers.

This method provides an approximation of simple random sampling. However, the researcher has to be aware of two potential problems. First, the individuals in the sampling frame may be ordered in some way and reflect a trend: for example, a factory orders employees by their income. The sample could then be systematically biased as a result. Second, the sampling interval might correspond to a particular characteristic in the population. If you are sampling every eighth house and it turns out that they are all at the end of a street and you wish to interview people about their neighbours, this could be problematic. Nevertheless, as Blalock notes (1984: 559), both of these are rare occurrences in social research.

In simple random sampling, it is possible to over-represent one category, for example, selecting more men than women in the sample. To correct for this you could identify a group by certain characteristics (age, ethnicity, gender etc) and then draw a sample from each group. This is called *stratified random sampling* and is particularly useful if the aim is to compare groups. This then reduces any variation between the groups, although there can still be variation within the groups among other characteristics.

Cluster or multi-stage sampling is a useful procedure when the population you wish to sample is geographically dispersed. First, you select clusters and then sub-sample within the clusters. Let us take the example of a random sample of police officers. The spread of officers in numerous police stations is problematic in terms of the time and resources at your disposal. In other words, there is too much spread in the population. Therefore, you undertake a two-stage process. First, you select the stations, and second, the officers. If you require a sample of 2,000 officers, this would vary between five officers in each of 400 stations to 1,000 stations each with two officers. In terms of precision and cost, this would vary between low precision and low cost to high precision with a high cost. Your optimum, therefore, would be 40 stations with 50 officers in each or 50 stations with 40 officers in each. It is worth remembering that if you select a small number of stations, you might miss out certain types, for example, those in particular inner city or rural areas.

Random sampling is an expensive method of conducting research and based upon statistical theory whose mathematical proof is beyond the aim of this book (for an introduction see Jolliffe 1974; Rowntree 1981; Gwilliam 1988; more advanced readers are referred to Blalock 1984; Freedman et al 1991). A quicker method which is widely used by market researchers, as well as social researchers, is known as *quota sampling*. This is not strictly a random, but a *non-probability* or *purposive* sampling method.

Quota sampling attempts to approximate or represent the population characteristics by dividing the sample along dimensions of, say, race, class, housing, gender, disability etc. Their distribution in the population is ascertained by using the Census data and the interviewers are then issued with a *quota target* which approximates these distributions. Hence, when you see people with clipboards in the street (and everyone is avoiding them!) and they approach some people, but not others, they are doing so on the basis of quotas. However, herein lies one problem. The interviewer may interview only those who appear to be approachable or who are not in a hurry. While from their point of view this is understandable, such considerations may bias the results.

In considering which method to use and how many to sample, the researcher can be left in something of a dilemma. Alan Bryman and Duncan Cramer (1990) usefully summarize the points that researchers should consider. First, quite simply, it will depend upon the time and resources at your disposal. Second, the larger the sample size, the more accurate the sample will be. Third, non-response should be considered in selecting a sample size. If, for example, you require a final sample size of 100 in a mail questionnaire (see below), it may well be advisable to mail out 250 questionnaires. Fourth, social researchers, although aware of the advantages of random or probability sampling, often do not use such techniques and resort to samples which are broadly representative (Bryman and Cramer 1990: 103–4).

The process of questionnaire construction

Moving away from the place of questionnaires in social research and methods of sampling, this section looks at the practical ways in which a questionnaire is constructed. This will depend upon the type of questionnaire being used. There are three types: the mail or *self-completion* questionnaires; the *telephone* survey and the *face-to-face* interview schedule. The choice of which to use will depend on the aim of the research and the resources available.

Questionnaire types

The mail or self-completion questionnaire offers a relatively cheap method of data collection over the personal interview. As their name implies, they are intended for the respondent to fill out themselves. As a result, once the questionnaire is sent out after the pilot work (see below) the researcher has little control over the completion of the survey. A covering letter explaining the purpose of the questionnaire stressing the need for co-operation and the anonymity of replies is therefore required. At the same time, they provide people with a medium for the anonymous expression of beliefs: for example, in researching an organization in times of rapid change where feelings ran high, this method provided an outlet for the anonymous expression of strongly held views (May 1991). That said, unless people have an incentive, either through an interest in the subject which the survey is covering or some other, then response rates will be low and the figure of 40 per cent, or four out of every ten people sent a questionnaire, is not uncommon.

Interest in the survey will affect the response rate and this will depend on the *target population*. The return rates of a random sample of the general population might well be lower than a specific targeting of people with similar interests. It is possible that only some groups will reply and not others. The replies might then be systematically biased towards one part of the population. For instance, in one health survey, people appeared more healthy than was generally thought the case. An examination of replies found that those in more deprived areas had a low response rate. As there is a relationship between health and income, this biased the results showing a more healthy population than was actually the case (Mawby 1991). While this bias may be checked against the Census data, as this occurs only once every ten years, the data may be up to nine years out of date.

Once the questionnaire is sent to people's addresses or distributed for self-completion, the researcher then has no understanding of the considerations which people make in answering a question. The layout, instructions and questions must therefore be clear and unambiguous. That said, mail questionnaires are cheap to administer, but you need to send reminders to people to raise response rates. Stamped addressed envelopes are required and reminders may be sent two and four weeks after posting the initial questionnaire:

A rule of thumb is that 300 to 400 envelopes and stamps and 160 questionnaires may be needed for every 100 people in the sample (200 envelopes – outward and return – being used in the first mail-out).

(Hoinville and Jowell et al 1987: 138)

We can now summarize the main strengths and weaknesses of mail questionnaires. First, they have a lower cost than face-to-face interviews. Second, if dealing with ethically or politically sensitive issues, their anonymity may be advantageous. Third, people can take their own time to fill in the questionnaire and consider their responses. Fourth, as interviews are not used this could lead to less bias which results from the way in which different interviewers ask the questions. Finally, it is possible to cover a wider geographical area at a lower cost. The disadvantages, on the other hand, include the need to keep questions relatively simple and straightforward as the researcher has no control over how people are interpreting the question once it has been mailed. Second, the possibility of probing beyond the answer that people give is absent. Third, there is no control over who answers the questionnaire; you may wish to target women in the household, but men fill it out instead. Fourth, the response rate may well be low and it is possible that you cannot check on the bias of the final sample.

Telephone surveys are a growing part of the researchers' methodological armoury. By the mid-1980s in the United States

telephone surveying had become commonplace, and in many instances it is the most preferred approach to surveying. It is a methodology that has achieved a respected status as a valid means of gathering information to aid effective decision making in both the public and private sectors. In fact, much more money is spent on telephone surveys by market researchers than by public opinion pollsters and academic researchers combined.

(Lavrakas 1987: 10)

At one time, this method was considered to be highly problematic due to its inbuilt bias. If you used a telephone directory (your sampling frame) several problems arise. First, people will, for various reasons, opt to be ex-directory. Second, in phoning someone you may get the wrong person or the right person at the wrong time, thus causing problems in response. Third, in Britain there is an inbuilt class and gender bias in telephone directories. It is likely that it will be the males in the household whose names will be in the phone book. Further, the distribution of phones between classes is disproportionate: Professional (98 per cent); Employer/Manager (97 per cent); Other Non-Manual (92 per cent); Skilled Manual (83 per cent) and Unskilled Manual (63 per cent) (source: Social Trends 1990). A random sample would not fully represent those in the skilled and unskilled manual bracket (the distributions are different in the USA). On the other hand, if the aim of the research is to target professional groups only, then biases may be of a different order: for example, along race and gender lines as particular groups of people are under-represented in this strata.

The advantages of telephone surveys, as with postal surveys, are that they are convenient and relatively cheap:

> Postal surveys and telephone interview surveys can both cost roughly half as much as surveys using personal interviews, but telephone surveys have the additional advantage of greater speed.
>
> (Hakim 1987: 59)

Further, response rates may be high as people might be less concerned about talking to someone on the phone, rather than opening a door to them. In addition, the monitoring of the work of telephone interviewers can be done from a central office where the dialling takes place. However, people may 'break-off' an interview more frequently, compared to a face-to-face situation, and the information may not be so detailed, for instance, the interviewer's ability to describe the environment of the interviewee in terms of their housing, area, life style, and so on.

Whether the researcher administers the questionnaire, or whether a team of researchers do, the theory is still one of standardization. However, in the face-to-face interview schedule the interviewer is also able, if required, to record the context of the interview and the non-verbal gestures of the respondent. As a result, unlike the other methods, there is a visual-interactional component between interviewer and interviewee. This has both advantages and disadvantages. As Fowler notes:

> Because of the central role they play in data collection, interviewers have a great deal of potential for influencing the quality of data they collect. The management of interviewers is a difficult task, particularly in personal interviewer studies. Furthermore, the role of the interviewer is a somewhat neglected topic in many survey texts.
>
> (Fowler 1988: 107)

From this, he considers three roles which the interviewer has to perform in the collection of data. First, to locate and secure the co-operation of the respondents, second, to motivate and guide the respondent through the questionnaire, and finally, to ask questions in a clear, standardized and concise way, to record the answers carefully in accordance with the survey instructions and maintain a rapport with the respondent (Fowler 1988: 107).

In comparison with the two other methods, this method yields a high response rate, at a high cost (depending on how many interviewers are used), with a higher control of the interview situation, but at a slower speed. The actual mechanics of this process will be elaborated upon in the next section noting that the design of the questionnaire will depend upon its aims, the audience to which it is directed and the amount of resources available for conducting the research.

Preliminary work and focusing the aim of the questionnaire

My purpose in this section is to draw the attention of the reader to the main points which are worth considering when designing a questionnaire and there are texts available whose sole focus is survey research and questionnaire design (Oppenheim 1973; Moser and Kalton 1983; Hoinville and Jowell et al 1987; Fowler 1988). That said, the following are particularly important given that design is so influential to the quality of the resultant data.

At this stage there are several points to bear in mind. First, the final questionnaire is designed only after the researchers have conducted the necessary reading of literature around the topic(s); second, its aims have been decided; third, the group to whom it will be administered chosen, and finally, pilot work has been undertaken. Basically, the questionnaire is an instrument for measuring the ideas which go into its design. For this reason, the questions not only reflect the survey's aims, but also must be understood by respondents in a clear and unambiguous way:

> A good questionnaire has to be designed specifically to suit the study's *aims and the nature of its respondents*. It needs to ... be clear, unambiguous and uniformly workable. Its design must minimize potential errors from respondents, interviewers and coders. And, since people's participation in surveys is voluntary, a questionnaire has to help in engaging their interest, encouraging their co-operation, and eliciting answers as close as possible to the truth.
>
> (Hoinville and Jowell et al 1987: 27, emphasis added)

Having decided that a questionnaire is the most suitable method for gathering data, researchers then need to ask themselves several questions in order to focus their inquiries. First, what is the aim of the questionnaire? Second, what types of information are required as a result? Third, who will form the sample and how will it be devised? Fourth, what type of questionnaire is most suitable, given the resources and time at your disposal as well as the aims of the research? Fifth, how will the questionnaire be analysed? Finally, when is the information required by and for what purpose?

In order to fulfil these criteria, it is helpful to concentrate upon the actual mechanics of construction, for the aim of the questionnaire will clearly depend upon the nature of the research, the researcher's interests, the reasons why it is being undertaken and who, if anyone, is sponsoring the research and with what purpose in mind. As a result, the earlier discussions on values and ethics and those on perspectives and social theory need to be borne in mind. In concentrating solely upon the techniques of design, the value, theoretical and ethical considerations which go into its production are easy to forget – even though they influence its outcome.

Designing questions

The most important part of the actual design of questions is to construct them unambiguously and to be clear in your own mind what the question is for, who it is to be answered by and how you intend them to interpret it. You might think that the meaning of a question is clear enough, but it does not follow that the people answering the question will agree with your interpretation. This is why it is essential to undertake preliminary reading around the topic and, if possible, conduct some initial fieldwork based either on interviews and/or observation work with the sample. This assists the researcher in understanding the concerns of the people who are being questioned and how they might interpret particular questions:

> The exploratory interviews and observation that often precede social surveys yield valuable information about the receptivity, frames of reference, and span of attention of respondents. Since a great part of the value of systematic pretesting resides in the gathering of such intelligence, it is justifiable to consider this aspect of pretesting under the rubric of qualitative fieldwork.
>
> (Sieber 1978: 365)

Even if initial fieldwork is possible, the questionnaire stills needs to be piloted on a subsample before it reaches the full sample. During this stage, after people have answered the questions, it is worth having a chat with them concerning their opinions on the order of the questions, the types of questions themselves and any difficulties they experienced in answering them. Following this, it is then possible to revise the layout, question wording and design to take account of any criticisms and problems. Piloting aims to see how the survey

> works and whether changes are necessary before the start of the full-scale study. The pretest provides a means of catching and solving unforeseen problems in the administration of the questionnaire, such as the phrasing and sequence of questions or its length. It may also indicate the need for additional questions of the elimination of others.
>
> (Kidder 1981: 162)

Questions also need to be asked which the target population population will not only understand, but also possess the knowledge to answer. Asking students, for example, about their experience of drug-taking during the Second World War is not likely to elicit a uniform response, for this question assumes that they would have lived during this period in history. Most, but not all answers, are likely to be blank. However, even if you interviewed those who lived through and remembered this period, you would also be presupposing that the sample were either aware of drug-taking or engaged in it themselves.

While this appears to be an extreme example, it is still possible to build in presuppositions in the design of questions which are less apparent, but which still have a direct effect upon the answer. Let us consider the types of questions you could ask.

Classification questions are the 'personal' section of the questionnaire and are often referred to as 'demographic' or 'face sheet' information such as age, income, housing, etc. The problem is that if you ask these questions at the beginning of the questionnaire, it may put people off. If you ask at the end after eliciting their opinions and the person then refuses to answer, this may jeopardize your chances of analysing the answers according to what are known as these *explanatory variables*: to return to an earlier example, age as an explanation for a conservative outlook on life. Quota samples use these questions at the beginning of the questionnaire, otherwise it may be a waste of time if the person is not in the quota group the interviewer wishes to target.

The use of classification questions needs a word of explanation to the respondents otherwise they may fail to see the need of them. You might need to stress how opinions need to be related to the kinds of people answering the questionnaire. For instance, you might be interviewing a student population and ask which course they are registered for. A general word of explanation for such questions not only adds to the chances of a good response, but also assists with the important aim of communicating the need for research and enhancing its participatory, rather than parasitic nature.

Most surveys concern themselves with either facts or opinions. With *factual questions*, as opposed to opinions, more latitude can be given to the interviewer to probe, explain and possibly even vary the question wording in a way which would bias an opinion question. These would be designed to elicit, for example, the newspapers which people read. However, while apparently easy to ask, without careful design, ambiguity can still arise. For instance, asking someone how many newspapers she has bought in the last week appears simple. However, you are not only relying on her memory, but also assuming she reads newspapers. You have also used the word 'bought'. Again, this appears simple, but according to the 'golden rule' of question design, is there a correspondence between the intention behind the question and the way in which the person will interpret it? As Oppenheim notes: 'Does this include buying for others? Does it include buying on account? Does it include things paid for by and bought on behalf of someone else?' (1973: 53). Good pilot work and an understanding of the 'frames of reference' of the sample can help correct such ambiguities.

With *opinion questions*, wording alternations can easily elicit different answers. According to the theory of standardization, each respondent must reply as a result of unambiguous questions and not as the result of poor question wording, the way in which the question is asked, or as a result of the context of an interview. On this latter point, administering a face-to-face questionnaire to a person in front of a group of friends may well elicit a different answer from when the person is interviewed alone. Unlike questions of fact, the interviewer can only repeat the question and not elaborate upon it as this would bias the answer.

There is also the decision to use *open* or *closed questions*. Open questions give respondents a greater freedom to answer the question because they answer in a way that suits their interpretation. The interviewer then records as much as possible of the answer, which is analysed after the interview. Closed questions, on the other hand, limit the number of possible answers to be given and therefore can be pre-coded so that each answer may be given a specific number for the purposes of analysis:

> The purpose of coding in surveys is to classify the answers to a question into meaningful categories, so as to bring out their essential patterns.
> (Moser and Kalton 1983: 414)

For instance, you have a question which has five possible answers; these would then be given a number from one to five (perhaps using 9 for a missing answer and 6 for a 'don't know' reply) and a column on the right-hand side of the page is used for recording the answer given (see the example under attitude scales, p. 80). Pre-coding of this nature makes the questionnaire much easier to analyse. However, in deciding to use such questions careful pilot work is required and the answers should fulfil two criteria: they should be not only *mutually exclusive* but also *exhaustive*. In other words, it should not be possible for someone's answer to fall into two of the categories used (exclusive), and all possible answers should be encompassed by the categories chosen (exhaustive): for example, if you are asking people about the type of housing they live in (house, flat, rented or owner-occupier, etc), the categories used should cover all possible replies from the sample and no reply should be able to be categorized by any more than one answer. The findings of a comparison between open and closed questions stressed the importance of this point:

> the failings of closed questions are more likely to be due to omissions of an important choice category (i.e., poor design) than to the use of the form in the first place.
> (Social and Community Planning Research 1981: 7)

In summary, the advantages of closed questions are that they are cheaper to use and analyse relative to open questions and they also permit comparability between people's answers. However, they also compartmentalize people into fixed replies (often considered an advantage) and they are problematic if people have not thought about the question which is asked. One report, comparing the two, suggests that open questions are a useful 'follow-up' to closed questions (eg 'you answered "X" earlier – could you tell me why you thought that?') and

> When situations are changing very quickly . . . open questions may prove the better form. Finally, as survey responses are increasingly used as a basis for

historical research, open responses have the value of enabling researchers to explore raw data and to devise new coding categories.

(Social and Community Planning Research 1981: 7)

Within question design *attitude scales* play an important role. They consist of a set of statements which the researcher has designed and the respondent is then asked to agree or disagree with the pre-coded answers. It is then possible to test a series of attitudes around a particular topic and not to rely upon one question as an indicator:

> Since so much depends on the way the issue is put into words, a single item or single question is often unreliable and, because it usually approaches an attitude from one particular direction only, may give rather one-sided results. Thus, agreement with the statement 'Divorce should be made easier' can hardly, by itself, be a reliable index of a broader attitude, such as the respondent's radicalism ... agreement may, in any case, be due to personal circumstances; but by having many items we can reduce the effects of one-sided responses.
>
> (Oppenheim 1973: 120)

Figure 1 is an example of what is known as a *Likert* scale, which places people's answers on an 'attitude continuum'. Statements are devised to measure a particular aspect in which the researcher is interested; the respondent is normally invited to agree strongly, agree, neither agree nor disagree, disagree or disagree strongly with these statements. Figure 1, however, was designed to measure the extent to which probation officers believed that different groups influenced the policy changes they were experiencing. Its design followed an examination of the organization's history, a preliminary interviewing of officers and observations of their work, during which time considerable disquiet was expressed at the lack of consultation over organizational changes.

Despite the length of the final mail questionnaire, by spending some time learning of the issues in which officers were interested, explaining the purpose of the research and ensuring the confidentiality of replies, the response rate was 70 per cent (May 1991). Note that the researcher was interested in the concept of influence and then had to devise questions which were indicators of this, bearing in mind the frames of reference of the target population. The number of groups who could have influenced this process were also identified in order that the questions covered all possible responses (exhaustive). Note also that the questions are pre-coded (from 1 to 4); the use of the margin on the right-hand side of the questionnaire for placing the codes into a computer for analysis; the introduction to the question resolving any ambiguities over interpretation of the categories and the box in the top right-hand corner which enables a code to be attributed to each questionnaire in order to assist with analysis.

The following questions concern your beliefs and opinions on various aspects of probation work. Please consider your answer to each question before <u>placing a circle around the answer that most approximates your opinion.</u> (The numbers are for coding purposes only)

Please Note: Where the term 'Probation Management' is used this refers to members of the Chief Officer's Management Team

Question 1
How influential do you believe the following are in the forming of Treen Probation Service policies?

	Very Influential	Influential	Not Very Influential	Not Influential	
The Treen Probation Ctte	1	2	3	4	(4)
The Home Office	1	2	3	4	(5)
The Goverment	1	2	3	4	(6)
Public Opinion	1	2	3	4	(7)
Probation Management	1	2	3	4	(8)
Treen Magistrates	1	2	3	4	(9)
NAPO	1	2	3	4	(10)
Assoc. of Chief Officers of Probation	1	2	3	4	(11)
Senior Probation Off.	1	2	3	4	(12)
Maingrade Officers	1	2	3	4	(13)
Ancillaries	1	2	3	4	(14)

Figure 1   An example of questions using a scaling method

Other scaling methods include the Osgood Semantic Differential scale; the Guttman scale; the Thurstone scale and Factorial scales (see Oppenheim 1973; Henerson, Lyons Morris and Fitz-Gibbon 1987).

The Semantic Differential scale was developed as a quantitative measure of meaning on subjective dimensions. In this technique, people are asked to tick a box between pairs of opposite adjectives. This yields rating scales, for example, between good/bad; fast/slow; mild/strong; cool/hot, and so on. Of course, their use will depend upon the aims of the research. However, this is said to provide not only matters of opinion, but also rate the images which people have of particular topics or items. One such example is the use of this method to evaluate people's images of a product in market research.

Having decided upon the nature and types of questions to be used, the process of actual question wording itself is of central importance:

> In reality, questioning people is more like trying to catch a particularly elusive fish, by hopefully casting different kinds of bait at different depths, without knowing what goes on beneath the surface!
>
> (Oppenheim 1973: 49)

There are, approximately, ten points that you might consider when actually writing your questions. First, they should not be too general or insufficiently specific. Second, bearing in mind the audience, they should use the simplest language possible to convey the meaning of the question and should avoid the use of prejudicial language. Simple items can be, unwittingly, sexist or racist in their assumptions.

This is illustrated by Margrit Eichler (1988) who takes the following two questions from an interview schedule from which a person is asked to either agree or disagree:

> It is generally better to have a man at the head of a department composed of both men and women employees.
>
> It is acceptable for women to hold important political offices in state and national governments.

Both of these questions assume a male norm against which women are measured. Indeed, it is not possible to express a preference for a female head of department – just to agree or disagree with the statement. On the other hand, the questions could be phrased as:

> What do you think is generally better: To have a women or a man at the head of a department that is composed of both men and women employees?
>
> What do you think is generally better: to have women or men hold important elected political offices in state and national government?
>
> (Eichler 1988: 43–4)

Answers might then range around the preference which the person answering the question has for women and men in such posts.

The third point that you might consider when writing the questions is they should avoid any possible ambiguity, otherwise they can be interpreted in a different way from the designer's intention. Fourth, avoid using vague words as they encourage vague answers. Fifth, avoid leading questions such as 'You don't think that . . . do you?' People replying will either react negatively to your presumption or answer in accordance with what they believe to be your wishes when the aim is to discover their opinions. Sixth, as noted in the example of student knowledge of drug-taking in the Second World War, avoid presuming that people have the information or the patterns of behaviour you wish to know about. If you are interested in how many cigarettes people smoke a day don't ask this straight away. You could begin with a *filter* question (no pun intended!) 'Do you smoke cigarettes?' If the answer is 'Yes', you could then ask 'And how many cigarettes do you smoke per day?' Seven, hypothetical questions elicit hypothetical answers. People may simply shrug their shoulders and say 'Who knows?' Eight, exercise some caution in the use of personal questions for both ethical and practical reasons. Insensitive use can lead to a termination of the interview or a refusal to answer the rest of the questionnaire. It is better to ask such questions, if needed, from a third party point of view: 'People think X, what is your opinion?' Nine, avoid embarrassing questions, which you should decide either to ask with due regard to the rights of the person or not ask at all. Tenth, an element of caution is required in the use of memory questions. Quite simply, people may not remember the information which is required, or it may not have had the significance in their lives which you presuppose. Once again, good pilot work can correct for these problems.

   Finally, the order of your questions needs to be well planned and the questionnaire well laid out and neatly typed; instructions on its completion to either the respondent (mail questionnaire) or interviewer (face-to-face) should be clear, unambiguous and easy to follow. The purpose of the questionnaire should normally be explained at the outset so that people feel involved with what you are doing. The opening question should also put people at their ease. Beginning a questionnaire with personal information concerning a person's sexual orientation is not a good start. This may seem like an obvious point, but prejudice and insensitivity can operate in less obvious ways. The questions themselves should be interesting and not simply personal; they should also relate to each other. One method is to start with broader questions and then move to more specific ones. Therefore, the order of the questionnaire is not the best logical sequence, but the best social-psychological sequence.

   In summarizing this section, Table 4 is designed to assist you in considering and remembering the procedures in questionnaire construction.

   In this process we move from the conceptual aims of the questionnaire through to its operationalization, to the results. These can then be analysed to see whether the original theoretical propositions require modifying or new information has come to light. Thus, to go back to the discussion in Chapter 2, this process is a combination of both inductive and deductive techniques of social research.

The analysis of questionnaires

The methods of analysis depend upon the data produced. In order to legitimately use some statistical methods it is necessary to argue that the data

Table 4 An outline of stages in questionnaire construction

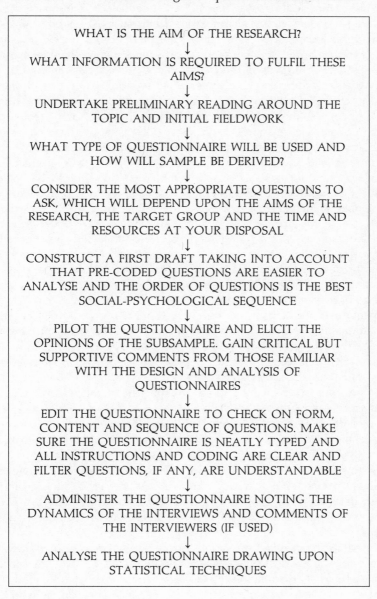

WHAT IS THE AIM OF THE RESEARCH?
↓
WHAT INFORMATION IS REQUIRED TO FULFIL THESE AIMS?
↓
UNDERTAKE PRELIMINARY READING AROUND THE TOPIC AND INITIAL FIELDWORK
↓
WHAT TYPE OF QUESTIONNAIRE WILL BE USED AND HOW WILL SAMPLE BE DERIVED?
↓
CONSIDER THE MOST APPROPRIATE QUESTIONS TO ASK, WHICH WILL DEPEND UPON THE AIMS OF THE RESEARCH, THE TARGET GROUP AND THE TIME AND RESOURCES AT YOUR DISPOSAL
↓
CONSTRUCT A FIRST DRAFT TAKING INTO ACCOUNT THAT PRE-CODED QUESTIONS ARE EASIER TO ANALYSE AND THE ORDER OF QUESTIONS IS THE BEST SOCIAL-PSYCHOLOGICAL SEQUENCE
↓
PILOT THE QUESTIONNAIRE AND ELICIT THE OPINIONS OF THE SUBSAMPLE. GAIN CRITICAL BUT SUPPORTIVE COMMENTS FROM THOSE FAMILIAR WITH THE DESIGN AND ANALYSIS OF QUESTIONNAIRES
↓
EDIT THE QUESTIONNAIRE TO CHECK ON FORM, CONTENT AND SEQUENCE OF QUESTIONS. MAKE SURE THE QUESTIONNAIRE IS NEATLY TYPED AND ALL INSTRUCTIONS AND CODING ARE CLEAR AND FILTER QUESTIONS, IF ANY, ARE UNDERSTANDABLE
↓
ADMINISTER THE QUESTIONNAIRE NOTING THE DYNAMICS OF THE INTERVIEWS AND COMMENTS OF THE INTERVIEWERS (IF USED)
↓
ANALYSE THE QUESTIONNAIRE DRAWING UPON STATISTICAL TECHNIQUES

are of a certain type. Broadly speaking there are three levels of measurement applicable to the social sciences: *nominal, ordinal* and *interval*. Nominal variables are simply those which are identified by names such as 'religious affiliation'. Ordinal variables, on the other hand, rank the differences in replies, for example, answers to the degree of difficulty of a particular undergraduate course or the agree–disagree continuum of the Likert scale. Ordinal scales cannot, however, specify that the differences between each of the scores will be identical (agree and agree strongly is the same as the difference between disagree and disagree strongly). For this purpose, measurement at an interval scale is required.

In the social sciences, most variables are of an ordinal form and for that reason statistical techniques which require an interval level of measurement are frequently invalid: *'a particular mathematical model presupposes a certain level of measurement'* (Blalock 1984: 20; original emphasis). Researchers have therefore devised statistical techniques specifically for social research such as log-linear analysis (see Gilbert 1981). In this section I shall concentrate only upon a general outline for analysing the relationship between two variables and the reader should be aware that other, more sophisticated techniques are available. If you wish to pursue this further, there are some excellent texts on data analysis specifically designed for social scientists (Erickson and Nosanchuk 1983; Marsh 1988; Bryman and Cramer 1990), as well as texts on how to present data (Sprent 1988) and how not to (Huff 1981)!

I mentioned the above not only for those who wish to seek further information, but also because it is often the case that researchers use statistical techniques which, quite simply, cannot be justified by the data they produce. It is also worth remembering that despite the use of a dazzling array of sophisticated statistical techniques, facts do not speak for themselves. Value, ethical and theoretical considerations are still part of the research process – regardless of the mathematical skills of the researcher.

One of the characteristics of questionnaires discussed earlier involved the relationships between variables, the example used being that between age and conservatism. The aim of questionnaire analysis is to examine patterns among replies to questions and explore the relationships between variables by explaining them in terms of what are known as *independent* variables. This takes the form of seeing to what extent one variable is influenced by another. This can be achieved through using computer packages such as Minitab and SPSS (Statistical Package for the Social Sciences).

If the aim is to examine the relationships between variables, then there must also be some means of deciding which variables to choose. It then becomes necessary to *specify* the relationship in terms of which variables are influential. Age may be related to conservatism, but people's occupations might also influence their outlook on life. Thus, it is possible that people of different socio-economic groups have a different outlook on life. To return to an example used in Chapter 2, there could be a relationship between class and voting behaviour, *independent* of age. A younger person who is a member of a profession may be more conservative than an older person who is a manual worker. In this instance it may not be age, but class, which influences a particular outlook on life. In order to analyse this relationship, the questionnaire would have to contain replies to questions on the respondent's age, occupation and voting behaviour.

The process of specifying the exact relationship between variables is achieved by *elaboration* (see Rosenberg 1968; 1984; Moser and Kalton 1983). An independent variable (class) is then deemed to have an effect on a dependent variable (conservatism) in what is known as a *bivariate* relationship. An exploration of these using the results of a questionnaire

> are of interest because they can suggest hypotheses about the way in which the world works. In particular, they are interesting when one variable can be considered a cause and the other an effect ... they are termed independent and dependent variables respectively.
>
> (Marsh 1988: 97)

Bivariate relationships are constructed by this process and other variables introduced to see the effect of this on the pattern of the relationship. In the above example, the results of age might be *cross-tabulated* with voting behaviour to produce a bivariate relationship. When the respondent's occupation is introduced into the equation, the relationship might become even stronger. It is then the task of the researcher, sitting at the computer terminal, to discover exactly what variables are influential and in what manner. How is this decided?

There are two tests which can be used for this purpose: first, tests of significance, and second, tests of association. One test of significance is known as chi-square (χ^2). For this to be reliable 'the data must consist of randomly selected, independently measured cases' (Erickson and Nosanchuk 1983: 255) and the number of people in each category must not be too small as this measure is sensitive to fluctuations in sample size.

The result of such a computation gives a particular value for chi-square which is then checked by using a table of chi-square values. If the test of a relationship between a person's occupation and his or her voting behaviour is significant at a 1 per cent level, this means that there is only a 1 in 100 possibility that this happened because of chance; we can therefore say that we are 99 per cent confident in this result. A test of significance, however, tells us only of the probability that the relationship between two variables happened because of chance and how legitimate it then is to generalize to the population (one of the aims of a sample-based questionnaire). It does not tell you what the *strength* of the relationship between the observed variables in your sample is. For this purpose, a measure of association is used which computes a value depending upon the strength of the association: common measures are 'phi' and 'Cramer's V'. Both produce results which vary between 0 and 1 depending on the strength of the association.

Together, tests of significance (to see to what extent it is legitimate to generalize from the sample to the population) and association (which tells you how strongly the sample variables are related), allow you to infer that one variable is related to another after testing the relationship by introducing third variables (eg age and voting behaviour and then introducing occupation in our above example).

Should you decide to use a questionnaire for your own research, you are now aware of the basic ideas which underline survey analysis and the techniques which are employed for this purpose. However, more sophisticated methods also exist to analyse questionnaires, bearing in mind the earlier comments on levels of measurement.

It remains to consider the criticisms of questionnaires. In reading this, it might appear like climbing down from the heady heights of statistical analysis, but this is just the point. Statistics are only a tool and when it comes to a critique of survey research, its opponents are not impressed by numbers, whether they be percentages, proportions, means or chi-square values.

Criticisms of questionnaires

Let us re-cap on some of the characteristics of questionnaires: the idea of causality; the empiricist concern with measurement; the concept of standardiz-ation and the testing of hypotheses. Each of these has been addressed, albeit indirectly, in the earlier chapters. The idea of causality has been criticized as an import from the natural sciences which is simply not applicable to the realm of human action which is rule-following, not 'caused'. Age or occupation, for example, does not simply *cause* opinions. Two variables may vary together, but this *correlation* does not mean that one variable causes a change in another. To say that there is a correlation between age and conservatism does not mean that age *causes* conservatism. For critics of surveys, we have to understand the process by which people come to adopt particular values.

Having presuppositions, such as the relationship between age and voting behaviour, leads researchers to ask particular questions. Because these restrict the way in which people can answer, it becomes inevitable that the theories are 'proven'. By the very design of questionnaires, it has already been decided what are important questions to ask. This deductive method fails precisely because the theorists' presuppositions have guided the research. The survey researcher might reply it is also inductive because the results of the answers generate relationships between variables which either lead to new ideas, as in the use of bivariate analysis, or refute the theories themselves. How can this be so? By using the concept of standardization, people do not have the opportunity to challenge ideas on their own terms. Furthermore, the myriad of differences in people's attitudes and the *meanings* which they confer on events can hardly be accommodated by compartmentalizing them into fixed categories (closed-questions) at one point in time (the actual completion of the questionnaire).

Differences are accommodated in questionnaires by the 'fixing' of complex answers within a series of simple categories. Yet not only is this a simplification of a complex social world, but also it takes no account of change in opinions across time. To correct for this, some surveys are *longitudinal*. Of these, a *panel study* takes a group or 'cohort' of people and interviews them across time: for example, groups of children born at a particular time are then interviewed at five yearly points in their life cycles to see how their attitudes, opinions, values and so on change over time. However, these are expensive and therefore not a common form of research, while it still remains the case that if the researcher is relying only on a questionnaire method of research, people's opinions are still represented by a fixed number of categories.

The above problems are thought to be overcome by an attention to design, measurement and good pilot work. However, this simply becomes an empiricist concern with measurement. The central issue in social research for the critics of questionnaires is a hermeneutic one: how can researchers legitimately understand the ways in which people interpret the world around them and act within their social universe? How can survey researchers guarantee that their questions will be interpreted by the respondent in the manner in which they intended when there is no opportunity for dialogue? This point is well made by John Hughes (1980) in a discussion on attitude scales:

> The open-textured quality of ordinary language which the investigator tries to remedy, in part at least, by the provision of forced-choice answers and such like, places a question mark against the assumption that the researcher and respondent share 'the same community of meaning structures for assigning cultural significance' to the items. If this assumption of meaning equivalence cannot be upheld then it is no longer clear in what sense it can be said that the attitude measure is a measure at all.
>
> (Hughes 1980: 96–7)

Even if 'meaning equivalence' between researcher's intention and respondent's interpretation can be upheld, as some research suggests (Social and Community Planning Research 1981), this still leaves questionnaire research with another problem: attitudes and actions are two different things, or what people say they do is very different from what they actually do.

The problematic relationship between attitudes and actions was considered by Richard Lapiere as long ago as 1934. Having surveyed hotel proprietors with the aim of obtaining 'comparative data on the degree of French and English antipathy towards dark-skinned peoples' (1934: 230), he found a widespread prejudice against letting rooms to those who fell into this category. However, he then had the opportunity to travel with a 'young Chinese student and his wife' (1934: 231). In a hotel with a reputation for its prejudiced attitude he noted the receptionist's 'raised eyebrow', but they were admitted without hesitation:

> Two months later I passed that way again, phoned the hotel and asked if they would accommodate 'an important Chinese gentleman'. The answer was an unequivocal 'No'.
>
> (Lapiere 1934: 231–2)

From this point on, despite the widespread prejudice uncovered by the questionnaire, there was only one incident in a total of 251 in which they were refused accommodation. As he concludes:

> If social attitudes are to be conceptualized as partially integrated habit sets which will become operative under specific circumstances and lead to a particular pattern of adjustment they must, in the main, be derived from a study of human beings in actual social situations.
>
> (Lapiere 1934: 237)

Lapiere neatly encapsulates the difference between attitudes and actions and the problem of tapping what people 'mean' when answering questionnaires. However, his concluding comments also appear to be a recommendation for good pilot work. For this reason, there are those who would argue that questionnaires can tap meanings if adequately designed and piloted and that the divide which is often thought to exist between quantitative and qualitative research, actually 'impoverishes' the aim of understanding and explaining human relations (McLaughlin 1991). Indeed, Marsh (1982) argues that questionnaires can adequately deal with meaning. While she acknowledges that ambiguous questions must be avoided, people will answer in a different way depending upon the meanings they attribute to a question. Other questions built into the questionnaire can enable the researcher to capture the reasons for this variation, as she argues in discussing the work of Brown and Harris (1978).

Broadly speaking, Brown and Harris studied a series of life events, to which women reacted, which then produced such feelings of hopelessness they induced clinical depression. The dimensions of this study therefore included both the understanding of these reactions *and* these events as 'casual' factors leading to depression:

> We have looked at two ways of achieving this in this chapter. The first involves asking the actor for her reasons directly, or to supply information about the central values in her life around which we may assume she is orientating her life. The second involves collecting a sufficiently complete picture of the context in which an actor finds herself that a team of outsiders may read off the meaningful dimension ... the mistake is to think that it is only action that is human and understandable – reactions are too.
>
> (Marsh 1982: 124)

Brown (1984) was also later to show how it was possible to capture both the meanings which actors attributed to an event and explain those in causal terms.

As quantitative researchers have argued (Husbands 1981; Marsh 1984), the use of questionnaires in these various ways then distances them from their positivist legacy upon which many critics focus.

In the quest to compartmentalize questionnaires within a positivist orientation and to produce a dichotomy between qualitative and quantitative methods of social research, their broad appeal can be easily overlooked. For instance, Ken Young (1981) argues that the outcome of policy is governed by two issues: first, the degree of control an organization exercises over its discretionary officials, and second, the extent to which the officials and policymakers' definitions of the situation inhabit common ground (Young 1981: 45). By the study of what he calls 'assumptive worlds', or 'definitions of the life situation' (Young 1977: 4), it is possible to begin to understand the 'subjective factors' and 'situational determinants' that different actors, at different levels of an organization, have and experience. These 'assumptive worlds' can be tapped through the use of questionnaires.

Within the tradition of critical theory, Karl Marx also made use of questionnaires in his research on the dynamics of capitalism (see Harvey 1990: 39–49). Further, another group of researchers, who included the German critical theorist Theodor Adorno, produced a study entitled *The Authoritarian Personality* (1950). In this study, they built up profiles of 'personality types'. People scoring highly on their tests were viewed as possessing a type of personality which is prone towards stereotypical and anti-democratic beliefs: in particular, disciplinarian and rigid patterns of behaviour based upon childhood upbringing. Feminist critics of positivism, often persuaded by more qualitative forms of research, have also employed statistical and survey analysis. Some research of this type has challenged the androcentric nature of behavioural research (Shibley Hyde 1990); attempted to overcome the tendency of surveys to compartmentalize or 'fracture' women's experiences (Graham 1984); tapped cultural norms on family obligations (Finch 1987) and shown how statistics are useful, but often used to intimidate people:

> They are only numbers: they are constructed, as words are in an ethnography; and they reflect their construction *even if outsiders do not know enough about the context of their production to recognise this.* Equally it is important not to be frightened by statistics, to let them intimidate you, or naïvely believe that 'statistics = bad'. Counting is an everyday action basic to many activities. Statistics need to be demystified.
>
> (Pugh 1990: 110, original emphasis)

Summary

Despite this broad appeal, a debate still remains over the place and applicability of questionnaires in social research. There are those researchers who would not, under any circumstances, countenance their use. There are those who would slavishly apply its methods without due regard to its weaknesses, and then hide behind a mask of elaborate statistical analysis. There are also those who know of the weaknesses of particular methods of research and make a judgement of which method to use based upon this information and the aims of their research. They may even decide to *triangulate* their inquiries which is 'the combination of methodologies in the study of the same phenomena' (Denzin 1978a: 291). The results of survey research may then 'be used to direct the researchers to individuals as instances for depth observation' (Fielding and Fielding 1986: 84). Nevertheless, while triangulation might appear attractive, it is not a panacea for methodological ills, nor does it avoid the issues covered in the first three chapters.

To make these types of judgements, the researcher has to understand the place of particular methods in social research and their strengths and weaknesses. Towards this end, the next three chapters are devoted to interviewing, participant observation and documentary research.

CHAPTER 5: QUESTIONS FOR YOUR REFLECTION

1   What is the purpose of conducting pilot studies?

2   What are the stages which should be considered in designing a questionnaire? What are the problems which you envisage at each stage and what should the researcher be aware of during these?

3   'Questionnaires measure only attitudes; they tell us nothing about the way that people behave'. Evaluate this criticism of questionnaires as a method of research.

4   If you were asked to devise a questionnaire which examined the relationship between race and crime, what ethical, political and theoretical questions would this raise for you as a social researcher?

6

Interviewing: methods and process

The aim of this chapter is to introduce the subject of interviewing. For this purpose, it is divided into four sections. First, a consideration of the various forms of interviewing which are employed in social research. Second, an account of the ways in which interviews are conducted and the issues which inform this process. Third, an overview of the main ways in which the resultant data can be analysed and finally, an examination of the critiques of interviewing in social research.

Interviews in social research

The methods of entering and maintaining conversations with people and the theoretical interpretations which social researchers make as a result, constitute the fundamentals of interviews defined as

> encounters between a researcher and a respondent in which the latter is asked
> a series of questions relevant to the subject of the research. The respondent's
> answers constitute the raw data analysed at a later point in time by the
> researcher.
>
> (Ackroyd and Hughes 1983: 66)

They can yield rich sources of data on people's experiences, opinions, aspirations and feelings. In order to achieve this, social researchers need to understand the dynamics of interviewing and sharpen their own use and understanding of the different methods of interviewing, together with an awareness of their strengths and limitations.

Broadly speaking, there are four types of interviews used in social research. However, while these characterizations appear to strictly demarcate one method from another, a research project may not simply be one of the following, but a mixture of two or more types. They are the structured interview, the semi-structured interview, the group interview and the unstructured or focused interview.

In moving from the structured interview to the unstructured interview, we shift from a situation in which the researcher attempts to control the interview and 'teach' the respondent to reply in accordance with the interview-schedule instructions (standardization), to a situation in which the respondent is encouraged to answer a question in her or his own terms. We may therefore characterize interviews along a quantitative–qualitative dimension, varying from the formal standardized example (surveys), to an unstructured situation of qualitative depth which allows the respondent to answer without feeling constrained by the pre-formulated ideas of the researcher. I shall expand on each of these types in turn.

Structured interviews

The use of structured interviews is associated with survey research. This is probably the technique which most people are familiar with. While the other techniques, particularly focused interviews, may directly involve the researcher as a subject and co-participant in the data collection process, this method relies upon the use of a questionnaire as the data collection instrument. As noted in Chapter 5, the theory behind this method being that each person is asked questions in the same way so that any differences between answers are then assumed to be real ones and not the result of the interview situation itself.

This method is said to permit *comparability* between responses. It relies upon a uniform *structure*, while a calculated number of people are interviewed so that they are representative of the population for the purposes of generalization. The resultant aggregated data are then examined for patterns of responses among the target population which are explained in terms of causal analysis. Its success is dependent upon good pilot work and the training of interviewers in order that the range of possible responses are covered by the interview schedule and the replies result from questions which are asked in a uniform and non-directive manner. They also depend upon the interviewer being similar to the target group, who, in turn, need to share a similar culture in order that the interpretation of the questions and the dynamics of the interview do not vary to a great extent. Therefore

> Where languages are too diverse, where common values are too few, where the fear of talking to strangers is too great, there the interview based on a standardised questionnaire calling for a few standardised answers may not be applicable. Those who venture into such situations may have to invent new modes of interviewing.
>
> (Benney and Hughes 1984: 216)

These alternatives include the semi-structured and focused interviews.

The semi-structured interview

In between the focused and structured methods sits one which utilizes techniques from both. Questions are normally specified, but the interviewer is more free to probe beyond the answers in a manner which would often seem prejudicial to the aims of standardization and comparability. Information about age, sex, occupation, type of household, and so on can be asked in a standardized format. Qualitative information about the topic can then be recorded by the interviewer who can seek both *clarification* and *elaboration* on the answers given. This enables the interviewer to have more latitude to *probe* beyond the answers. As Nigel Fielding notes in using the semi-structured method when researching police socialization: 'They were semi-structured by a thematic guide with probes and invitations to expand on issues raised' (Fielding 1988a: 212).

These types of interviews are therefore said to allow people to answer more on their own terms than the standardized interview permits, but still provide a greater structure for comparability over the focused interview. As with all of the interviewing methods, the interviewers should be not only aware of the content of the interview, but also able to record the nature of the interview and the way in which they asked the questions. However, in this type of interview, in comparison with the structured method, the context of the interview is an important aspect of the process. In its literal sense, to which few but the most crude behaviourists would subscribe, the standardized method is assumed to elicit information untainted by the context of the interview. Given this greater degree of latitude offered to the interviewer and the greater need to understand the context and content of the interview, while trained interviewers may be used, researchers themselves often conduct the interviews.

The focused interview

The central difference of this form of interviewing from both the structured and semi-structured interview is its open-ended character. This is said to provide it with an ability to challenge the preconceptions of the researcher. Some might regard this as a licence for the interviewee to simply talk about an issue in any way they feel like. This apparent disadvantage is turned into an advantage:

> a phenomenon like rambling can be viewed as providing information because it reveals something about the interviewee's concerns. Unstructured interviewing in qualitative research, then, departs from survey interviewing not only in terms of format, but also in terms of its concern for the perspective of those being interviewed.
>
> (Bryman 1988a: 47)

Sometimes called the 'informal', 'unstandardized' or 'unstructured' interview, this method achieves a different focus for the following reasons. First, it provides qualitative depth by allowing interviewees to talk about the subject in terms of their own 'frames of reference'. This allows the meanings and interpretations that individuals attribute to events and relationships to be understood. Second, it thereby provides a greater understanding of the subject's point of view.

This technique includes what are known as 'life-history' or 'oral history' interviews. Therefore, in asking women about their experiences, as opposed to assuming that they are already known, this approach is said to challenge

> the 'truths' of official accounts and cast doubt upon established theories. Interviews with women can explore private realms such as reproduction, child rearing, and sexuality to tell us what women actually did instead of what experts thought they did or should have done. Interviews can also tell us how women felt about what they did and can interpret the personal meaning and value of particular activities.
>
> (Anderson et al 1990: 95)

We are now squarely at the qualitative end of the research spectrum. Structured interviews are thought to allow very little room for the person to express their own opinions in a manner of their choosing. They must fit into boxes or categories which the researcher has predetermined.

The focused interview obviously involves the researcher having an aim in mind when conducting the interview, but the person being interviewed is more free to talk about the topic. Thus *flexibility* and the discovery of *meaning*, rather than standardization, generalization or a concern to compare through constraining replies by a set interview schedule, characterize this method.

Group interviews

Group interviews constitute a valuable tool of investigation, allowing the researcher to focus upon group norms and dynamics around issues which they wish to investigate. The extent of control of the group discussion will determine the nature of the data produced by this method. In the words of one text on this subject:

> The contemporary focus group interview generally involves 8 to 12 individuals who discuss a particular topic under the direction of a moderator who promotes interaction and assures that the discussion remains on the topic of interest ... A typical group session will last one and a half to two and a half hours.
>
> (Stewart and Shamdasani 1990: 10)

A balance must therefore be struck between the group being too small for interactive study or too large thus preventing all group members from participating in the discussion. However, as with all research guidelines, this will depend on what is possible in circumstances over which the researcher may have no control, as well as the aims of the investigation and the resources available.

Group interviews have been used in studies of steel workers who had experienced changes in working practices (Banks 1957) and in research on the effects of long-term imprisonment (Cohen and Taylor 1972). In Banks' study, steel workers were interviewed both individually and as a group. While a degree of consistency was found between the data yielded by both methods, the group responses tended to take account of the situations of others present and there was a greater tendency to express grievances with the management. Thus, it appeared to be possible to gain different results from using group and individual interviews. However, it does not follow that one result is 'true' and another 'false'. Group and individual interviews may produce *different* perspectives on the *same* issues. This comparison demonstrated that interaction within groups (such as on the factory floor) affects us all in terms of our actions and opinions. As most of our lives are spent interacting with others, it comes as no surprise that our actions and opinions are modified according to the social situation in which we find ourselves. For this reason, group interviews can provide a valuable insight into both social relations in general and the examination of processes and social dynamics in particular.

Conducting interviews in social research

The above has covered four methods of interviewing which have different ideas and methods underlying their practice. For this reason and by way of an introduction to the process of conducting interviews, I shall concentrate in this section on the main points which you might consider if adopting one or more of these techniques. However, the actual use of these pointers will clearly depend upon the interviewing method which is to be employed. This part of the chapter is also demarcated as texts on social research tend to adopt a particular perspective when it comes to the interviewing process. The first part will consider textbook prescriptions for interviewing which are mainly, but not exclusively, applicable to structured and semi-structured forms. The second part will then move on to consider the process of conducting focused or unstructured interviews. As will become evident, feminists have criticized textbook accounts of interviewing as both impractical and undesirable. Given this, the third part of this section will outline the main issues to consider when conducting feminist-based interviewing.

Textbook prescriptions for interviewing practice

Commonly, a tension is thought to exist between subjectivity and objectivity in the interviewing process. On the one hand, interviews are said by many to elicit knowledge free of prejudice or bias; on the other, a self-conscious awareness must be maintained in order to let the interview 'flow':

> There is a tension in the biographical interview between, on the one hand, the need of the interviewer to establish and maintain a rapport and a trusting relationship in which the interviewee will disclose significant personal information and, on the other, the practical demands and constraints of any research enquiry . . . what transpires is inevitably something of a balancing act.
>
> (Gearing and Dant 1990: 152)

The interviewer and interviewee therefore need to establish an intersubjective understanding. At the same time, the pursuit of objectivity requires a 'distance' in order to judge the situation. We seem to have two polar opposites – full engagement to detached analysis:

> The problem is clear. The more the interviewer attempts to sustain a relationship with the subject . . . the more he feels the interview is 'successful'. The more standardized the interviewers are in their relation with the subject, the more reliable the data presumably becomes.
>
> (Cicourel 1964: 77)

In order to achieve this 'balance', several issues arise in texts on interviewing which need to be considered by the researcher. First, there is the question of the interviewer's role: what effect is the interviewer having on the interviewee and hence the type of material collected? Is the interviewer's role during the interview one of impartial scientist or friend and how does this affect the interview? Related to this are discussions on the characteristics of interviewers: what is their age, sex, race and accent? This is an important issue which directly affects the type of information elicited. For instance, a study was conducted in Tennessee among black respondents using white interviewers. The idea was to consider the attitudes of black people and the extent to which they were satisfied with their social, political and economic lives. When interviewed by white interviewers, the people's attitudes were classified as expressing a 'high' level of satisfaction. However, when interviewed by black interviewers, attitudes changed and a more radical opinion was expressed. Therefore, before conducting interviews, it is important to consider a match of characteristics, on the basis not only of race, but also of age, sex and accent. This helps to guard against the substitution of the interviewer's words for the respondents. Thus, texts speak of 'blending-in'. Quite simply, it may not be appropriate for a grey-suited person more familiar with the deviants of city financial life to interview Hell's Angels about their beliefs and actions.

Following Cannell and Kahn, Claus Moser and Graham Kalton (1983) suggest that there are three necessary conditions for the successful completion of interviews. While they are specifically discussing survey interviews, they raise issues which are worth more general consideration. The first necessary condition is a question of *accessibility*. This refers to whether or not the person answering the questions has access to the information which the interviewer seeks. This may seem a simple point yet, as noted when discussing questionnaires in particular, there may well exist a 'gap' between the understanding of the interviewer and the interviewee. Of course, depending upon the interviewing method used, the interviewer may possess the flexibility to clarify the questions.

A lack of information may result from other reasons: for example, the person once knew the answer, but has now forgotten; for someone to disclose certain types of information involves emotional stress; a certain type of answer or method of answering is expected which the person is not familiar with (the 'frames of reference' are discrepant) or, quite simply, people may refuse to answer for personal, political or ethical reasons, or a combination of any of these. In such situations, the interviewer must make a judgement concerning the continuation of the interview.

The second necessary condition is *cognition*, or an understanding by the person being interviewed of what is required of him or her in the role of interviewee. Interviews are social encounters and not simply passive means of gaining information. As with all social encounters they are rule-guided and the parties bring with them expectations of their content and the role they may adopt as a result. It is important, therefore, that interviewees not only know the information that is required, but also understand what is expected of them. Without this, the person being interviewed may feel uncomfortable and this affects the resultant data. For these reasons, clarification is not only a practical, but also an ethical and theoretical consideration. Once again, this will depend on the type of interview being used. In a structured situation, the nature of the answer is guided by the interview schedule. On the other hand, the focused interview rests its strength upon eliciting answers which are, as far as possible, in the person's own words and frame of reference.

Related to the above is the third concept of *motivation*. The interviewer must make the subjects feel that their participation and answers are valued, for their co-operation is fundamental to the conduct of the research. This means maintaining interest during the interview (Moser and Kalton 1983: 271-2).

Once these matters are considered and acted upon, during the actual course of the interview, there are certain techniques for asking questions. First, a distinction is made between 'directive' questions, which require a 'Yes' or 'No' answer, and 'non-directive' questions, which allow more latitude for the response. Thus, an interviewer may directly ask for a reply to be framed in a particular way, or the interviewer may be less directive and ask, for example, 'Could you tell me a little more about that?' Another recommended method is to repeat what the person has said, but with a rising inflexion in your voice. For instance, if the answer is, 'I enjoyed meeting them', the interviewer then says, 'You say you enjoyed meeting them...?' This is presumed to gain an elaboration of the person's statement.

In everyday life we sometimes find ourselves in conversation where a person either is hostile to the line of conversation or becomes embarrassed for one reason or another. The interview is no exception to this. Of course it may be wrong to pursue the line of questioning, but one method of preventing embarrassment or hostility is to ask by way of 'generalization'. Instead of posing a direct question: 'What do you think about X?', you might ask: 'Many people consider that . . . do you have an opinion on this?' This use of 'probes' is widely recommended. Probing is defined as 'encouraging the respondent to give an answer, or to clarify or amplify an answer' (Hoinville and Jowell et al 1987: 101). These vary from so-called 'neutral' probes in standardized situations, to more open types in unstructured interviews. The ability to probe is reduced as the interview becomes more structured, for any variations in probing may not permit comparability. However, a change in the emphasis of a question, or a similar question posed in a different way, can not only provoke further thought on the subject, but also perhaps offer a catalyst enabling the interviewee to make links to other answers they have given. This allows elaboration by a method of using information subsequently gained during the interview and applying it to a later stage in the conversation. There are some parallels here with the idea of 'retrospective–prospective interpretation' (Garfinkel 1967). Along these lines, it is also possible to ask people about *future* possibilities in relation to *past* experiences. This enables the interviewer to gain an idea of *how* people think about issues or come to terms with events in their lives, allowing them to build up a picture of the event or issue which is being considered in order that it is not 'compartmentalized', but related to other factors that people consider important.

Another technique commonly urged is probing for comparable and codeable answers which falls more in to the structured and semi-structured methods. In interviewing people they may make similar responses to those previously interviewed. As a result of this knowledge, you may decide to pursue the line of questioning in order to understand the extent to which the answers are similar and may therefore be coded, for analysis, in the same way.

Without due consideration to the interviewee as a person in their own right, they can easily be left with the impression that the researcher is doing them a favour – a bizarre twist of circumstances! Practically speaking, if people feel valued then their participation is likely to be enhanced – as well as their attitudes towards future participation in social research. One idea which can help researchers is to imagine themselves in the same position in similar circumstances. Would they be prepared to co-operate and answer their own questions?

In order to assist in placing the person at ease, attention is given to the issue of *rapport* which 'means that a basic sense of trust has developed that allows for the free flow of information' (Spradley 1979: 78). This brings us round to a discussion of focused interviews and the establishment of rapport using this method.

The practice of focused interviews

In terms of focused interviews, Spradley (1979) views the establishment of rapport as a four-stage process. First, there is the initial apprehension that both the interviewer and interviewee have of the process. This is perfectly understandable if the parties are strangers and the interviewer should not feel it is a personal weakness on their part. To overcome this, both parties must begin to talk to each other which is assisted by the use of what he calls *descriptive questions*. These include, for instance, the amount of time that a person takes to perform a task in which the interviewer is interested. These could take the form of 'grand tour' questions such as asking someone to give an account of his 'average day' at work, whether in the home or elsewhere. This could be reduced to 'mini-tour' question by asking someone what she does in a particular role, for example, what her tasks actually involve in the performance of a given role. It is also possible to ask people about particular things that have happened to them. The example Spradley uses is an interviewee saying that someone gave him a 'hard time'. He then asked what he meant by this? More generally, you could ask people what experiences they particularly remember surrounding the topic in which you are interested or, finally, asking people what terms they use for particular places or things. In Spradley's example he learns that a jail is called a 'bucket' and this enabled him to ask questions around that topic using the language of the interviewee.

The use of such questions also helps in the second stage of establishing rapport: *exploration*. Here each party to the interview begins to discover what each is like and how the interview will proceed and for what reason. Again, this is assisted by asking descriptive questions which leads to the third stage of *co-operation* where each party to the interview 'knows what to expect of one another' (Spradley 1979: 82). The final stage could take many weeks to arrive at and will depend upon the time at the disposal of the researcher and respondent. This stage is called *participation*:

> a new dimension is added to the relationship, one in which the informant recognizes and accepts the role of teaching the ethnographer. When this happens there is a heightened sense of cooperation and full participation in the research. Informants begin to take a more assertive role. They bring new information to the attention of the ethnographer and help in discovering patterns in their culture.
>
> (Spradley 1979: 83)

The focused interview is therefore a process of building up trust and co-operation. It utilizes not only descriptive questions, but also what Spradley calls *structural* questions (1979: 120). These enable the interviewer to explore areas of a person's life and experiences in greater depth; they can also be used to explore and disconfirm particular ideas the researcher has. These 'verification' questions might take the form of asking what types of people the interviewee tends to socialize with. However, there is a need to be aware of the sensitivity of some issues and how to phrase such inquiries.

As with all research, interviews do not begin simply when the first actually commences. Preparation by reading and initial exploratory work, understanding the situation into which you are going, clarifying any ambiguities which people might have of the research and eliciting their co-operation and being sensitive to ethical, political and theoretical considerations in the process, form a central part of its practice. It may be the case that the people whom the researcher wishes to interview are not amenable to direct approaches or are difficult to trace. In these circumstances, the technique of *snowball sampling* may be employed:

> This approach involves using a small group of informants who are asked to put the researcher in touch with their friends who are subsequently interviewed, then asking them about their friends and interviewing them until a chain of informants has been selected.
>
> (Burgess 1990: 55)

This form of non-probability sampling is very useful in gaining access to certain groups. However, researchers also have to be aware that they inherit the decisions of each individual as to whom is the next suitable interviewee. This may not present a problem, but it may also lead to the researcher collecting data which reflect a particular perspective and thereby omitting the voices and opinions of others who are not part of a network of friends and acquaintances.

Another method of assisting in the process of rapport and recall is called 'sequential interviewing'. This may be applicable to all three methods of interviewing, but is of particular interest to those which permit a greater flexibility for the person to answer in his or her own terms and involves interviewing people about events in the way they unfolded. By using this chronological format, it enables people to reflect on their experiences and the event in which the researcher is interested, as it unfolded. If an unstructured format is used, its flexibility allows people to return to a point previously made and elaborate upon it. Further, as the account of the event unfolds, it also enables the interviewer to ask about a previously stated belief in terms of the new information gained. This method of 'reflecting back' allows interviewers to confirm their interpretations and to seek elaboration of the person's account. It also allows interviewees either to elaborate upon the information given or to correct and/or modify their accounts.

The chronological method of interviewing is associated with the idea of a person's 'career'. Originating in the work of the Chicago School of social research (see Bulmer 1984a; Kurtz 1984), this does not mean changes in a person's occupational status, but focuses upon the transformations which people undergo in adopting particular roles as the result of new experiences. Thus Erving Goffman (1968) spoke of the value of the idea of career in terms of its 'two-sidedness:'

One side is linked to internal matters held dearly and closely, such as image of self and felt identity; the other side concerns official position, jural relations, and style of life, and is part of a publicly accessible institutional complex.

(Goffman 1968: 119)

While Goffman is making a point regarding the use of observation of people's actions to check their accounts of those actions through interviews, this method has been used by Howard Becker (1963) in his study of marijuana users.

Becker (1963) examined, through the use of fifty interviews, the process by which people learnt to become marijuana users. According to Becker, people built up an identity as users of this drug. The simple fact of smoking the drug, in itself, was not enough. People had to develop the habits, techniques and patterns of behaviour of others before they were able to fully enjoy its effects. The novice was therefore

curious about the experience, ignorant of what it may turn out to be, and afraid it may be more than he has bargained for. The steps outlined below, if he undergoes them all and maintains the attitudes developed in them, leave him willing and able to use the drug for pleasure when the opportunity presents itself.

(Becker 1963: 46)

The stages through which people had to pass were then mapped in his account by using extracts from the interview data collected. These then illustrated how each stage was an important part of learning to become a marijuana user. They were: 'learning the technique', 'learning to perceive the effects' and 'learning to enjoy the effects'. Through this method, Becker was able to chart a person's socialization into a subculture from their initial willingness to try a drug, to a first experience of it, to learning the techniques to get a 'high' and finally, learning to enjoy what was likely, at first, to be an unpleasant experience (dizziness, thirst, tingling of the scalp and misjudgement of time and distance). By adopting the concept of a 'career' in the interviewing process, Becker ends up with a fascinating insight into what many people regard as deviant behaviour.

We are now firmly at the qualitative end of the interviewing spectrum where life history and biographical interviews rest. Both types seek qualitative depth. Typically, they are detailed conversations which attempt to gain a fuller insight into a person's biography. Clifford Shaw's (1930) work uses a life history method which relates the story of a teenage boy who was in prison for Jack Rolling (a similar type of offence to the mugging of drunks). Shaw focuses on the early childhood of Stanley (the Jack Roller) and the death of his mother. After this period, he ran away from home and spent time in various institutions, before finally living on the streets and becoming a Jack Roller. The data upon which his life story was based took six years to collect. The flexibility of this method enabled Shaw to return to Stanley from time-to-time when he was asked to expand on his accounts. Shaw was then able to build up a picture of his life and the circumstances which led to his actions.

Feminist approaches to the process of interviewing

Ann Oakley (1979) interviewed women about their experiences of the transition into motherhood. The research itself involved the conducting of 233 interviews which generated a total of 545 hours and 26 minutes of tape-recorded data (Oakley 1979: 309). The women whom she interviewed were at a critical stage in their lives (the prospect of giving birth) and wished to know the answers to questions or simply be comforted in the ordeal ahead of them. As a result, she was asked a total of 878 questions, 76 per cent of which were requests for information on medical procedures, physiology and baby care, etc. The remainder of these questions were divided into 'personal' and 'advice' questions and those concerning the research. Personal questions included being asked of her own experiences of motherhood and childbirth (published in her own autobiography: see Oakley 1984).

In the face of these requests, how could she then entertain the prescriptions of textbook interviewing? For example, it is supposed to be a one-way process of gaining answers from people, but not answering their questions. Disengagement in the interviewing process is therefore not regarded as

> a realistic description of what occurs, but an idealized and wishful set of statements and prescriptions which we construct after the event and around our account of this. In other words what we present is a 'doctored' account ... a researcher who behaves in textbook ways ... would render them immediately noticeable because it would be so unnatural.
> (Stanley and Wise 1983: 155–7)

Ann Oakley (1990) lists three reasons why disengagement could not, nor should, be entertained. First, it was not reasonable to adopt this exploitative relationship with the women she interviewed. As a feminist faced with questions such as 'Does an epidural ever paralyse women?' an answer such as 'That's a hard one, I have never thought of that' (Oakley 1990: 48) is in line with textbook prescriptions, but hardly satisfactory. Second, given that one aim of feminist research (as noted in Chapter 1), is to counter the public–private divide by giving a voice to women's issues and experiences, she

> regarded sociological research as an essential way of giving the subjective position of women not only greater visibility in sociology, but, more importantly, in society, than it has traditionally had.
> (Oakley 1990: 48)

Third, the idea of not answering questions posed by the interviewee was not conducive to the traditional aim of establishing rapport. A refusal to answer, or an evasive answer, is not a genuine reciprocation of information as most interactions imply. To expect someone to reveal important and personal information without entering into a dialogue is untenable. For these reasons, *engagement*, not disengagement, is a valued aspect of the feminist research process.

Disengagement is argued to reflect a 'masculine paradigm' of research (Oakley 1990). The idea of 'controlling' the social distance or familiarity between interviewer and interviewee, or controlling for the dangers of 'over-rapport' as some texts put it, is a contradiction in terms:

> I think that a female interviewer who is interviewing women and who is aware of the way in which women are treated and the position of women, is going to be aware of this contradiction between what the textbooks say interviewing is all about and how a feminist feels she should treat other women.
>
> (Oakley, in Mullan 1987: 194)

Establish 'rapport', being 'disengaged' and conducting the interview in a hierarchical relationship between the parties is rejected in both theory and practice.

In contrast to the need to establish rapport, in her study of clergy wives, Janet Finch was 'startled by the readiness with which women talked to me' (1984: 72). This, she considers, is not simply the result of using an in-depth interviewing technique, but that a woman interviewing other women is 'conducive to the easy flow of information' (Finch 1984: 74) for three reasons. First, women are more used to intrusions into their private lives through visits from doctors, social workers, health visitors, etc. and are therefore less likely than men to find questions about their lives unusual. Second, in the setting of their own homes, the interviewer becomes more like a 'friendly guest' than an 'official inquisitor'. Third, the structural position of women in society and their 'consignment to the privatised, domestic sphere...makes it particularly likely that they will welcome the opportunity to talk to a sympathetic listener' (Finch 1984: 74).

Other considerations in feminist-based interviewing are interactions between men and women and the ways in which everyday conversations are structured, thus affecting any dialogue involving the two sexes. Are everyday conversations between men and women a genuine and mutual exchange of views without social power operating in such a way as to bias the exchanges in the male's favour? According to the results of one study, men tend to dominate conversations. Pamela Fishman (1990) concludes how men and women differ in the way that they maintain interaction:

> The women seemed to try more often, and succeeded less often than the men. The men tried less often and seldom failed in their attempts. Both men and women regarded topics introduced by women as tentative; many of

these were quickly dropped. In contrast, topics introduced by the men were treated as topics to be pursued; they were seldom rejected. The women worked harder than the men in interaction because they had less certainty of success. They did much of the necessary work of interaction, starting conversations and then working to maintain them.

(Fishman 1990: 233-4)

In other words, if we take-for-granted the 'normal' manner of conversation in our work with other researchers and those who are part of our research, the chances are that it will exclude many women from equal participation; a particularly important point if conducting group interviews which contain both men and women. Therefore, once again, the reflexive examination of research practices becomes a fundamental part of the interviewing process.

The analysis of interviews

In this section, I wish to outline the ways in which interview data can be analysed, as opposed to the actual mechanics of analysis. However, these are only some of the ways in which analysis can be performed. During the course of the discussion, I shall therefore refer to works on data analysis in order that you are aware of alternative sources should you wish to pursue this topic further. As the use of analysis for questions using structured interviewing has already been covered in Chapter 5, I shall concentrate on the other methods.

Benney and Hughes (1984) speak of two conventions which characterize interviews: *equality* and *comparability*. The former operates to the advantage of the respondent in so far as it aims at participatory dialogue in the interviewee's own terms – as some exponents of the focused techniques, particularly feminist researchers, would advocate. At the same time, there is a lack of structure in such interviews. This makes the task of comparison between interviews more difficult because the responses to particular questions, except in the case of some semi-structured forms, will not be uniform. For some researchers, the structured and to some extent also the semi-structured format, are preferred because of the greater ease of analysis. However, interviews have different *aims* and the convenience of analysis should not be a reason for choosing one rather than another.

The first point to consider is the use of a tape recorder or notes on the interview. While attractive, recording has advantages and disadvantages. These fall under three headings: interaction, transcription and interpretation. At an interactional level, some people may find the tape recorder inhibiting and not wish their conversations to be recorded. Transcription itself is also a long process – a one-hour tape can take eight or nine hours to transcribe fully depending upon your typing ability. Nevertheless, tape recording can assist interpretation as it allows the interviewer to concentrate on the conversation and record the non-verbal gestures of the interviewee during the interview, rather than spending time looking down at his or her notes and writing what is said. Further, once the conversation is started, many people can forget the tape is on (including the interviewer when the tape shuts off noisily in the middle because the recording time was not long enough). Plus, editing the tapes according to theoretical categories in which the analyst is interested, assists in the comparative analysis of interview responses. Finally, tape recording guards against interviewers substituting their own words for those of the person being interviewed, but it can also make the analyst complacent as it is frequently believed that once the data are collected most of the work is done.

Following the interview, the work is only just starting. Not only does the writing up of notes or transcription of tapes have to take place, but so does the analysis. As Paul Atkinson notes, researchers, once they have collected their data,

> often expect, if only at a subconscious level, to 'find' educational, sociological or psychological concepts staring them in the face or leaping out at them from the data. It is a common enough misconception to expect to stumble across 'authoritarianism', 'social control', or whatever, and to be disappointed − even to feel betrayed.
>
> (quoted in Silverman 1985: 50)

In moving away from the structured format, it becomes necessary to employ techniques which can make some analytic 'sense' of the raw data. Conventional methods of achieving this involve the *coding* of open-ended replies in order to permit comparison. Coding has been defined as

> the general term for conceptualizing data; thus, coding includes raising questions and giving provisional answers (hypotheses) about categories and about their relations. A code is the term for any product of this analysis (whether a category or a relation among two or more categories).
>
> (Strauss 1988: 20-1)

Strauss's prescriptions in his detailed monograph on qualitative analysis follow the method of grounded theory (see Glaser and Strauss 1967). Yet even if analysts are not a follower of this method, the ways in which they begin to categorize data will still depend upon the aims of their research and theoretical interests. These, in turn, should be open to modification and challenge by the interview data analysed. It could be, for example, that a researcher is interested in the ways in which people negotiate their roles or performances in particular contexts (see Strauss 1978). The researcher would then focus upon the data in order to understand the ways in which people go about their daily lives and compare each interview in this way to see if there are similarities. If replies are similar, then they can be categorized under particular headings such as 'methods of negotiation', which allows the analyst to index the data under topics and headings.

Whyte (1981) used two methods to 'index' interview materials in his study of the social organization of 'street corner society': first, the respondents and their relationships to each other, and second, their references to events in terms of what actually happened and how important it was to the person being interviewed (Whyte 1984: 118). By focusing upon the ways in which people spoke of one another and made sense of the events which they experienced, this enabled him to build up a picture of the meaning of relationships to people and the language that people used to describe each other and the events which took place. This is a form of what is known as *ethnographic* analysis, which is achieved by becoming familiar with the interview data in order to understand the culture that people inhabit and their relationships to each other (Spradley 1979).

The important analytic stage of becoming familiar with the data is assisted by writing up notes or transcribing tapes and simply listening to the conversations. This is further assisted if the technique of 'developmental interviewing' has been employed. By moving, chronologically, through a person's account of an event and their experiences of it, a picture is constructed. A comparison of people's accounts is enhanced by focusing on the ways in which different people relate their experiences according to the circumstances they found themselves in. If a tape recorder was used, this can be achieved by editing each tape according to various topic headings which the analyst chooses. Each tape would then comprise a part of the interview with people which is relevant to these categories. These, together with notes on the course of the interview and any significant non-verbal gestures employed, assist the researcher in becoming familiar with the data and the particular nuances of each interview. On the other hand, if written notes were used, once they are fully written up, they simply have to be ordered in the same way (this is assisted by writing up the interviews on a word-processor and using the 'cut and paste' facility). There are now computer packages for the analysis of qualitative data which search for key phrases and the frequency with which people use certain words and in what context (see Fielding and Lee 1991).

From this, analysts can ascertain what Mills (1940) has called people's 'vocabularies of motive'. These may be given during the interview as reasons why people performed various actions within particular situations in which they found themselves. Other researchers have also argued that the accounts that people give of their actions are either 'justifications' or 'excuses'. These, in turn, may be viewed as indicative of how people identify themselves and routinely negotiate their social identities (Scott and Lyman 1968). An account given during an interview is 'the presentation not only of reasons but of oneself' (Harré 1988: 167). Thus, in a study of domestic fires and the methods which they used to analyse the interview data, two researchers note how

> the individuals normally recounted their actions in an explanatory context. In other words, they qualified the description of their actions by the reasons why they behaved as they did, generally without any prompting.
>
> (Brown and Sime 1981: 182)

The analysis of interviews can not only examine people's motivations and reason for actions, but also see these in terms of people's social identity and how their identities and reasons are constructed within the social settings in which they live and work. In this context, Dorothy Smith and Alison Griffith examined the relationship between mothering and schooling influenced by a feminist standpoint epistemology. They were interested in

> the social relations in which the work that mothers do in relation to their children's schooling is embedded. Their ongoing practical knowledge of the concerting of their activities with those of others is expressed in how they speak about those activities.
>
> (Smith 1988: 189)

To express it another way, how the relationship between mothering and schooling is constructed and reflected upon within the settings in which a mother enters (the school, home, workplace, etc).

Finally, there are also those who have moved away from the idea that interviews tell researchers the 'truth' about the actions or events which people engage in (a positivist orientated position) or that they demonstrate the structural constraints under which people routinely act and interpret events and relationships (a realist orientated position). Simply expressed, the assumption that there exists something beyond the accounts that people give is abandoned. Instead, what is examined are regularities and features of the account; this method was employed by Nigel Gilbert and Michael Mulkay in a study of scientists' accounts (Gilbert and Mulkay 1984). This has been referred to as a form of 'discourse analysis' (Wetherell and Potter 1988; Dant 1991). I mention this for the interested reader and in order to show the variety of ways in which interview data are interpreted. However, the idea that interviews are interesting only for the ways in which people use language to produce accounts is highly contested (see Gilbert and Abell 1984; Silverman 1985).

Interview analysis, whatever the focus of study, can be a long process in which perseverance, theoretical acumen and an eye for detail is paramount. It is often said that the hard work starts only when the data are collected and analysis begins: that is frequently the case. The success of its execution, in turn, lies in the hands of the researcher. In this section I have simply given an overview of its main elements and the different approaches employed. Yet to be faced with many hours of tapes or pages of transcripts can be a daunting sight. However, if you choose to use interviewing yourself, don't think the hours of frustration you might experience are the result of problems peculiar to you. They are not likely to be. The process can be alleviated by experience, reading around the subject and seeking supportive individuals for their opinions on the data and your coding.

Criticisms of interviews

I have covered a range of perspectives on interviewing. In this process it has been noted how structured interviewing does not simply reflect positivism, nor unstructured interviewing a social construction approach associated with idealism. In terms of the latter method, the section on analysis covered an ethnographic approach using cultural analysis, to a form of discourse analysis which focuses upon language use. As the result of covering such a broad spectrum I have, implicitly at least, covered many of the criticisms. However, consider the following.

Interviews are used as a resource for understanding how individuals make sense of their social world and act within it. However, the variant of discourse analysis I mentioned is interested in interviews as topics in their own right. It is thereby assumed that the link between a person's account of an action and the action itself cannot be made: it tells the social researcher little about a reality 'external' to the interview. Instead, an interview is a social encounter like any other. The prescription of interviewing books to 'control' the situation are just attempts to produce a false social situation which has no validity beyond the interview as a social encounter. Interviews cannot be assumed to produce data which reflect a 'real world'. For this reason, interviews are a *topic* of social research, not a *resource* for social research:

> interview data report not on an *external* reality displayed in the respondent's utterances but on the *internal* reality constructed as both parties contrive to produce the appearances of a recognisable interview.
>
> (Silverman 1985: 165)

The focus moves to the methods that people employ in constructing the interview, not the interview data themselves. This leads to a form of conversation analysis (see Heritage 1984; Schegloff 1988) which has been used to study such topics as embarrassment (Heath 1988), doctor–patient interactions (Heath 1981), as well as the interviewing of job applicants (Button 1987). Note, however, that we have taken a methodological route back into the discussion in Chapter 2, where so-called practical reasoning and the methods that people use to make sense of the social world around them were considered topics for social research and theorizing. The same criticisms of this perspective apply to this focus on interviewing as a topic for social research.

Again, the issues of qualitative depth in focused interviews and quantitative patterns of relationships which emerge from structured interviewing raise their heads. In Chapter 5 we saw how it was argued that questions of 'meaning' could be understood using a structured format. Yet more instrumental and less theoretical considerations also place a schism between these methods. In-depth qualitative interviewing with a large number of people is both expensive and time-consuming and this frequently dictates the methods employed. However, this does not prevent the researcher from understanding that the aims and limitations of different methods still apply, nor from lobbying sponsors for the use of the method(s) which would best suit the aims of the research. Researchers therefore have a duty to themselves and to others to reflect upon and acknowledge both the strengths and weaknesses of the methods they employ.

There are also the feminist criticisms of interviews which have been briefly covered. The spurious distinctions between reason and experience and of objectivity as detachment, are just some of the underlying arguments which inform this critique. However, as noted in Chapter 5, feminists have also used structured interviewing and in that section I concentrated on focused methods. Thus, while sharing the critiques of malestream research, there also exists a debate around interviewing methods among those who would regard themselves as feminist researchers. Further, some have argued that Ann Oakley's characterization of textbook prescriptions is an inaccurate representation (Malseed 1987). However, in reply, she argues this does not detract from the substance of her argument (Oakley 1987).

In a final criticism, I examined the contention that interviews rely on people's account of their actions as representing something beyond the interview situation. Several possibilities arise from this. First, accounts may simply be inaccurate for one reason or another. Second, while accounts may be a genuine reflection of a person's experiences, there might be circumstances or events which surrounded these of which the person was not aware. Third, a fuller understanding can be achieved only by witnessing the context of the event or circumstances to which people refer. The only way in which the researcher could examine these is to be there at the time. This, not without an element of contrivance on the author's part, brings us round to the subject of observation.

Summary

In many walks of life, interviews are used on a daily basis to understand and appraise individuals in particular and gain information in general. While the aims of such interviews are different in form from those used in social research, this common usage is a point often lost on those who concentrate solely upon their validity, instead of the way they are used as instruments for gaining information and, often, employing social power. At the same time, interviewing utilizes particular skills. For these reasons, researchers need to maintain an interest in their interviewing practices, as well as what is said and done as a result of the interview. Lastly, it is worth emphasizing that the data derived from interviews are not simply 'accurate' or 'distorted' pieces of information, but provide the researcher with a means of analysing the ways in which people consider events and relationships and the reasons they offer for doing so. If both the strengths and weaknesses of different methods of interviewing and approaches to their analysis are understood, they provide a way of understanding and explaining social events and relations.

CHAPTER 6: QUESTIONS FOR YOUR REFLECTION

1   What are the different methods of interviewing used in social research and how do they differ in their aims and process?

2   You are asked to devise an outline for an 'interviewer handbook'. The aim of this is to explain the different skills which are required for different types of interview methods. What do you consider are the essential attributes of an interviewer and why?

3   Choose a topic in which you are interested and would want to interview people about. Which method would you choose and what do you think its strengths and weakness might be?

4   'The Interview: Topic or Resource?' What perspectives inform this debate and what is your opinion on it?

7

The method of participant observation

To the contemporary postmodern French theorist Jean Baudrillard, our ideas of the world have become a set of media images through which reality is constructed. We are no longer able to simply differentiate between appearance and reality. Adverts persuade us to consume goods by employing a visual media which often has nothing whatsoever to do with the product; we become sold on and by images.

Such ideas, as with postmodernism in general, have not been received without some degree of scepticism. In examining the work of Baudrillard, the social theorist Zygmunt Bauman (1992) concludes with a recommendation for him: 'It becomes a philosopher and an analyst of his time to go out and use his feet now and again. Strolling still has its uses' (Bauman 1992: 155). To 'stroll' in this sense is to listen, observe and experience and to expose theories and biographies to new and unfamiliar social settings and relations, with a view to enhancing an understanding of them. This and the ideas upon which it is based are the subject of this chapter which, first, introduces the ideas and place of participant observation in social research, second, examines the process of conducting research using this method, third, considers the methods of analysing observations, and finally, discusses the problems associated with this method of social research.

Participant observation and social research

Participant observation has a quite distinct history from that of the positivist (or variable centred) approach to research. While its origins may be sought in social anthropology, it was the Chicago School of social research, particularly Robert Park, who encouraged his students to study, by observation, the constantly changing social phenomena of Chicago in the 1920s and 1930s. This led to a wide body of research on areas such as crime and deviance, race relations and urbanism (see Bulmer 1984a; Kurtz 1984).

The Chicago School and participant observation

Its aims, as well as its history, are also different: for example, the design of questionnaires involves the researcher in developing ideas and testing or exploring these using questions. Critics argue that researchers using this method assume that they already know what is important. In contrast, participant observation is said to make no firm assumptions about what is important. Instead, the method encourages researchers to immerse themselves in the day-to-day activities of the people whom they are attempting to understand. In contrast to testing ideas (deductive), they may be developed from observations (inductive).

In the Chicago tradition of research, we see a merging of two intellectual traditions. First, there is the tradition of *pragmatism* from the work of the American philosophers such as William James, Charles Peirce, John Dewey and George Mead. Within this tradition, it is emphasized that social life is not fixed, but dynamic and changing. In the words of Paul Rock (1979), social life is both 'incremental' and 'progressive'. Therefore, if people's social lives are constantly changing, we must become part of their lives in order to understand how it changes; we must participate in it and record our experiences. Knowledge of the social world does not then come from the propositions of logic upon which the theorist then descends upon the world to explain it. Knowledge can come only from undertaking detailed and meticulous inquiries through which we generate understanding.

Practitioners shun what is known as the *a priori* (a proposition that can be known to be true or false without reference to experience), preferring the *a posteriori* (knowing how things are by reference to how things have been or are):

> They attempt to make their research theoretically meaningful, but they assume that they do not know enough about the organization *a priori* to identify relevant problems and hypotheses and that they must discover these in the course of the research.
>
> (Becker 1979a: 312)

This is not an assumption of interviews in so far as if someone is asked for an account, the researcher does not consider it necessary to have personally experienced the event or relationship to which it refers in order to analyse or understand it. Similarly, positivists who use questionnaires are not immersing themselves in the social world in which people are busy experiencing, perceiving and acting according to their interpretations of that world. Instead, it is important to participate in social relations and seek to understand actions within the context of an observed setting. Why? Because it is argued that people act and make sense of their world by taking meanings from their environment. As such, researchers must become part of that environment for only then can they understand the actions of people who occupy cultures, defined as the symbolic and learned aspects of human behaviour which include customs and language. This technique, it is argued, is least likely to lead to researchers imposing their own reality on the social world they seek to understand.

The second strand informing the Chicago School tradition is known as *formalism*. While social relationships may differ from each other, they take forms which display similarities. In this way, we do not simply talk about one setting or group being 'unique', but ask the extent to which it displays similarities or it is typical of other groups or settings. Therefore, the focus of social inquiry is upon the interactions of people within social settings, not upon individuals as such. An advocate of this idea, George Simmel, argued that

> in order to discover and elucidate the general features of human interaction . . . the investigator must proceed, as in all other sciences, on the basis of methodical abstraction. For Simmel this constitutes the separation of the form from the content of social interactions, the forms by which individuals and groups of individuals come to be members of society.
>
> (Frisby 1984: 61)

Formalism as a perspective is also concerned with the ways in which particular social and cultural forms of life emerge. In keeping with pragmatism, they are argued to come from the practical concerns of people's everyday lives 'but that once established they take on a life of their own' (Hammersley 1990b: 37). These forms may actually conflict with each other, but the task of the researcher is to understand how they evolve. It is not surprising that Robert Park, a student of Simmel's, encouraged his students to 'stroll'.

These strands of thought also combine with the idea of *naturalism* which emphasizes that 'the social world should be studied in its "natural state" undisturbed by the researcher' (Hammersley and Atkinson 1983: 6). However, this does not mean that people simply react to their environments. According to this view, influenced by a number of theoretical and philosophical traditions, people are busy interpreting and acting within a social world infused with meaning. Thus, any concern with change and process must take this as its starting-point:

> I wish to point out that any line of social change, since it involves change in human action, is necessarily mediated by interpretation on the part of the people caught up in the change – the change appears in the form of new situations in which people have to construct new forms of action.
>
> (Blumer 1972: 191)

The process of learning behaviour, which this approach emphasizes, is argued to be absent from other forms of research: for instance, a questionnaire asks questions at one particular time. It is a 'static-causal snapshot' of attitudes; how and why people change is not understood. In practice, observers then record their own experiences in order to understand the cultural universe which people occupy. Participant observation may therefore be defined as

> The process in which an investigator establishes a many-sided and relatively long-term relationship with a human association in its natural setting, for the purposes of developing a scientific understanding of that association.
>
> (Lofland and Lofland 1984: 12)

Ethnography, as it is also referred, leads to an empathic understanding of a social scene. It excludes, over time, the preconceptions that researchers may have and exposes them to a new social milieu which demands their engagement. In this way, according to one view (Glaser and Strauss 1967), theory is generated from data. Glaser and Strauss have two criteria for theory. First, it should 'fit' the data and not be forced on to it. Second, it should be meaningfully relevant to the behaviour under study. As the researcher is exposed to each new social scene, this is a control on hasty theoretical conclusions (Silverman 1985). The more varied the scenes that one views or circumstances that one experiences, the more one can understand actions in social context.

Muddying the waters

The above tradition has had a considerable impact on the aims and method of participant observation. However, in Chapters 5 and 6 we have also seen that perspectives do not simply dictate methods and different perspectives frequently use the same methods or combination of methods. Participant observation is no different in this respect and no introduction to its place in social research can fail to acknowledge this.

We have encountered a number of dichotomies in social research which, on closer examination, have tended to be less clear than the doctrinaire posturing of much literature on social research would suggest. I am thinking, in particular, of the strict separation between quantitative and qualitative social research and theory and fact. While the methods which we use will obviously influence the nature of the data which we collect,

> Qualitative and quantitative methodology are not mutually exclusive. Differences between the two approaches are located in the overall form, focus, and emphasis of study.
>
> (Van Maanen 1979: 520)

Qualitative researchers therefore frequently resort to the language of quantification in their work and while surveys are argued by researchers to tap questions of meaning, they must first understand people's frames of reference and for this reason have a qualitative dimension to their design and interpretation.

The idea that there are facts which we can gather on the social world is also highly questionable, for it is theory which mediates our interpretations. Yet the emphasis of the above approach to participant observation has been upon induction and naturalism. Data are assumed to be collected and are somehow 'naturally occurring' – without being mediated by the theoretical concerns and biography of the researcher – while theory is derived from observations.

Again, these assumptions have been subjected to scrutiny and found wanting. For these reasons, researchers influenced by other perspectives have employed the method of participant observation and it would be an error to gloss over them and present the method as if its practice reflected a unified perspective (Stanley 1990c). However, two features certainly differentiate it from positivist-orientated research. First, the subject matter of the social sciences differs from the natural sciences, and second, to assist in understanding social reality, we must also directly experience that reality (Bryman 1988a: 52).

Willis (1977) used the method within the realist tradition. Spending time with a group of 'lads', he charted their progression from school to work. From his observations on their everyday lives, he derived a theory which argued that capitalist relations structured not only their actions, but also their expectations. However, this was not to assume that the 'lads' were simply cultural puppets. On the contrary, they were active in their resistance to oppressive social structures by not only understanding, but also questioning and mocking, the authority of teachers.

Ethnographers influenced by Marxism have also studied West Indian life styles in Bristol (Pryce 1986) and youth cultures more generally (Jefferson 1975). Cicourel (1976) has worked in the ethnomethodological tradition in order to show how juvenile justice was the product of negotiation between officials, parents and the juveniles. Feminist researchers, of differing theoretical orientations, have used observation methods to study women quantity surveyors (Greed 1990), relations within Chinese restaurants (Kay 1990), women and social class (Webb 1990), sexism in courtroom decisions (Eaton 1986) and women and delinquency (Campbell 1981; 1984).

I am now in a position to summarize the positive aspects of this method. First, it is least likely to lead researchers to impose their own reality on the social world they seek to understand. Second, the process of understanding action is omitted from other forms of research and how and why people change is not understood. Third, during interviews, there may be language or cultural differences expressed. In this case, observers may record their own experiences in order to understand the cultural universe which people occupy (subjective experiences) and convey these observations to a wider audience (from field notes) within the context of explaining their data (theoretical framework). The process by which these are achieved is the subject of the following sections.

The practice of participant observation

This method is one that those new to social research believe they can undertake with little effort. On first glance, it appears to be just about looking, listening, generally experiencing and writing all this down. This possesses more than a grain of truth. However, it is equally plausible to argue that participant observation is the most personally demanding and analytically difficult method of social research to undertake. Depending on the aims of the study and the previous relationship of researchers to those with whom they work, it requires them to spend a great deal of time in surroundings with which they may not be familiar; to secure and maintain relationships with people with whom they may have little personal affinity; to take copious notes on what would normally appear to be everyday mundane happenings; to perhaps incur some personal risk in their fieldwork and then, if that is not enough, weeks or months of analysis follow after the fieldwork. To those who are prepared and willing, however, it is also one of the most rewarding methods which yields fascinating insights into people's social lives and relationships and, more generally, assists in bridging the gap between people's understanding of alternative life styles and the prejudice which difference and diversity frequently meets.

The researcher's role

Participant observers may work in teams, which assists in sharpening insights and generating ideas. More often, however, researchers work alone. In the process they witness the 'reflexive rationalization' of conduct, that is the continual interpretation and application of new knowledge by people (including themselves) in their social environments as an ongoing process. The ethnographer then becomes the instrument of data collection (Brown 1984). Ethnographers gather data by their active participation in the social world; they enter a social universe in which people are already busy interpreting and understanding their environments:

> The condition of 'entry' to this field is getting to know what actors already know, and have to know to 'go on' in the daily activities of social life.
> (Giddens 1984: 284)

It does not then follow that researchers comprehend the situation as though it were 'uncontaminated' by their social presence and for this reason, naturalism, in its literal sense, is regarded as 'dishonest' by denying the effect of the researcher on the social scene (Stanley and Wise 1983: 160). On the contrary, the aim of understanding is actually enhanced by considering how they are affected by the social scene, what goes on within it and how people, including themselves, act and interpret within their social situations – hence the term *participant* observation.

In 'doing' ethnography, engagement is used to an advantage. Furthermore, being part of the social world which we study 'is not a matter of methodological commitment, it is an existential fact' (Hammersley and Atkinson 1983: 15). In this process, ethnographers have explicitly drawn upon their own biographies in the research process: for example, having been personally and politically engaged in protest as part of a group, before deciding to turn attention to its analysis (see Roseneil 1993). Our own cultural equipment is thereby used reflexively to understand social action in context. For this reason

> Rather than engaging in futile attempts to eliminate the effects of the researcher, we should set about understanding them.
> (Hammersley and Atkinson 1983: 17)

Depending upon the aim and history of the research, the particular roles which researchers adopt will vary and this, in turn, will affect the data produced. However, we may wish to adopt a particular role, but the circumstances do not permit it. As the experiences of Buchanan, Boddy and McCalman (1988) suggest, while organizational researchers, for example, should be 'opportunistic' in their fieldwork, if the possible and desirable clash, the former will always win through! The reasons why we are not able to adopt a particular role, while frustrating, might also become the topics of our research for they may tell us a great deal about the operation of social power and relations in the setting or organization under study.

In what is now becoming a standard reference on fieldwork roles, originally written in 1958, Gold (1969) identifies four roles of field research which assist in the process of analysing field notes. A central part of the analytic process being a reflexive consideration of the 'relations between and among investigator and research participants' (Gergen and Gergen 1991: 93) and the types of data subsequently generated.

The first role that Gold identifies is the *complete participant*. The researcher employing this role attempts to engage fully in the activities of the group or organization under investigation. Their role is also covert for their intentions are not made explicit. This is the role that Humphreys (1970) adopted in his work (discussed in Chapter 3). Among its advantages, it is argued to produce more accurate information and an understanding not available by other means (for example, see Festinger, Riecken and Schachter 1956; Ditton 1977; Rosenhan 1982).

Second, there is the *participant as observer*. This person adopts an overt role and makes her or his presence and intentions known to the group (for example, see Campbell 1984; Hobbs 1988; May 1991). In this process, they attempt 'to form a series of relationships with the subjects such that they serve as both respondents and informants' (Denzin 1978a: 188). Despite traditional concerns with 'establishing rapport' or what is called 'going native' and hence not being 'objective', for many researchers who possess the capabilities to understand, listen and learn, these are not problems and reflect a particular view of scientific inquiry which has been subjected to critical scrutiny and found wanting.

This role often means becoming a 'fan' (Van Maanen 1978) who desires to know and understand more from people within the setting. It does not, however, mean attempting to act as one of the group studied. This is particularly the case when it comes to research on crime and deviance. Polsky puts this forcefully: 'in doing field research on criminals you damned well better *not* pretend to be "one of them", because they will test this claim out' (Polsky 1985: 117). At the same time, attention to the accurate recording of events is still paramount and problems with this, or the previous role, may focus on the researcher's recall. This is graphically illustrated by Dick Hobbs (1988) in his study of the police and working-class crime in the East End of London. Being with the 'men' of the metropolitan police had its drawbacks in terms of focused analysis and the writing-up of field notes:

> for the most part I spoke, acted, drank and generally behaved as though I was not doing research. Indeed, I often had to remind myself that I was not in a pub to enjoy myself, but to conduct an academic inquiry and repeatedly woke up the following morning with an incredible hangover facing the dilemma of whether to bring it up or write it up.
>
> (Hobbs 1988: 6)

Indeed, feminist ethnographers have also turned their attention to relations within public houses (Hey 1986).

Third, we move away from the idea of participation to build up, over time, an understanding of a social setting, to the role of *observer as participant*. Strictly speaking, this would not be regarded as participant observation:

> The observer-as-participant role is used in studies involving one-visit interviews. It calls for relatively more formal observation that either informal observation or participation of any kind.
>
> (Gold 1969: 36)

Due to the lack of any lasting contact with people, Gold notes the possibility in this role of misunderstanding due to unfamiliarity with the culture and the language employed. It is more of an encounter between strangers which does not utilize the strengths of spending time in the field and getting to understand the rules, roles and relationships within the settings observed. Similarly, the *complete observer* is a non-participant role. At this end of the spectrum, the role completely removes the researcher from observed interactions and is epitomized by laboratory experiments which simply involve the mechanical recording of behaviour through, for instance, one-way mirrors.

Access

If participant observation involves becoming part of a group or organization to understand it, then it is obviously not simply a case of 'hanging around'. To become part of a social scene and participate in it requires that the researcher is accepted to some degree. This period of 'moving into' a setting is both analytically and personally important. Those aspects of action which are 'strange' to the observer may be 'familiar' to the people who are part of the study. However, how people manage and interpret their everyday lives is an important condition of understanding a social scene. In this sense, the experiences of the observer are central. As we experience a new scene it feels 'strange'. After a time, it becomes more familiar and it is understanding 'how' people achieve this which is one legitimate concern of participant observation:

> We learn what we can in advance about this relatively unknown territory, but once we are there, the first requirement is to gain some initial familiarity with the local scene and establish a social base from which we can continue our exploration until we are able to study some parts of that territory systematically.
>
> (Whyte 1984: 35)

It becomes important to regard the normal as unfamiliar. Further, if negotiating access into, for example, an organization, the researcher should be aware of the power relations within the organization. As Severyn Bruyn notes:

> The participant observer who studies a complex social organization must be aware of the fact that clearance at one level of the organisation does not insure clearance at another level. It is very important that the researcher takes into account the levels of power and decision-making extant in the group.
>
> (Bruyn 1966: 204)

If management are your level of entry into an organization, that could mean that others in the organization will be suspicious of your intentions. After all, they may consider that you are part of a management strategy of change. In such situations, the researcher must address these issues. However, while initial suspicion may be experienced, it is important not to regard this as a personal weakness, for it may be an understandable reaction on the part of the people within the setting or organization. Of course, this could block your entry, but access is not a stage, as many texts suggest, through which an observer passes before 'uncontaminated' data are supposedly derived (see May 1993).

Initial reactions to your presence can cause a sense of personal discomfort, but tell you a great deal about relations and concerns of people and should be recorded and not simply regarded as personal problems or weaknesses. For instance, only two days after starting research on changes in a public sector organization (May 1991), I was questioned by two people who were apparently suspicious of my intentions. The questions were forcefully put and difficult to answer at the time. Yet I learnt from this episode. I learnt that suspicion was understandable due to the politically charged atmosphere surrounding organizational change. I learnt that my credibility as an impartial researcher was to be a central issue as I moved through the different levels within the organization. My level of entry was management and not to have positively acted in the light of this initial suspicion would have meant, by default, carrying this suspicion with me. I also learnt that the two people who did the questioning had a vested interest in the changes taking place within the organization and, as such, any research associated with it.

Frequently in literature on the practice of participant observation, questions of access are regarded as methodological and/or theoretical inconveniences to be overcome. Researchers actual experiences of fieldwork are then reserved for separate volumes (see Bell and Newby 1977; Bell and Roberts 1984; Bryman 1988b; Roberts 1990; Hobbs and May 1993). On the contrary, experiences gained during negotiations for access to a group or organization, as well as the researcher's reflections on the research in general, are fundamental to the aims of enhancing understanding and explaining social relations.

Utilizing flexibility

One of the main advantages of participant observation is its flexibility:

> If you're half-way through a survey and one of the questions isn't working, you're worried, what are you going to do? You can't change it. Whereas if I learn today something useful from my field research, my observation, I can go out tomorrow and use it.
>
> (Becker, in Mullan 1987: 120)

Fieldwork then becomes a continual process of reflection and alteration of the focus of observations in accordance with theoretical developments. It also permits researchers to witness people's actions in different settings and routinely ask themselves a myriad of questions concerning people's motivations, beliefs and actions. Here are just a few for your reflection which could preoccupy any fieldworker: why did that happen and to whom? What are people supposed ordinarily to do in this setting and why? What would happen if people did X? What do they think about Y? What are the usual rules of the social scene? How are the rules negotiated? What are the verbal and non-verbal gestures employed? Who said what to whom and why? What do they mean and how do they relate to particular relationships and actions? Why is X not done? What would happen if something different happened? Finally, how does physical space relate to the setting and the interactions which take place within it? (These questions are adapted from Lofland and Lofland 1984.)

These are just a small number of possible questions that ethnographers would routinely ask themselves during the course of fieldwork. It is then possible to focus the next series of observations on answering these questions and thereby utilizing the flexibility of the method. In addition, participant observation often employs the unstructured interview technique as a routine part of its practice. The comparison of data derived from these two methods is not assumed to be incompatible. The very opposite is the case for such comparisons illuminate the researcher's understanding and provide information which is simply not available through observation:

> Observation guides us to some of the important questions we want to ask the respondent, and interviewing helps us to interpret the significance of what we are observing. Whether through interviewing or other means of data gathering, we need to place the observed scene in context, searching for the potential positive or negative sanctions, which are not immediately observable but may be important in shaping behaviour.
>
> (Whyte 1984: 96)

The questions to which we are directed are formulated according to an exposure to the social scene over time and an observation of people's everyday actions. This, together with an explicit analytic framework and aim of the study, enables researchers to focus their research inquiries. For this purpose, Whyte uses what he calls an 'orientating theory' which 'simply tells us in the most general terms what data we are likely to need at the point of analysis' (Whyte 1984: 118). Data are then collected under two headings (also mentioned in Chapter 6 under analysis): first, the identification of relationships within the social setting, and second, a description of events and situations which took place. Observation and the writing up of notes under these headings, together with any relevant interview data, provides a rich insight into social relations, events and processes. Data collection and analysis and the decision as to when to withdraw from fieldwork then take place together in what Glaser and Strauss (1967) refer to as 'theoretical sampling' and 'theoretical saturation', the latter referring to the time when observations no longer serve to question or modify the theories generated from earlier observations, thus rendering the theory 'saturated' with data.

Field notes

The 'data logging process', as Lofland and Lofland (1984) call it, is often regarded as boring but 'if the researcher lacks any personal emotional attachment to the concerns of the research, project quality (even completion) may be jeopardized' (1984: 47). This relies not only upon commitment, but also on the quality of the researcher's observations, the field notes and analytic abilities. In relation to field notes, there are a series of guidelines which can be given which I shall briefly overview in this section, but researchers do vary in their methods. Some prefer to use school exercise books with wide margins on the left-hand side. These margins enable you to highlight particular observations in which you are interested, make analytic notes, or notes to yourself to investigate an event or relationship in more depth and read other literature on a topic or theme which you have observed or which has arisen from your observations. (I use a particular pencil, with a rubber on top, which enables me to write fairly quickly and make corrections – we all have our quirks!)

The notes which you make will depend upon the focus of your inquiries. As noted, the flexibility of this method is a considerable advantage and some time will be spent in familiarizing yourself with the social setting and the people within it (and they with you). Following this initial period, to take notes on anything and everything which happens is not only impossible, but also analytically undesirable; your observations will be guided by your theoretical interests and they, in turn, modify or alter those. You will also need to minimize the time from observations to full notes and in the initial stages of your research, make a running description of events noting those questions for the ethnographer outlined above, and any others which may arise or you wish to pose.

While the nature of relationships are noted, the order and setting in which events unfolded are important to note, as are the rules employed and your reflections upon the events observed (the latter being for the left-hand margin). Over time, a picture is built up of the roles, rules and relationships between people. For instance, Bob Burgess, in his study of a school, moved from a general description to more detailed and focused records:

> in the staff common room my first set of fieldnotes begin by locating the position of the individuals with whom I sat. Gradually my notes detail a wider group of individuals, their names and their positions in the school until I could subdivide the groups in the staff common room according to their major characteristics.
>
> (Burgess 1990: 169)

A particular notation and filing system for your notes is important: for example, key words to jog your memory; different quotations marks to indicate paraphrased and verbatim quotes; files on individuals, topics and events; theoretical 'memos' (see Strauss 1988) to yourself on the research, plus any supplementary data in the form of documents or previous literature and research on the subject. Whatever method you devise, the important issues are *consistency* and *accessibility*.

Subjective adequacy

In writing notes, the feeling often arises that the observer may have missed something or is being too selective in their observations or even too general. Severyn Bruyn (1966) assists in this concern by listing six indices of what he calls 'subjective adequacy' to enhance the understanding of the researcher and thereby the validity of the research. These are time, place, social circumstances, language and intimacy. As authors on validity and qualitative research have noted (Kirk and Miller 1986), while this concept is often couched in terms of a positivist approach to research, Bruyn's ideas do assist in the continual process of reflexivity.

Time is the first of the indices. Quite simply, the more time that the observer spends with a group, the greater the adequacy achieved. As 'process' is a focus of inquiry,

> It is time which often tells us how deeply people feel about certain subjects. It is time that tells us how long it takes an outside influence to become a meaningful part of the lives of people in a culture. Those social meanings which really count in people's lives cannot be calculated by reference to the temporally limited, stimulus–response framework of the experimentalist. Cultural influences have an incubation period which takes time and close association to study.
>
> (Bruyn 1966: 207)

Second, there is *place*. A concentration on this dimension enables the researcher to consider the influence of physical settings upon actions. The researcher should record, therefore, not only the interactions observed, but also the physical environment in which it takes place. Closely related to this are *social circumstances*. The more varied the observer's opportunities to relate to the group, in both terms of status, role and activities, the greater will be his or her understanding. In work on the probation service (May 1991), I spent time with officers in prisons, organizational meetings and courtrooms, allowing me to observe probation work in different settings and the relationship between officer's actions and social environments.

Fourth, there is *language*. The more familiar that researchers are with the language of a social setting, the more accurate will be their interpretations of that setting. Bruyn is using the term language in its 'broadest sense' (1966: 212) to encompass not only words and the meanings that they convey, but also non-verbal communications such as facial expressions and bodily gestures in general. As researchers become more familiar with this aspect of the social setting they learn the language of the culture and record their impressions and any changes in their own behaviour: 'language threads through subject and object, creating, expressing, and representing the life and character of the people studied' (Bruyn 1966: 213).

Fifth, there is *intimacy*. The greater the personal involvement with the group and its members, the more the researcher is able to understand the meanings and actions they undertake. This not only links in with social circumstances, but also provides access to a more private or 'backstage' world, which underlies the comments of one of the greatest observers of human action, Erving Goffman. He speaks of the 'front' and 'backstage behaviour' of people which the observer can witness:

> there tends to be one informal or backstage language of behaviour, and another language of behaviour for occasions when a performance is being

presented. The backstage language consists of reciprocal first-naming, co-operative decision-making, profanity ... The frontstage behaviour language can be taken as the absence (and in some sense the opposite) of this.

(Goffman 1984: 129)

Finally, there is *social consensus*. This is the extent to which the observer is able to indicate how the meanings within the culture are employed and shared among people. This ability is clearly assisted by being exposed, over time, to the culture and noting under what conditions and in what settings the meanings are conveyed. This links into what is known at the 'principle of verifiability' which enhances the reliability of the study. As Hughes (1976) describes it, social researchers achieve 'understanding' when they know the rules of a social scene and can communicate them to another person who could then 'become a member of the actor's group' (Hughes 1976: 134). In other words, not only familiarity, but also the ability to communicate to another person the nature and rules operating within the setting so that they could then enter that setting and feel part of it. This, of course, is an ideal which researchers should aim at, not something which can be routinely and easily achieved.

In this section I have sought to present an overview and introduction to the main issues involved in the process of undertaking participant observation: from the researcher's role, through access to a social scene, to the flexibility of the method and finally, questions of subjective adequacy. During each of these elements of the research process, the question of reflexivity has been raised. While this is applicable to all forms of research, with participant observation in particular, researchers and their experiences and observations are the means through which the data are derived. For this reason, a process of constant questioning takes place whether in the form of considering explicit theoretical formulations or reflecting upon personal experiences which form such an important component of those. Seeing these as a central part of the process also greatly assists when it comes to the final analysis and writing-up of the research. Therefore, I shall elaborate upon these in the next section, while also considering the different ways in which the data may be analysed at the final stage of the research.

The analysis of observations

The concept of reflexivity and the advantages of flexibility both emphasize the process of analysis as part of fieldwork itself. At the same time, it was noted that researchers will also be constrained by the setting itself which may limit their abilities to conduct in-depth analysis at that stage. Therefore, the opportunity for reflection on experiences and a detailed analysis of the data may not come until the researcher has decided to withdraw from conducting any further fieldwork.

Howard Becker (1979a) lists four distinct stages of analysis whose overall aim is the categorization of collected data in order that the events, relationships and interactions observed may be understood or explained within the context of a developed theoretical framework. The first of the stages towards this aim is the 'selection and definition of problems, concepts and indices'. At this stage, researchers seek problems and concepts within the field setting which enable them to develop their understanding of the social setting; to determine the types of data which may be available by this method and to what extent observed social phenomena are related. Once established, such phenomena as may be observed are then placed within a theoretical framework for further investigation. Thus, in his research on medical students, Becker et al (1961) observed them referring to particular patients as 'crocks'. By focusing upon the interactions between students and patients, a theory of how some groups within the hospital classified other groups and for what reasons, was developed by further observations.

The second stage is a check on the 'frequency and distribution of phenomena'. This means focusing the inquiry in order to see what events 'are typical and widespread, and by seeing how these events are distributed among categories of people and organizational sub-units' (Becker 1979a: 317). It is at this point that the distinction between quantitative and qualitative work also breaks down (but not between good and bad research), because the researcher enters the realm of probability; in other words, how likely it is that a given phenomenon is frequent in the social setting and for what reason. It is possible to check such observations through interviewing and utilizing these forms of data, together with, say, documents on events – if available. This enables a check to be made against observations but, as Becker notes, this may not always be possible in the field so observers have to consider what other evidence they may need at the final stage of analysis and collect it accordingly: for example, collecting the minutes of organizational meetings and comparing these with your notes at those meetings if observing the policy process in an organization (May 1991). It is not infrequent to find yourself confronted by enormous amounts of data, much of which may not be of help in your theoretical formulations. However, it is better to have it at your disposal.

Third, he notes the 'construction of social system models' as the final stage of analysis 'in' the field, which 'consists of incorporating individual findings into a generalized model of the social system or organization under study or some part of that organization' (Becker 1979a: 319). This is similar in form to Glaser and Strauss's (1967) movement from substantive to formal theory. In each setting, one may derive a concept of substantive theory grounded within observations. In analysing different contexts, the researcher can then move to more formal theory composed of abstract categories. I shall give two examples.

Glaser and Strauss (1967) studied the concept of loss in the case of nurses dealing with dying patients. In each setting, nurses understandably experienced social loss which manifested itself in various ways. However, this in turn depended on the general concept of what social value was attached to individuals. So they moved from the particular (observed experiences of social loss) to the more general (how people attach social value to each other and how that affects their experiences of loss). Similarly, Becker's (1963) work on marijuana use led to an interest in the process through which people redefine experiences in order to 'neutralize' their deviant status. Yet in his eagerness to show how wrong previous literature on drug use was, he ignored a larger and more general question: that is, 'how do people learn to define their own internal experiences?' (Becker 1986: 148). This focus led to a whole series of empirical studies leading towards a general theory of self-identifying activity. As Becker notes, in using literature on the topic to help you generate theory, the moral of this story is: 'Use the literature, don't let it use you' (Becker 1986: 149).

Aside from the use of previous literature, this method also requires the constant comparison of data on the phenomena in which the researcher is interested. Thus, triangulated inquiry allows a comparison of data from interviews, observations, documents and even surveys (see Jick 1979; Whyte 1984; Fielding and Fielding 1986). The important point to remember is the level of generality at which you are operating for this obviously differs with substantive and formal theory:

> Both types of theory exist on distinguishable levels of generality which differ only in degree. Therefore in any one study each type of theory can shade at points into the other. The analyst, however, needs to focus clearly on one level or the other, or on a specific combination, because the strategies vary for arriving at each one. Thus, if the focus is on the higher level of generality, then the comparative analysis should be made among different kinds of substantive cases and their theories, which fall within the formal area.
>
> (Strauss 1988: 242)

The need to make comparisons between substantive cases to generate formal theory makes the task of using a consistent method of filing notes, theoretical ideas and secondary sources (other studies, books and documents on the topic) all the more important.

Assisting at this and the other stages of analysis is the use of 'units'. A 'unit is a tool to use in scrutinizing your data' (Lofland and Lofland 1984: 71). In their outline of qualitative analysis, John and Lyn Lofland note that they emerge as the scale of organization increases and each new one contains past ones. Thus, you start with *meanings* such as cultural norms and people's definitions of the situation and the variations in the scope of rules in the social scene. You may then focus on *practices* such as recurrent categories of talk and action which you consider have analytic significance. You might then consider *episodes*, for example, the remarkable and dramatic such as crowd disorder and sudden illness. Then move on to *encounters* (see Goffman 1961) where two or more people in each other's presence strive to maintain a single focus of mutual involvement. While how people 'get on' with each other appears mundane, it is also part of the social fabric which is observed and is worthy of attention in its own right. You then have a unit of analysis called *roles* and the focus here is directed towards the labels that people and organizations use to organize their own activities and describe those of others. How are these used? What are the issues in performing a role and what difficulties are encountered in their execution? These are just some of the questions to be asked. Then there are *relationships*. Noting Whyte's suggestion above on dividing data in terms of events and relationships, we would note how people regularly interact over time. From relationships we move to *groups* defined as those who conceive of themselves as a social entity (the 'we') having hierarchies, cliques and the means to cope with circumstances by mutual support or adaption. How and why these come about would be one focus of study of this social unit.

The units increase in abstraction with a focus upon *organizations*. The questions to ask yourself at this point and how this unit is defined are summarized by John and Lyn Lofland as

> Consciously formed collectivities with formal goals that are pursued in a more or less planned fashion. Some major aspects of the analysis of organizations include the circumstances of their formation, how they recruit and control members, the types and causes of goal-pursuit strategies they adopt, and the causes of their growth, change, or demise.
>
> (Lofland and Lofland 1984: 87–8)

Continuing with the theme of more general social units which encompass previous ones, there are *settlements*. These are beyond the grasp of the participant observer given their complex history and abstract nature. They comprise complex encounters, roles, groups and organizations within a defined territory which perform a range of functions. A classic example of this type of settlement analysis would be Whyte's *Street Corner Society* (1981).

A more general and abstract social unit is that of *social worlds* which manifest themselves in terms of modern transportation and communication systems providing the means for the proliferation and rise of social units. However, these are 'sprawling, shapeless entities' (Lofland and Lofland 1984: 91) which are not reducible to any one of the other units they contain. Thus, we speak of 'business worlds' or 'political worlds'. Finally, there are *life styles* considered as global adjustments to life by large number of similarly like-minded and situated individuals. Here we might consider the social forces that create or channel our tastes and structure our cultural lives (for example, see Williams 1981; Williamson 1987).

Each of these different units may have different questions asked of them by the analyst. However, as we move away from what can be observed to more abstract entities, so too we move away from substantive to more formal theories. Yet this method of analysis is very useful for orientating the researcher to data which may, on first glance, appear unmanageable. This is where the development of an analytic framework during fieldwork renders the data both manageable and intelligible.

Becker (1979a) notes a final stage: the withdrawal from the field to a final analysis and writing-up of the results. At this stage there might be a search for data which does not appear to represent your emerging theoretical consider-ations. If so, it requires your consideration and explanation. At the same time, evidence is systematically collected in order to illustrate a particular theme which arises from the data or to illustrate the particular way in which an episode, encounter or relationship unfolded and the practices and the meanings utilized by the people concerned. This may lend itself to a *sequential* analysis whereby the chronological unfolding of a particular topic or event is examined. This goes back to the methods described in Chapter 6 for analysing focused interviews.

Aside from the suggestions of Glaser and Strauss (1967), Becker (1979a), Lofland and Lofland (1984) and Strauss (1988), there have been a number of interesting innovations in the analysis of qualitative data, one of which, as noted, employs computer programmes for the mechanical indexing of the data (Fielding and Lee 1991). Others have specifically explored the relationship between feminism and fieldwork (Williams 1990) and qualitative analysis and semiotics (Manning 1987). This latter method focuses upon codes and signs used in social interaction whose analysis can be used for interpretative understanding of human relations and, for the purposes of policy analysis, organizational actions. Researchers may then focus upon the relationship between the use of language and human actions or study how language is employed in the social setting. Either way, what is often a difficult area of study may be employed in interesting new directions for qualitative researchers.

Writing ethnography

Clearly, no matter how well the data are analysed, the results must be presented and communicated in a way which is both persuasive, well argued and accessible to the audience, although the actual witnessing and recording of actions can cause problems when it comes to publication (see Becker 1979b). The final result of your work is a text which attempts to persuade the audience of the authenticity of your descriptions and their analyses. In this sense, writers have focused on texts not only as reporting a reality 'out there', but also in terms of their abilities to construct social reality (Atkinson 1990). Therefore, I would like to conclude this section with a brief look at the writing of ethnography, noting that many of these points are equally applicable to other methods.

Harry Wolcott (1990) suggests several points which need to be borne in mind when writing-up fieldwork. First, maintain a focus on the topic and continually ask the question: 'What is this (really) a study of?' (Wolcott 1990: 46). However, don't let yourself suffer from writer's cramp:

> you have already made many choices when you sit down to write, but probably don't know what they were. That leads, naturally, to some confusion, to a mixed-up early draft. But a mixed-up early draft is no cause for shame. Rather, it shows you what your earlier choices were, what ideas, theoretical viewpoints, and conclusions you had already committed yourself to before you began writing. Knowing that you will write many more drafts, you know that you need not worry about this one's crudeness and lack of coherence. This one is for *discovery* not *presentation*.
>
> (Becker 1986: 17, emphasis added)

Second, Wolcott suggests that data must be 'ditched' as you home in on the topic. While interesting to you, a long rambling description of an event, without analytic mileage, may not be to the audience. Third, if you do not have the evidence for some issues, don't let it grind you down. Check your materials and if it is not available, then there is little you can do. Remember, researchers cannot claim to know everything! Fourth, unless otherwise prevented, write in the first person. Don't overdo it with constant 'I's', but you were centre stage in this method of data collection and reflexivity and biography is a legitimate part of its practice. Fifth, Wolcott suggests the past tense for writing to prevent the use of present and past tenses together (Wollcott 1990: 47). Sixth, to illustrate analytic points, utilize specific instances from field notes. This is part of Clifford Geertz's (1973) notion of 'thick description' as it aligns the analytic framework with the imagination of the reader and a description of people's relationships and the events observed. Seventh, consider the audience for whom you are writing. Wolcott's suggestion is to write for those who know little of the area of study. This is a good discipline as it enables a degree of general accessibility to areas of academic study and is particularly important when considering action or evaluation research on behalf of an organization to whom you have to report. Finally, there is the brevity of your writing. While it is important to get it first written and not just 'right', the craft of writing remains of central importance. Corrections, additions, revising and editing of the text are all part of the writing process through which everyone has to travel. Again, a supportive and knowledgeable friend or supervisor can always be asked for their opinions in cases of doubt.

Criticisms of participant observation

As with Chapter 6 on interviewing, I have characterized the method of participant observation as not being the preserve of one school of thought and in so doing have again pre-empted some of the criticisms which are made by one perspective on the practice and theory of another. Interactionist researchers focus upon the operation of rules in social interaction, but not upon how these rules are formulated by people in context and so are criticized for presupposing their existence. Yet I have noted that how rules are formulated, negotiated and employed within interaction is a legitimate area of inquiry for observation. This point made, the ideas which inform 'naturalism' are worth some further consideration for they are often apparent, in various guises, in the process and production of ethnographic research. Martyn Hammersley (1990b; 1990c; 1992), in particular, has turned his attention to the problems of naturalism and those of ethnography in general.

As noted in relation to interviewing, the idea of disengagement to produce 'untainted data' is something of a myth and is based upon a particular view of 'scientific procedure' challenged by both feminists and those who emphasize the importance of reflexivity in the research process. Naturalism, although different in history and aim, often becomes translated as positivism by concentrating upon the production of data about the social world whose validity is based upon it being 'untainted' by the medium of its collection. Hence a lot of material on observation is devoted to 'reactivity', 'going native', and so on. On the other hand, naturalism focuses upon social life as a process in direct contrast to the positivist viewpoint. Given this state of 'flux', the positivist criteria of being able to replicate a study in order to justify its scientific status is rendered problematic (see Marshall and Rossman 1989).

The issues surrounding data collection as mediated by the researcher is not peculiar to observation, but as it relies so heavily upon the researcher's powers of observation and selection, then it is directly reliant upon his or her abilities. It is therefore possible that researchers will omit a whole range of data in order to confirm their own pre-established beliefs, leaving the method open to the charge of bias. Further, the observation of small-scale settings leaves it open to the charge that its findings are local, specific and not generalizable: it lacks *external validity*. This may be challenged by arguing that the observed social scene is 'typical' or by using a variety of data sources. However, on the latter point, Denzin's (1978a) prescriptions for triangulation often read like a positivist desire to mediate between sources of data in the search for some 'truth' about the social world *independent* of people's interpretations and creations of it:

> Underlying this suggestion is, ironically, once more, elements of a positivist frame of reference which assumes a single (undefined) reality and treats accounts as multiple mappings of this reality.
>
> (Silverman 1985: 105)

The distinction between fact and value which often characterizes interpretations of naturalism is therefore problematic. In the actual practice of this method (as noted in Chapter 1), feminist researchers have argued that women may view the social world from a greater vantage point, given their exclusion from its dominant ways of working (Smith 1988), while practitioners of ethnography have noted how it often 'embodies implicitly masculine perspectives' (Atkinson 1990: 148).

Realists, while utilizing this method, have also criticized the idea that we can observe events or relationships free from theories or concepts. Thus, any distinction between theory on the one hand, and empirical data through neutral observation on the other, must be challenged for we mediate our observations through concepts acquired in everyday life (Sayer 1992). The difference between 'natural' and 'artificial' settings as presupposed by naturalism must therefore be highly questionable (Hammersley and Atkinson 1983; Silverman 1985). Reflexivity, biography and theory lie at the heart of research practice in general and ethnography in particular. This emphasis recognizes that we are part of the world we study; that we bring to any setting our own experiences; that there is a constant interaction between theory and data; and that these issues cannot be separated from each other as methodological literature frequently implies.

Aside from the assumptions of naturalism, the problems of external validity and a masculine bias in its practice, participant observation has, for want of a better phrase, practical limitations. It demands that researchers spend time with relatively small groups of people in order to understand fully the social milieu which they inhabit. Hammersley and Atkinson (1983), while advocates of this method, note that

> like all methods, ethnography also has important limitations; it cannot be used to study past events; its ability to discriminate among rival hypotheses is weak by comparison with the experiment; and, in contrast to the social survey, it is poor at dealing with large-scale cases such as big organizations or national societies.
>
> (Hammersley and Atkinson 1983: 237)

Once again, we are left with not one single method as being the answer to all the methodological problems of social research: the use of a method or combination of methods will depend upon the aim of our research, the practical difficulties which are faced in 'the field', and the money and time available for research. Its successful execution depends upon the skills of the researchers and their understanding of the issues which inform research practice.

Summary

Participant observation is about engaging in a social scene, experiencing it and seeking to understand and explain it. The researcher is the medium through which this takes place. By listening and experiencing, impressions are formed and theories considered, reflected upon, developed and modified. Participant observation is not an easy method to perform or to analyse, but despite the arguments of its critics, it is a systematic and disciplined study which, if performed well, greatly assists in understanding human actions and brings with it new ways of viewing the social world.

CHAPTER 7: QUESTIONS FOR YOUR REFLECTION

1   What are the strengths and weaknesses of participant observation compared to other methods of social research?

2   What are the issues that participant observers should be aware of when conducting their research?

3   What different roles of participant observation are there and how do they affect the data which are collected?

4   In your opinion, what is the relationship between social theory and data collected by observational methods?

8

Documentary research

The use of documents alongside observational data was raised in Chapter 7, allowing comparisons to be made between the observer's interpretations of events and those recorded in relevant documents. These sources may also be utilized in their own right. They can tell us a great deal about the way in which events were constructed at the time, the reasons employed, as well as providing materials upon which to base further research investigations. As such, the method is deserving of attention and, as we shall see, covers a wide variety of sources including official statistics. The cautionary comments in Chapter 4 on using secondary sources for research should therefore be read alongside the following account.

The place of documents in social research

There are a wide variety of documentary sources at our disposal for social research. Documents inform the practical and political decisions which people make on a daily and longer-term basis and may even construct a particular reading of past social or political events. They can tell us about the aspirations and intentions of the period to which they refer and describe places and social relationships at a time when we may not have been born, or were simply not present. Nevertheless, despite their importance for research purposes and in permitting a range of research designs (Hakim 1987), this is one of the least explained research techniques in the literature. Why should this be so?

Ken Plummer (1990) offers one answer to this question. The twin influences of positivistic methodologists and abstract theorists on social research lead either to documents being dismissed as 'impressionistic', or to the use of any type of data being regarded as crude empiricism. Thus, despite the richness of documents, research reports based upon these sources are often 'relegated to the dustbins of journalism and the most marginal social science journals'

(Plummer 1990: 149). In contrast to these tendencies, it is clear from his book that social research has much to learn from these sources.

A further reason focuses upon the use of documents for historical research. History is often thought to sit uneasily alongside social science disciplines (see Goldthorpe 1984). Another possibility focuses upon the method itself. Documentary research is, in comparison to the other methods we have covered so far,

> not a clear cut and well-recognized category, like survey research or participant observation ... It can hardly be regarded as constituting a method, since to say that one will use documents is to say nothing about *how* one will use them.
>
> (Platt 1981a: 31, original emphasis)

To take each of these three points in turn. Positivism has been criticized as based upon a limited concept of science which, upon examination, cannot live up to its own canons of scientific inquiry, while its methods reproduce and reflect biases already contained within society. As for the debates on the relationship between history and social research, space precludes a detailed discussion. However, history as a discipline in its own right provides us with a sense of our 'past' and with that, the ways in which our 'present' came about. The nature of past social, political and economic relations are there for us to see through the acts of historical research which enable us to reflect on contemporary issues. For instance, Geoff Pearson (1983) examines the view that hooliganism is symptomatic of a contemporary moral decline following a 'permissive age'. By employing a range of documentary sources going back to Victorian times, he examines what are often thought to be these 'golden ages', only to find identical fears being expressed in each period considered. This study therefore demonstrates that this phenomenon is not peculiar to contemporary times, as is widely believed.

On a more instrumental level, the ambiguities and tensions surrounding documentary research are changing as more researchers utilize documents due to the increasing availability of data in modern information societies. As such, researchers need to be aware of the documentary sources which may be used, as well as the ways in which they are used (Jennifer Platt's 'how'). The next section therefore considers various documentary sources for social research; the second part of the chapter examines the perspectives and processes which inform their use and collection.

Sources of documentary research

These include historical documents, not only laws, declarations and statutes, but also secondary sources such as people's accounts of incidents or periods in which they were involved. However, while many definitions of documents are narrow in scope, John Scott (1990) offers a broad definition for research purposes which is worth quoting at length:

> a document in its most general sense is a written text...Writing is the making of symbols representing words, and involves the use of a pen, pencil, printing machine or other tool for inscribing the message on paper, parchment or some other material medium...Similarly, the invention of magnetic and electronic means of storing and displaying text should encourage us to regard 'files' and 'documents' contained in computers and word processors as true documents. From this point of view, therefore, documents may be regarded as physically embodied texts, where the containment of the text is the primary purpose of the physical medium.
>
> (Scott 1990: 12–13)

A report based on official statistics would be covered by this definition. To these we could add other government records: for example, Hansard, ministerial records, debates, political speeches, administrative and government committee records and reports, etc. In addition, the content of the mass media, novels, plays, maps, drawings, books and personal documents such as biographies, autobiographies, diaries and oral histories; the latter being used in work and life history analyses (Samuel 1982; Anderson et al 1990; Plummer 1990; Dex 1991). Photographs, although existing on the borderline between the 'aesthetic' and 'documentary' (Scott 1990: 13), may be records of events and for that reason, attention has also been turned to these with interesting results (Sontag 1978; Farran 1990; Spence and Holland 1991). It is not surprising, given such a catalogue of sources, that Scott's book aims 'to recognise this diversity in documentary sources as a valuable feature of social research' (Scott 1990: 13). Let us further consider both physical and documentary sources available to researchers.

According to Webb et al (1966) researchers may use 'physical traces' as part of what they call 'unobtrusive measures' of social research. Sherlock Holmes used 'physical' evidence in his deductions which they define as

> those pieces of data not specifically produced for the purpose of comparison and inference, but available to be exploited opportunistically by the alert investigator.
>
> (Webb et al 1966: 36)

Into this category would fall evidence left at the scene of a crime such as hair, or a piece of fabric from clothing. These are further subdivided into 'erosion' and 'accretion' measures. Erosion measures are defined as those 'where the degree of selective wear on some material yields the measure' (Webb et al 1966: 36). One example might be the degree of wear on a carpet to determine the frequency of its use, or the wear on library books for a similar purpose. Indeed, the wear on vinyl tiles surrounding an exhibit in a museum in Chicago provided an indicator of its popularity with visitors (Webb et al 1966: 36). While in terms of the popularity of library books, this can be ascertained by using the library records whether in manual or computer format. Indeed, it might even be possible to determine the times when people attend their places of work by whether they have collected their mail!

Accretion measures, on the other hand, are deposits of materials (Webb et al 1966: 36). One such example, to continue with the detective analogy, is the deposit of mud on shoes. The mud can be analysed and its likely location established, telling detectives where the suspect or victim may have come from. In a similar way, archaeologists estimate the populations of ancient sites by the size of the floor area of excavated buildings.

Literature on the classification of documents (Webb et al 1966; Denzin 1978a; Burgess 1990; Scott 1990; Calvert 1991) tends to fall into three main groups: first, primary, secondary and tertiary documents; second, public and private documents; and third, unsolicited and solicited sources. Primary sources refer to those materials which are written or collected by those who actually witnessed the events which they describe. In Bertrand Russell's (1912) terms they represent knowledge by *acquaintance*. It is therefore assumed that they are more likely to be an accurate representation of occurrences in terms of both the memory of the author (time) and their proximity to the event (space). However, as Burgess notes (1990: 124), these sources must also be seen in social context and for this purpose, the researcher might employ secondary sources. These are written after an event which the author had not personally witnessed and the researcher has to be aware of potential problems in the production of this data. Tertiary sources enable us to locate other references. They are 'indexes, abstracts and other bibliographies ... There are even bibliographies to help us find bibliographies' (Calvert 1991: 120). Libraries often possess collections of abstracts and reference manuals which assist in this process.

The distinction between public and private documents is an important one. The fact that materials may exist says little about whether the researcher may gain access to them. For this reason, Scott (1990) divides documents into four categories according to the degree of their accessibility. They are closed, restricted, open-archival and open-published. In his study of the life and thought of Sydney Olivier (an early Fabian thinker), Frank Lee (1988) found it necessary to seek the permission of the guardians of the private 'Olivier Family Papers', whose access is restricted.

In terms of public documents, the largest category are those produced by national and local governments and would include, for example, registrations of births, marriages and deaths and also police, taxation and housing records. Some of these documents may be protected by the Official Secrets Act and are therefore 'closed'. Few official records, as Scott notes, fall into the restricted category; one example is the British royal papers whose access may be granted only by the monarch (Scott 1990: 17). Open-archived records are stored in the

Public Records Office (PRO) at Kew, in Richmond, Surrey, or, in the case of the United States, the Library of Congress. Open-published documents include many of those covered in Chapter 4, plus Acts of Parliament and Hansard records of parliamentary debates.

Finally, we come to the third group: solicited and unsolicited documents. Burgess (1990) makes this distinction on the grounds that some documents would have been produced with the aim of research in mind, whereas others would have been produced for personal use. Diaries, for example, may be used in social research by asking participants to record particular events and/or express their opinions upon them. However, even if they are for personal consumption and are accessible to a researcher, they are still 'addressed to an audience' (Thompson 1982: 152), or what has been called a 'model reader' (Eco 1979). It is this sense of social context and to whom a document or text may be addressed, which brings us round to a discussion of the perspectives in and processes of documentary research.

The process of documentary research

Conceptualizing documents

There are several ways in which researchers might conceptualize a document and frame their research questions accordingly. In one guise or another, we have encountered most of them in our discussions of other methods. Thus, for some researchers, a document represents a reflection of reality. It becomes a medium through which the researcher searches for a correspondence between its description and the events to which it refers. Yet if we can 'read off' the accounts of a document, separate from the methods we employ to achieve this, are we not suggesting, once again, that there are social facts which exist independently of interpretations? We have already encountered the problems of this positivistic approach.

In contrast, other approaches consider documents as representative of the practical requirements for which they were constructed. In this focus, we consider what Cicourel (1964) has called the 'unstated meaning structures' of documents. The document itself is taken to stand for some underlying social pattern or use value. Thus, in his classic study on juvenile justice (Cicourel 1976), he examined the translation of oral conversations between juveniles and police and probation officers into written reports. These reports attempted to justify the procedures adopted for this purpose, but were also open-ended in their translation. This provided for 'various constructions of "what happened"' (Cicourel 1976: 17). They were thereby based upon a form of 'practical reasoning' which rendered the social order of juvenile justice accountable and comprehensible and yet open to negotiation and manipulation by interested parties. There are parallels here with the discussion on official statistics as 'accomplishments' and interviews as topics and not resources. Let us take one further illustrative example.

Research by Zimmerman (1974) on caseworkers' use of documents in a welfare agency firmly places the use of administrative documents within what he calls 'practical organizational purposes'. On most occasions, information contained within them is accepted without question as 'fact'. If it is questioned by, for example, a welfare claimant, the document then stands as the arbitrator of these 'facts'. Indeed, the suggestion that the document may be false was regarded by agency staff as 'incredible':

> For them, the possibilities opened up by such a doubt, including the possibility of a conspiracy between the applicant and the document-producing organization, were not matters for idle speculation. The possibility of error was admitted, but only as a departure from ordinarily accurate reportage.
>
> (Zimmerman 1974: 133)

Moving away from the idea that a document independently reports social reality, or its production is yet another method by which people accomplish social order, we now utilize our own cultural understandings in order to 'engage' with 'meanings' which are embedded in the document itself. Researchers do not then apologize for being part of the social world which they study but, on the contrary, utilize that very fact. A document cannot, therefore, be read in a detached manner. Instead, we must approach documents in an engaged manner. This emphasis on *hermeneutics* (discussed in Chapter 1 and elsewhere), submits the analyst to consider the differences between their own frames of meanings and those found in the text. A researcher might then begin with an analysis of the common-sense procedures which came to formulate the document in the first instance, but their analysis need not end there. The document may be located within a wider social and political context. Researchers then examine the factors surrounding the *process* of its production, as well as the social *context*.

According to one version of this view, what people decide to record is itself informed by decisions which, in turn, relate to the social, political and economic environments of which they are a part:

> fields of learning, as much as the works of even the most eccentric artist, are constrained and acted upon by society, by cultural traditions, by wordly circumstance, and by stabilizing influences like schools, libraries, and governments ... both learned and imaginative writings are never free, but are limited in their imagery, assumptions, and intentions.
>
> (Said, in Easthope and McGowan 1992: 59)

Documents might then be interesting for what they leave out, as well as what they contain. They do not simply reflect, but also construct social reality and versions of events. The search for the documents' 'meaning' continues, but with researchers also exercising 'suspicion'. It is not then assumed that documents are neutral artifacts which independently report social reality (positivism), or that analysis must be rooted in that nebulous concept practical reasoning.

Documents are now viewed as mediums through which social power is expressed (Giddens 1976; 1984; Habermas 1984; 1987). They are approached in terms of the cultural context in which they were written and may be viewed 'as attempts at persuasion' (Sparks 1992). Approaching a document in this way 'tells us a great deal about the societies in which writers write and readers read' (Agger 1991: 7). It might, for example, reflect the marginalization of particular groups of people and the social characterization of others: for example, in her study of the way in which the media represented the Greenham women who protested against nuclear weapons, Alison Young (1990) did not take their reports at 'face value':

> This strategy of rejection and repudiation I take to be axiomatic for any critique of representational forms such as the press, which continually foster the desire for consensual world views, unifying and objective underlying orders, monolithic structures and the obscuring of differences.
>
> (Young 1990: 164–5)

Within this approach, the very act of reading a text may become the revision of its premises. Thus, for Adrienne Rich, a feminist reading of a text is also an act of refusal. The researcher concentrates on the way in which it constructed the contribution of women to an event, but the strategy of refusal enables women to see their contemporary social and political situation in a new light:

> the act of looking back, of seeing with fresh eyes, of entering an old text from a new critical direction – is for women more than a chapter in cultural history: it is an act of survival. Until we can understand the assumptions in which we are drenched we cannot know ourselves.
>
> (Rich in Humm 1992: 369)

Critical approaches to documentary sources are far from being unified bodies of thought. Michel Foucault's work, for instance, is a critical project which is not so concerned with the relationship between the author and the document, but with the 'hidden' meanings of the text:

> It is a very familiar thesis that the task of criticism is not to bring out the work's relationship with the author, not to reconstruct through the text a thought or experience, but rather to analyze the work through its structure, its architecture, its intrinsic form, and the play of its internal relationships.
>
> (Foucault 1984: 103)

The poststructuralist work of both Michel Foucault and Jacques Derrida (see Kamuf 1991) are influenced by a 'semiotic' approach to textual analysis (mentioned in Chapter 7). This is particularly represented in the work of Roland Barthes (1967). In contrast, Anthony Giddens (1979) is critical of this approach as it appears to suggest that a text does not refer to anything beyond itself nor to the intentions of its author. We return, once again, to the issue of whether a text (which would include an interview transcript or observation field notes) corresponds to the events which it describes: is it a topic *of* social research or a resource *for* social research? Giddens is not a positivist in the sense so far described but argues, contrary to Foucault, that a text must be approached in terms of the intentions of its author and the social context in which it was produced.

Following from Giddens' approach, Scott (1990) argues that a researcher should approach a document in terms of three levels of meaning interpretation. First, the meanings that the author *intended* to produce, second, the *received* meanings as constructed by the audience in differing social situations, and third, the *internal* meanings that semioticians exclusively concentrate upon. However, they cannot 'know' these 'independently of its reception by an audience' (Scott 1990: 34).

These are new directions in documentary research which move away from the positivist emphasis that Plummer (1990) identified as one impediment to their use in social research. Collectively, they represent various approaches to analysis and combine elements of realism, critical theory, feminism, postmodernism and poststructuralism. These are not easy ideas to grasp — particularly as positivism has held such a grip on social research for so long. However, to present the 'how' which Platt (1981a) referred to as being one perspective on documentary research would be an inaccurate representation of their contemporary use (as well as being counter to the philosophy underlying this book).

Using documents

Perspectives noted, I wish now to move on to the process of collecting documents. For this purpose I shall use two examples, one drawn from the use of past documents to understand events and relationships, the other being a media research project. In the process, it will become evident that the methods utilized depend upon not only the researcher's perspectives, but also the time and resources available, the aims of the research and the problems encountered in the collection of data. As we shall see with the first example, if we are relying solely upon this technique, we cannot rectify this by producing the data ourselves. Nevertheless, with Scott's (1990) broad definition of a document and the vast generation of information which now characterizes modern societies, this may not be a problem unless dealing with particular historical periods. A number of problems may then be encountered.

David Dunkerley's (1988) research account provides a useful summary of some of these problems in his 'case study research' (see Yin 1988) which examined the relationship between a naval dockyard and the local community. This account appears in a volume which deliberately aims to show how research was actually carried out, as opposed to the ideals of methodological procedure. It demonstrates that even the most experienced researchers are subject to issues associated with time and money and the availability and accessibility of documentary evidence. This study aimed to

> concentrate upon the origin of the dockyard labour force, the extent of intergenerational job transmission, internal work structure, job security and political attitudes, and the effect of mobility opportunities.
>
> (Dunkerley 1988: 85)

Three methods of documentary inquiry were chosen for this purpose. First, a sample of population censuses dated since 1851, which are kept at the Public Records Office (PRO). The aim with this set of materials was to gain information on levels of employment, birthplaces, and so on, across time. Second, the use of local histories, as well as Admiralty and Treasury Papers (also at the PRO) which would specifically relate to dockyard labour relations, employment opportunities and skills to be found within the locality. Third, the use of oral histories based on interviews with three generations of dockyard workers.

Three immediate problems arose in what the author notes was an ambitious exercise given the constraints of time and resources (Dunkerley 1988: 86). First, it was assumed that the historical records would be available. As it transpired, local information was either not available or no longer existed (due to bombing raids during the Second World War). In addition, what there was turned out to be catalogued in the PRO under obscure headings. Second, the type of material collected by the Census changed over the years, making its collection either a non-starter, or rendering the ability to compare changes, across time, untenable. Third, when it came to more recent and detailed information, it was 'subject to closure and simply not available to the bona fide researcher' (Dunkerley 1988: 86). What information there was also proved to take a considerable time to extract.

As a result of these problems and the distance that the researcher had to travel to get to the research site, the aims of the dockyard community study were altered and additional funding had to be sought. In the end, the study concentrated upon 'technological and historical development covering a period spanning the last century' (Dunkerley 1988: 87). This change of focus took account of cost and time, as well as the availability of documentary evidence.

This account demonstrates that researchers have to be aware of the possibility that the information which they seek is 'closed'. In researching people over the age of 90, for example, researchers were prevented by the Department of Social Security from obtaining sample names from records (Bury and Holme 1990). Furthermore, even if documents are available, if they are handwritten, the researcher may have problems in reading them, or they may have been damaged over time. Diaries and other personal documents, in particular, use abbreviations and coded references to individuals or events which may be difficult to interpret. One of the most famous diarists, Samuel Pepys, often used codes in his diary entries (Scott 1990: 179).

The second example is based upon a field of study which has examined the relationship between the media and their depictions of criminal or deviant activity (see Cameron and Frazer 1987; Caputi 1987; Young 1990; Ericson, Baranet and Chan 1991; Sparks 1992). While they differ in their methodological and theoretical approaches, they all employ documentary sources in one form or another. In order to consider this process, I shall concentrate on the works of Richard Ericson and his colleagues.

A study by Ericson, Baranek and Chan (1991) examined the content of news sources on crime, law and justice. Following their previous work (1987; 1989) their perspective viewed news as not only reflecting but also actively constructing our sense of the social 'reality' to which it refers. Journalists themselves are therefore implicated within society's apparatuses of social control by constructing news which visualizes and symbolizes crime and attempts to convince the audience of the authority of its descriptions. After all, most people learn of crime, law and order via the media:

> Through dramatized descriptions, metaphoric language, and pictures, news depicts events that are called up in the mind (visualized) even while they remain invisible to the eye. News representations are symbolic in the sense they embody, stand for, or correspond to persons, events, processes, or states of affairs being reported. News representation involves authorization of who can be a representative or spokesperson of a source organization, of what sources are 'authorized knowers'.
>
> (Ericson, Baranek and Chan 1991: 5)

The aim of this study was to examine the ways in which different media sources operated according to the markets they worked within. For this purpose, the authors took a sample of radio, television and newspaper outlets, covering issues of crime, legal control, deviance and justice in the Toronto region of Canada. This provided a comparison of the different ways in which news was depicted. These sources were also grouped into 'quality' and 'popular' so the variations between markets could be examined. However, this was a study of news 'content'. Yet it has been emphasized that social 'context' is fundamental to understanding the meanings contained within documents. The authors were only too aware of this point:

> News, like law and science, is a socially constructed product that is highly self-referential in nature. That is, news content is used by journalists and sources to construct meanings and expectations about their organizations.

This means that the analyst of news *content* must examine the meaning used by news producers in the *construction* of their product.

(Ericson, Baranek and Chan 1991: 49, emphasis added)

In order to locate the study of patterns of meanings in media texts by the use of *content analysis* (see p. 145), they drew upon their previous ethnographic work on journalists and the construction of news sources (Ericson, Baranek and Chan 1987; 1989). The texts themselves were sampled over a period of thirty-three days to study them across time. The aim was to compare quality and popular newspapers, with an evening broadcast on quality and popular television and an evening quality and popular radio broadcast. The newspapers were sampled by pages; the television broadcasts were videotaped and the radio broadcasts audiotaped. The radio and television reports were transcribed – verbatim – along with notes on the use of 'visuals' and the use of sounds other than words. The result was a vast number of data which were analysed in considerable detail and located within their previous studies on news construction.

Approaching a document

Having discussed these examples, it remains to consider in this section with what questions a researcher should approach a document? This is not an exhaustive list, but points to the main themes raised in the process of documentary research. Scott (1990) proposes four criteria for assessing the quality of the evidence available from documentary sources and this section considers each one: authenticity, credibility, representativeness and meaning.

The issue of a document's *authenticity* is clearly essential to the conduct of this form of research:

> Judgement of authenticity from the internal evidence of the text comes only when one is satisfied that it is technically possible that the document is genuine.
>
> (Calvert 1991: 121)

However, even an inauthentic document could be of interest because 'it cannot be fully and correctly understood unless one knows that it is not authentic' (Platt 1981a: 33). Platt therefore provides several guidelines for assessing their authenticity. First, it contains obvious errors or is not consistent in its representation. Second, different versions of the same document exist. Third, there are internal inconsistencies in terms of style, content, handwriting, etc. Fourth, the document has passed through the hands of several copyists. Fifth, the document has been in the hands of a person or persons with a vested interest in a particular reading of its contents. Sixth, the version derives from a suspect secondary source. Seventh, it is inconsistent in relation to other similar documents. Finally, it is 'too neat' in terms of being representative of a certain group of documents (Platt 1981a: 34).

Following the questioning of a document's authenticity, there is its *credibility*, which 'refers to the extent to which the evidence is undistorted and sincere, free from error and evasion' (Scott 1990: 7). One example of such an assessment relates to the use of Census and registration information. Questions to ask at this point include, Are the people who record the information reliable in their translations of the information that they receive? How accurate were their observations and records? To achieve this, as noted above, we may employ other sources on the life and political sympathies of the author. This will enable the researcher to establish the social and political context in which the document was produced.

Representativeness has been referred to as a question of 'typicality' in Chapter 7. The issue of whether a document is typical depends on the aim of the research. 'Untypical' documents may be of interest, so we should not become too obsessed with this issue. However, if we are concerned with drawing conclusions which are intended to argue that there is a typical document or a typical method of representing a topic in which we are interested, then this becomes an important theme in order to demonstrate how one interpretation of an event predominates to the exclusion of others. For instance, Calvert (1991) notes how some documents are deliberately destroyed and recent protests in the United States over the 'systematic bias' of a series entitled 'Foreign Relations of the United States'.

Finally, there is the question of a document's *meaning*, which refers to the clarity and comprehensibility of a document to the analyst. Two questions are of concern: 'what is it, and what does it tell us?' (Scott 1990: 8). However, these are far from easy questions to answer. Going back to the example of the media research of Ericson and his colleagues, meanings were set within a social context derived from previous studies. Thus, while meanings change and the use of words varies, an idea of social context enables understanding.

The method of documentary research, like all of those we covered so far, requires not only some practice, but also a reflexivity on the part of the researcher. So far, I have endeavoured to provide you with an introduction to a method which has, in the past, been subsumed under the dominance of the others we have discussed. This, I believe, is a shortfall. As I hope to have shown, it is also a valuable method in understanding and explaining social relations. It now remains for me to consider the analyses of documents and criticisms of documentary research.

The analysis of documents

We have now considered a document in terms of its authenticity, representativeness, credibility and meaning; Scott (1990) divides 'meaning' into intended, received and content meaning. Building on these themes, this section will follow the same pattern as in Chapters 5–7 in presenting an overview of approaches in order that readers may pursue their interests beyond the level covered here. This is particularly pertinent given that a number of theoretical issues have been raised, from mainstream positivism, through the interpretation of documents in terms of practical reasoning, to semiotics, feminist and critical approaches. Differences of theoretical emphasis certainly exist in the ways in which a document is considered. Thus, in terms of life histories, Plummer's (1990) approach to their analysis considers the intentions and purposes of the author. Yet to those influenced by Barthes (1967), the text takes on a life of its own, separate from the author. Given these differing perspectives, it is not surprising to find documents analysed in both quantitative and qualitative ways.

Quantitative and qualitative approaches

In terms of social research, documents do not stand on their own, but need to be situated within a theoretical frame of reference in order that its content is understood. For this purpose we can use *content* analysis. This focus considers the frequency with which certain words or particular phrases occur in the text as a way of identifying its characteristics. The resulting analytic framework then makes 'sense' of the data through generated theoretical categories. This method takes both quantitative and qualitative forms. Quantitative content analysis

> seeks to show patterns of regularities in content through repetition, and qualitative content analysis...emphasizes the fluidity of the text and content in the interpretive understanding of culture.
> (Ericson, Baranek and Chan 1991: 50)

As with interviewing and observation, the use of computer analysis of texts is helpful towards these ends. These assist in searching for individual words and phrases and their frequency or context in the text; they can also help in analysing connections between codes or categories of behaviour which the production of the document represents (see Fielding and Lee 1991). Content analysis is also employed on a commercial basis by, for example, the journal *Trend Monitor*, which is 'an in-depth study of the computing, communications and media sectors' (*Guardian* 25 May 1989).

As with the discussion on standardization in Chapter 5, the quantitative analyst would seek to derive categories from the data in order that it can be compared. Words or phrases in the document are then transformed into numbers. The number of times which a word occurs in the text is taken as an indicator of its significance. This is presumed to enhance both the reliability and verification of the classified data. It is therefore assumed 'that there exists a defensible correspondence between the transformed account and the way the information was meant in its original form' (Garfinkel 1967: 190-1).

In considering the problems of a quantitative count, the issues covered in previous chapters are again raised. First, this method considers product and says little of process. In the context of this discussion, it deals only with what has been produced, not the decisions which informed its production which tells us so much about its meanings. Second, an empiricist problem is raised for it deals only with information which can be measured and standardized and for this reason considers only data which can be simplified into categories. Third, in this preoccupation, it reproduces the meanings used by authors in the first instance, as opposed to subjecting them to critical analysis in terms of the political context of their production. Fourth, it fails to understand the practical organizational context of their production and interpretation as part of the methods by which people make sense of their social world (Benson and Hughes 1991). Fifth, it assumes that the audience who receive the message must translate it as the analyst does. By definition, it thereby negates the idea that a text is open to a number of possible readings by its audience. (Would all people read the same meanings into a diary account or newspaper report?) To return to our molecules in a test tube analogy in Chapter 1, this can so easily become a crude stimulus–response model of human behaviour: what people read is what they think. Analysts have only to read the text to know what the audience is automatically thinking.

The frequency with which words or phrases occur in a text (a quantitative emphasis) may therefore say nothing about its 'significance within the document' (a qualitative emphasis):

> It may be that a single striking word or phrase conveys a meaning out of all proportion to its frequency; and a non-quantitative approach may be better able to grasp the significance of such isolated references. The content analyst must engage in an act of qualitative synthesis when attempting to summarise the overall meaning of the text and its impact on the reader.
>
> (Scott 1990: 32)

Thus, to return to the points made earlier, the text (be it a document, diary, etc), the audience of the text and its author become three essential components in a process of Scott's meaning construction (intended, received and content meaning). According to Scott, for researchers to grasp its significance, they should concentrate upon what the author intended when he or she produced the document; the meaning given to it by the potential audience (including the analyst who, by an act of reading, is part of that audience and therefore needs to act reflexively) and finally, between these two, the text itself which the content analysts and semioticians concentrate upon. These components add up to a simple observation: 'A document's meaning cannot be understood unless one knows what genre is belongs to, and what this implies for its interpretation' (Platt 1981b: 53).

Qualitative content analysis, on the other hand, starts with the idea of process, or social context, and views the author as a self-conscious actor addressing an audience under particular circumstances. The task of the analyst becomes a 'reading' of the text in terms of its symbols. With this in mind, the text is approached in terms of the cultural equipment and understanding of the context of production by the analyst themselves; the latter which is derived either through the use of secondary sources or, as in the above example, other methods such as observational studies:

> In the process, the analyst picks out what is relevant for analysis and pieces it together to create tendencies, sequences, patterns and orders. The process of deconstruction, interpretation, and reconstruction breaks down many of the assumptions dear to quantitative analysts.
>
> (Ericson, Baranek and Chan 1991: 55)

The flexibility of this method, as with participant observation, is regarded as a prime advantage. It enables the researcher to consider not only the ways in which meaning is constructed, but also the ways in which new meanings are developed and employed. In the process, theory is generated, modified and tested from the particulars of the document to a general understanding of its context and ways of representing the social world. While Scott speaks of the importance of linking the text to its author (the writer's intended meanings, as a diarist, journalist or the writer of an autobiography), texts are also used in ways which depend on the social situation of the audience (the reader's received meaning). This allows, contrary to the emphasis of quantitative analysis, for a variety of readings.

Aside from this emphasis on intended and received meaning, there is also content meaning which content analysts and semioticians focus upon. As Manning (1988) notes, semiotics is concerned with

> the science of signs, and seeks to derive the principles of signification; to explain how the meanings of objects, behaviours, or talk is produced, transformed and reproduced... The interpretant connects an *expression* or signifier (a word, a picture, a sound) with a *content* or signified (another word, image or depiction).
>
> (Manning 1988: 82)

For this focus to be meaningful, in Scott's sense, the text must be located and analysed alongside intended and received meanings. In other words, the writer will assume a competence on the part of her or his audience and it is these assumptions which the analyst needs to engage with by employing, reflexively, their own cultural understandings and an understanding of the context in which the document was produced.

In practical terms, the questions asked of a document at the level of content meaning focus upon relationships *within* the text and its relationships to *other* texts:

> What is the relationship of a text's parts to each other? What is the relationship of the text to other texts? What is the relationship of the text to

those who participated in constructing it? What is the relationship of the text to realities conceived of as lying outside of it? What empirical patterns are evident in these intra- and intertextual relations and what do these indicate about the meaning?

(Ericson, Baranek and Chan 1991: 48)

A critical-analytic stance would then consider how the document may attempt to represent the events which it describes and close off contrary interpretations by the reader. This considers the ways in which a text attempts to stamp its authority upon the social world it describes. In so doing, the social world might be characterized by the exclusion of valuable information and the characterization of events and people in particular ways.

The above characterization has tended to assume a simple dichotomy between quantitative and qualitative approaches. While there are clear differences of emphasis, questions have continually been raised regarding this dualism. It is perhaps not surprising, therefore, to find researchers from different theoretical vantage points utilizing both methods with interesting results. However, they do not share the underlying assumptions of much content analysis outlined above. Indeed, Marsh, whose comments on meaning and quantitative analysis were noted in Chapter 5, has employed computer packages to examine work history data (Marsh and Gershuny 1991) in a volume which attempts to challenge the quantitative–qualitative divide (Dex 1991). In addition, both Silverman (1985) and Billig (1988), from different theoretical vantage points, have employed simple counting methods to analyse the speeches of a trade union leader and politician, respectively. While, according to Scott (1990), computer programmes for the analysis of documents can still be usefully employed if using his threefold criteria of meaning interpretation. Nevertheless, the use of quantitative analysis does not side-step the need for researchers to account for the interpretations they have employed in analysing the document(s).

A note on presentation of findings

In the second of two articles, to which John Scott's work is indebted, Jennifer Platt (1981b) notes the connection between the justification of the interpretative procedure used in the analysis of documents and how the research results are presented in an authoritative manner. As with research in general, the art of communication is fundamental to the research process. As she notes (Platt 1981b: 60), this differs when it comes to the presentation of a small number of cases or instances of a social phenomenon. The author then attempts to appeal to the authority of their interpretations in particular ways. One method is to resort to presenting all the data which substantiate a point that you wish to make. Another is to make liberal use of footnotes in order to elaborate upon the text. This is not an easy problem to solve. However, she suggests three ways in which to steer a middle course between total data display and an appeal to authority. Before moving on to criticisms of documentary research, I shall summarize these below.

The first strategy is to provide an account of the method utilized at the outset. This removes the obligation to elaborate on the procedure when you wish to make a particular point in the interpretation of the document(s). As Platt (1981b: 61) notes, however, the problem with this strategy is that the method is not demonstrated at each point in the analysis, but asserted at the beginning. As a result, it requires a high level of trust in the author. The researcher could then use a second strategy and give an account of the method as each conclusion unfolds, a method similar to the historian's use of footnotes. Each positive and negative instance in relation to the results would be reported in order to substantiate the inferences. However, 'the danger here is that it could become as cumbrous as giving all the data' (Platt 1981b: 61).

Finally, the researcher might employ an 'illustrative style' as a strategy. Data are then selected in terms of their ability to illustrate general themes which emerge within the data and which can be supported by the use of specific examples. Again, however, the reader must trust the authority of the interpretations. Not surprisingly, therefore, given the advantages and disadvantages of each strategy, Platt (1981b) advocates the use of all three depending upon the nature of the data used and the types of conclusions reached. For large amounts of data, a sampling and coding procedure would need to be explained. In terms of small-scale data, the sources and methods of inferences would need to be described. If examples are used to illustrate points and if others are available, how were they chosen? Finally, there is the possible use of a general account of the process of analysis and checks on the interpretative procedures employed:

> This amounts to saying that where a systematic procedure has been used it should be described, and the results reported will then carry the conviction which the procedure deserves. The issue thus comes back to that of devising satisfactory systematic procedures of analysis and interpretation.
>
> (Platt 1981b: 62)

Criticisms of documentary research

Criticisms of documentary research tend to stem from how they are used, as opposed to their use in the first place. Both implicitly and explicitly, many of these have been covered. Here, I shall consider the bias of documents and selectivity in their analysis.

The importance of seeing a document in terms of its potential bias has been emphasized. History itself and our understanding of it can be informed by a selective reading of documents or those documents themselves may also be selective. Thus, what people decide to record, to leave in or take out, is itself informed by decisions which relate to the social, political and economic environment of which they are a part. History, like all social and natural sciences, is amenable to manipulation and selective influence. In undertaking documentary research, we should be aware of these influences and not assume that documents are simply neutral artifacts from the past. Due to an often uncritical approach to this form of research, it has been criticized for marginalizing people along race, class, gender and cultural lines.

Another issue is the use of documents without due regard to the process and social context of their construction. Semioticians, for example, examine the text itself in terms of meaning 'content', without a consideration of Scott's 'intended' and 'received' components of meanings. This is because the author is of no little interest, as Foucault's quote (p. 139) makes clear. The tradition of social thought which underlies these comments stands in contrast to approaches, such as those of Giddens and Plummer, which regard the intention and purposes of the author as an important part of their analysis. All of these authors would, in contrast, not regard a document as simply reflecting the social 'reality' to which it refers, as some positivist approaches advocate.

Summary

The title 'documentary research' reflects, as we have seen, a very broad spectrum of both perspectives and research sources. Documents may well be part of the practical contingencies of organizational life, but as we have also seen, they are viewed as part of a wider social context. They have also been considered in terms of the centrality of their authorship, while others, particularly influenced by recent strands of French poststructuralist social theory, do not consider the author as being of such consequence. These latter influences have seen a move towards more literary styles of analysis which sits uneasily with the positivist legacy of social research. Whatever the merits of these perspectives, with the increase in information available through such means, this is becoming a more popular method of research which, alongside others, yields valuable insight into social and political life.

CHAPTER 8: QUESTIONS FOR YOUR REFLECTION

1 Outline the main ways in which documentary sources are categorized.

2 What are the disadvantages and advantages of using documentary sources?

3 You are asked to devise a study which employs 'unobtrusive measures' of police performance. Clearly, you would first have to define the idea of 'performance'. However, holding that aside, what sources would you use? To get you started, is the level of graffiti in public places an indicator? Or the number of pairs of boots an officer uses in a year?

4 Considering the three stages of meaning which John Scott argues that an analyst should consider in approaching a document, what is your opinion on the idea that the author is of no importance in its analysis?

9

Comparative research: potential and problems

Comparative research is an evolving topic. As a focus of research, it consists of a pluralist approach to methods and theories centred mainly, but not exclusively, around the theme of comparing countries under the umbrella term 'cross-national' study. While relevant materials are often contained in journals and works on comparative politics, sociology and social policy, attention is increasingly turned to the methodological sphere with sources appearing on the specific issues, methods and processes involved in cross-national comparison. Despite this, a discussion of its place in social research rarely appears in introductory texts.

This chapter is written in a less systematic and structured fashion than Chapters 5–8 for the above reasons. To assist in a general understanding of this topic, it begins with a discussion on the place and growth of comparison in social research. The second section then focuses upon the issues involved in cross-national research. Increasing sums of money are attached to comparative work and the pressures in social research institutions to attract funds, and then 'count' the number of publications which result, make it more fashionable. The intention of this latter section is to offer an overview of its potential and problems, as opposed to a wholesale and uncritical adoption.

The place and growth of comparison in social research

Globalization and the growth of comparative research

As nation-states developed, so too did the opportunities for cross-national research. Now, in contemporary times, with increases in communications and technological advances, the world is 'getting smaller'. News programmes keep us up-to-date on events on the other side of the globe and telephones enable those who can afford it to talk to friends, relatives or business people in other countries – almost in an instant. Documents are sent via telephone lines and video links cross national boundaries and oceans. This, of course, also has an effect on the organization of societies and people's lives.

Due to these changes, it becomes less possible to speak of a 'society', given that modern industrial societies are open to these influences and not hermetically sealed off from the world. To simply employ the idea of a 'society' can also ignore or stifle the differences which exist within it. These differences are, in part, generated by the development in mass communications which provide for the mediation of different cultural representations across national boundaries. As Poster observes, 'Electronically mediated communication to some degree supplements existing forms of sociability but to another extent substitutes for them' (Poster 1990: 154). Given this diversity, accompanied by increases in mass communications and the work of multinational companies and international markets, Anthony Giddens refers to a process of 'globalization':

> Globalisation can thus be defined as the intensification of worldwide social relations which link distant localities in such a way that local happenings are shaped by events occurring many miles away and vice versa.
>
> (Giddens 1990: 64)

Research has followed this process as an increased generation of information has accompanied these transformations. Insights into our own lives are thought to be enhanced by studying the ways in which different cultures and societies organize their social and political affairs and everyday lives. This underlies Butler and Stokes's comment that comparisons of political systems 'can extend our understanding of British politics and lead to still more general formulations of the process of change' (1969: 533). This optimistic-based impression is counter-balanced by the increased complication of social and political life that has accompanied globalization due to the differences and diversities which exist within and between nations. The consequence has been to question the goals of cross-national empirical generalizations and the possibility of what have been termed 'metanarratives' (Lyotard 1984) of theoretical explanation. An uncertainty as to the future, particularly given a resurgence of nationalism and the 'breaking-up' of previous nation-states, opens up the possibility of pessimism. At the same time, this ambivalence renders comparative research even more important. As past assumptions of similarity between and homogeneity within societies breaks down, an opportunity present itself:

> Understanding the reason why the complex conditions within which we live are bound to remain, in significant respects, beyond our control, paradoxically provides us with the opportunity of contributing more effectively to the shaping of social futures.
>
> (Smart 1992: 221)

One aim of comparative research, therefore, is to understand and explain the ways in which different societies and cultures experience and act upon social, economic and political changes. Institutions and governments, for different reasons and motivations, release funds to undertake research. This might take the form of 'applied' research where the desire is to collect information for governmental purposes or, on a more commercial basis, examine an economy in terms of the organization of its manufacturing, financial and service sectors. The collection of information and the subsequent decision-making based upon it can then have an effect on different cultures and nation-states: for better or worse, depending upon the vantage point from which such developments are viewed.

The place of comparison in social research

While cross-national comparative research is a growing phenomenon, we all use the idea of comparison when making judgements in everyday life and the practice of social and natural sciences is inconceivable without it (as with the discussion on value judgements and comparative assessment in Chapter 3). Methodologically speaking, nowhere is this more evident than in the experimental method of research. Here, the epitome of 'high science' is thought to find its representation among research practitioners. In pursuing a belief in the parallels between the natural and human sciences, there are those who emulate its techniques.

Broadly speaking, the experimental method randomly allocates people to particular groups and then subjects them to controlled stimuli. Behavioural or physiological changes can then be measured as the scientist monitors the effect of these controls. A sequence of *cause* and *effect* is then established in the observed pattern of events. Thus, in medical trials, one group may be given a 'test' drug and another group is given either no drug or a placebo (a drug without effect in order to act as a 'control' on the group). Differences between the two groups are measured and any 'real' physiological or biological effects of the new drug established. However, owing to the methodological and theoretical difficulties with the experimental method, as well as social life being more complicated than experiments can allow for, social researchers frequently resort to what are known as 'quasi experiments'. In these instances, the researcher has less control over 'outside' or *exogenous* variables which could influence the groups' 'internal' behaviour (see Kidder 1981; Moser and Kalton 1983; Shipman 1988).

These methods are still practised and appear to be enjoying a resurgence of interest with the growth of research which seeks to evaluate whether a particular programme of activity is achieving its stated ends. As one of a series of texts on *evaluation research* puts it:

> Without any *comparison* group, it is hard to know how good the results are, whether the results would have been as good with some other program, and even whether the program has any effect on the results at all.
>
> (Fitz-Gibbon and Lyons Morris 1987: 26, original emphasis)

Moving away from the narrow idea of comparison in experiment and design and evaluation research, there is a more general idea of comparison which social researchers constantly engage in. When they choose to study a part of human relations

> the choice always represents a comparison of the selected phenomenon under observation in relation to other social phenomena, whether this choice is made explicitly or implicitly. Normal behaviour and norms cannot be studied without acknowledging deviations from the normal. Actually, no social phenomenon can be isolated and studied without comparing it to other social phenomena ... Trying to understand and explain variation is a process which cannot be accomplished without previous reflections on similarities and dissimilarities underlying the variation'.
>
> (Øyen 1990b: 4)

At the level of analysis, we make comparisons between the influences of variables from questionnaire results, or accounts in interview transcripts, or documentary sources and field notes on observational settings. On a more general level, we compare within societies (*intra-societal* comparison) and between societies (*inter-societal* comparison). The former method might examine differences between the ways in which white and black people are processed through the criminal justice system (as per the example in Chapter 4). The latter method might compare societies which display both similarities and differences, for example, in relation to their provision of welfare. This idea is certainly not new. As one contribution to a reader on comparative policy research begins: 'States, kingdoms and principalities have been compared for approximately 2,500 years' (Deutsch 1987: 5).

In the field of politics, a particularly strong legacy of comparative work exists which can be traced back to the work of the Greek philosopher Aristotle (Blondel 1990; Rose 1991). Among more recent and well-known examples are the works of Emile Durkheim on suicide (1952), Max Weber on religion (1930; 1965) and Richard Titmuss on blood donation (1970). Indeed, the discipline of social anthropology studies the lives of people in 'non-industrial' or 'pre-modern' societies and therefore requires a comparative understanding from both its students and practitioners (La Fontaine 1985). Attention has focused on its importance for research purposes, teaching and disciplinary development in many other areas of study: for example, sociology (Marsh 1967; Vallier 1971; Armer and Grimshaw 1973); criminology and the study of deviant actions (Newman 1976; Mawby 1990); the city (Walton and Masotti 1976); the social effects of free-market policies (Taylor 1990); social policy (Higgins 1981; Jones 1985; Esping-Andesen 1990; Dominelli 1991; Room 1991) and policy analysis and social research in general (Warwick and Osherson 1973; Dierkes, Weiler and Berthoin Antal 1987; Øyen 1990a). This sample of available comparative work adds to an increasingly expanding area of interest with a long established history. As I write, no doubt, new volumes, research reports and articles are being produced and research grants applied for. In the next section, I therefore wish to concentrate on the questions which arise in comparing societies.

The process of cross-national research

Examining comparative research in terms of being 'cross-national' may enable us to focus upon a simple definition and compare along the dimension of demarcated national boundaries. However, within these societies there are ethnic and cultural differences which governments and the general public cannot afford to ignore, nor researchers gloss over if their aim is systematic understanding and explanation.

The central question which faces comparative research is 'Does it require a different practice from other forms of research?' Within the literature, there appear to be several responses to this question. First, there are those who consider that comparative work is no different from any other. The units of analysis, whether they be political parties or welfare systems, need no special theoretical accounts or methodological discussions. This group Øyen (1990a) calls the 'purists', adding the caveat that this is a tendency to which many researchers succumb. Second, there are those, like many researchers if they were honest, who are ethnocentric in their approach. They are not sensitive to social context and historical and cultural differences and simply 'add on' their findings to existing ways of understanding and explaining. The consequence is that cross-national data are not assumed to add to the complexity of social science research (Øyen calls this group the 'ignorants'). Third, there are those whom Øyen refers to as the 'totalists': this group appear to be aware of the issues involved in cross-national research and its methodological and theoretical pitfalls. At the same time, 'They consciously ignore the many stumbling blocks of the non-equivalence of concepts, a multitude of unknown variables interacting in an unknown context and influencing the research question in unknown ways' (Øyen 1990a: 5). Finally, there are the 'comparativists', who recognize the arguments of the purists and totalists, but believe that cross-national research is a distinctive topic. As a result, they undertake this work in a different manner and frame their research questions accordingly.

Clearly, these four groups are ideal types. However, many researchers now compete for the position of 'comparative expert'. This has desirable consequences, but the nature of what is meant by 'comparative study' is, as these different responses suggest, another matter. Simply 'tacking on' our preconceived ideas, or even prejudices, on the operation of societies does little to advance our understanding and counters the idea of a reflexive foundation for research practice. Thus, to be able to consider issues of practice and how these five approaches may be evaluated, the following sections provide an overview of the potential and problems associated with comparative research.

The potential of comparative research

There are several benefits in undertaking comparative research. Broadly, I shall refer to these as the *import-mirror* view, the *difference* view, the *theory-development* view, and finally, the *prediction* view. It will be clear from the following discussion that these are not distinct, but interrelated themes. However, their adoption assists in extracting the arguments from literature written by those who see comparative research as having the potential to enhance our understanding and explanation of human relations. We shall consider each of these in turn.

The import-mirror view suggests that the project of comparative analysis is worthwhile because in producing findings on the practices of other countries, we are better able to see the basis of our own practices. On an instrumental level, this means the borrowing of ideas from other countries: 'the goal is lessons rather than creating or testing theory. Countries that are similar are more likely to borrow from one another' (Teune 1990: 58). According to this view, the results generated by comparative study may permit the importation of different methods of organizing a society's affairs to improve their efficiency. On a less instrumental dimension, this also allows us to reflect upon our own social systems and cultural ways of behaving. It thereby possesses the potential to challenge our 'background assumptions' (Gouldner 1971) by producing findings on different social contexts and cultural practices.

At the same time, this can allow those who are studying other countries to have a particular insight into their practices. While it is advantageous to be an 'insider', 'outsiders' (as researchers) can raise questions which may not have been thought of by those who take their own practices for granted. Of course, we do not necessarily require cross-national research for this purpose as there is often sufficient diversity within our own societies. However, societies and the systems they devise reveal variable historical conditions leading to current practices and policies. Thus, and this brings us round to the second advantage, comparative analysis is undertaken to explain and understand difference.

By examining different societies, we can ask why some have developed in similar ways and others in diverse ways. This adds to an understanding and explanation of the complicated relationship between economic, social and political systems. For instance, Esping-Andersen's (1990) study is centred on a belief 'that only comparative empirical research will adequately disclose the fundamental properties that unite or divide modern welfare states' (Esping-Anderson 1990: 3). Further, the contributors to the volume by Taylor (1990) examine the 'cultural specificities' which any adoption of free-market policies has to take account of. Through comparative accounts of five western-style societies, the limits to market-based policies are illuminated. Differences within and between these societies expose the problem of adopting a philosophy of 'free markets' given the profound social costs which this entails.

Comparisons which reveal difference and diversity and, in the above example, cultural impediments to the implementation of policy, enable us to consider the macro factors which influence social and political change and the micro factors peculiar to each social setting. This relates to a third advantage, which sees an improvement in theoretical development resulting from the growth of comparative research. For those who consider that the goal of social research is the discovery of general theories which explain the way societies are organized: 'comparative studies are absolutely essential' (Holt quoted in Grimshaw 1973: 19). However, the problem here (as noted in the discussion in Chapter 2) is that these theories may be stated at such a level of abstraction they are not useful for the interpretation of data. Furthermore, such abstraction may ignore important differences between countries and cultures.

Given this problem, there are those who would steer a middle course between universalistic theories which are assumed to be generally relevant to societies across time and space and particularistic theories which are only applicable to particular social settings and not generalizable. This is said to take account of differences within societies, as well as similarities between them. Rose (1991) expresses this succinctly. Indeed, at the end of this quote, he links the 'theoretical' and 'difference' potentials of comparative research:

> Anyone who engages in comparative research immediately notices differences between countries. Yet anyone who persists in wide-ranging comparative analysis also recognizes boundaries to these differences: for example, among two dozen countries, the variations in methods of electing a Parliament are limited. Since the time of Aristotle, the first task of comparison is to observe the extent to which countries differ or are similar. The second task is to ask why. Under what circumstances do differences occur?
>
> (Rose 1991: 447)

To allow for the possibility of diversity and similarity, comparative analysis considers both *endogenous* and *exogenous* factors. The former are those which are peculiar to the country which is being studied, while the latter are those elements, such as international capital, gender and race relations, which while influencing that country's social and political relations, are not simply peculiar to it. However, as the discussion on Taylor's (1990) work indicated, comparative researchers need to be sensitive to the 'cultural specificities' which affect *how* exogenous factors influence each country.

Esping-Anderson's comparative study could also be summarized as an example of this middle-course genre. The need for theoretical generation was the second belief, aside from that of empirical comparison mentioned above, which informed his work:

> existing theoretical models of the welfare state are inadequate. The ambition is to offer a reconceptualization and re-theorization on the basis of what we consider important about the welfare state. The existence of a social program and the amount of money spent on it may be less important than what it

does. We shall devote many pages to arguing that issues of de-
commodification, social stratification, and employment are keys to a welfare
state's identity.

(Esping-Anderson 1990: 2)

I have deliberately included the latter part of this quote which refers to the
concepts which he employed to understand and compare the identity of welfare
states. This is a central point in theory development. The use of such concepts, it
is argued, enables the researcher to have a common point of reference in order
to group empirical data which is differentiated along both linguistic and
geographical dimensions (Ferrari 1990; Rose 1991). By approaching the
comparison of welfare states in this way, Esping-Anderson (1990) was able to
show, using a considerable amount of data and 'ideal-type' welfare regimes
(liberal, conservative and social democratic), how countries' welfare states
evolved as a result of different historical forces. Thus, he compares, but in so
doing does not ignore, differences between countries. The result is a novel
theoretical analysis of contemporary changes in welfare states (although it has
been criticized for the absence of gender as a significant social category in
comparative welfare-state analysis: see Langan and Ostner 1991).

Finally, we come to the fourth view: the prediction of programme outcomes
is enhanced through comparative work. According to this view, not only can
the potential for the success of particular policies, systems or practices in a given
society be understood, but also their outcomes can be predicted, once
experiences of their effects in other societies and social and cultural contexts is
examined. Therefore, organizations or governments may embark upon a
particular courses of action knowing their likely consequences.

Problems in comparative research

Comparative research is considered to have potential around one or more of the
above four themes. However, the picture is, as you can imagine, more
complicated than this simple characterization allows for. In both the process of
undertaking comparative research and in the potential for theoretical development a number of problems have been raised in the literature.

One of the primary problems with comparative analysis is not only the
ability of a researcher to adequately understand cultures and societies which are
different from their own, but more specifically, to generalize and explain social
relations across societies and social contexts. Following the work of authors
such as Winch (1958), it has been argued that in order to understand a culture,
we have to know the rules which are employed in that culture; only then can we
understand the ways in which the culture views the social world. So far, so
good. However, and this is the important point, there is nothing 'beyond' this
understanding: for example, establishing whether a culture or society beliefs are
valid through a comparison with other societies. As three sympathizers of this

view express it, Winch sees the creation of a comparative social research programme as requiring

> the comparison of like with like ... In order to decide which institutions of one society – our own in many cases – to compare with those of another we shall need to be able to match those institutions, to say what kind of part they play in their respective societies ... However, if we are in a position to say what part each institution plays in the life of its society then we have already achieved a very good understanding of it.
>
> (Anderson, Hughes and Sharrock 1986: 184)

In other words, this understanding is the aim of comparison and its finishing point. We cannot therefore explain its history and development in terms of social forces which are 'external' to this culture. This renders the ability to generate particular cross-cultural and societal explanations untenable.

The potential of comparative research in allowing the outsider to 'look in' and see things in a different way which is theoretically useful is also untenable, according to this view. Researchers can understand only from the 'inside' – from the social context which is peculiar and *relative* to that time and place. We have actually returned to the discussion in Chapter 1. Social research should look for and seek to understand the *meanings* within a social context where people act according to the rules of their social setting. This excludes, by definition, the search for *causal* explanations which are generalizable across societies. Instead, the 'stranger' must be prepared to grasp what Winch (1958) calls 'forms of life' which are fundamentally different from their own, but which can be evaluated only in terms of the indigenous culture. Beyond this, there is no way of establishing a general explanation of beliefs beyond their social context. As Ernest Gellner, a persistent critic of Winch's views, succinctly summarizes this position, people

> speak their own lives and pursue their manifold interests in the context of 'forms of life', cultural/linguistic traditions, and the concepts they employ derive their validity from, and *only* from, possessing a place in these forms of life.
>
> (Gellner 1974: 143, emphasis added)

Winch's arguments can be further located and based in relation to those arguments in Chapter 2 on common sense as a basis of theorizing. The researcher cannot legitimately consider, in theoretical or empirical terms, anything other than the practical use of language in everyday life or the methods which people use in interpreting the social world in *context*. This position has actually been raised in all the four previous chapters in one form or another, for it occurs throughout discussions on social research (on the meaning-equivalence of attitude scales in questionnaires, interviews as topics not resources and documents analysed in terms of practical reasoning). However, conflict around the exercise of power, within the same societies, questions the idea that there are beliefs which are beyond question in its own terms, let alone those of the outsider. The question to be formulated here is 'why' does this occur? These are questions to which Esping-Andersen (1990) and Rose (1991) address themselves. The influence of global capital on a culture or the development of whole societies affects that culture as an *exogenous* factor, particularly in terms of the relationships between western societies and the Third World. For this reason, among others, critical social researchers would not regard Winch's arguments as tenable.

The implications of Winch's arguments are reflected in the literature on comparative work. Both Esping-Anderson (1990) and Rose (1991) not only are aware of the importance of being sensitive to social context, but also note the similarities which are found between societies. Comparative researchers are also aware of the issue of comparing 'like with like' (see Marsh 1967; Armer 1973; Teune 1990). This finds its outlet in discussions on *appropriateness* and *equivalence* in comparative research. Appropriateness refers to the methods employed and the conceptualization of issues when undertaking comparative research. Researchers cannot assume that what is appropriate for their culture will necessarily be appropriate for another. A sensitivity and understanding of cultural context is thereby required:

> Appropriateness requires feasibility, significance, and acceptability in each foreign culture as a necessary (but not sufficient) condition for insuring validity and successful completion of comparative studies.
>
> (Armer 1973: 50–1)

Equivalence is a related issue. As Winch (1958) rightly suggests, meanings vary between cultures. This raises a particular problem in the use of surveys in cross-national research where meaning-equivalence is an important component of a questionnaire's validity (see Verba 1971; Scheuch 1990). In terms of the process of study, unless researchers have an understanding of the social context with which they are dealing, two samples, although random, may actually sample different age ranges or population characteristics which are not comparable. This often results from indigenous factors which the researcher either has overlooked or is simply not aware of or sensitive to. A survey might then measure different aspects of the phenomena under investigation and treat them as similar. For this reason

> a second major methodological task in comparative research is to devise and select theoretical problems, conceptual schemes, samples, and measurement and analysis strategies that are comparable or equivalent across the societies involved in a particular study.
>
> (Armer 1973: 51)

A more general problem relates to appropriateness and equivalence. As Marsh comments: 'the task of linguistic translation fall heavily upon the shoulders of the comparativist' (Marsh 1967: 272). Language differences, even if researchers have a proficient understanding of a language, require a cultural understanding of words to allow for the equivalence of meaning. This becomes particularly important when dealing with dialects where the meanings of words varies or entirely different words may be employed in referring to the same phenomena.

When it comes to examining available data on countries, it is worth bearing in mind that if not conversant with the language, the use of any English translations can be selective in their descriptions. Problems of language, together with a drive to increase comparative work and, as authors have noted, the high costs of comparative survey and observational research (Manis 1976) lead many researchers to rely on official publications. Any analysis based upon such documents may then produce partial and incomplete theories. In other words, the stereotype of English visitors abroad continuing to speak English, and simply raising their voice if not understood by 'those foreigners', has its research equivalent.

As researchers have pointed out (Lawrence 1988), the language issue is becoming less problematic as English comes to dominate as a world language. However, issues of meaning equivalence still remain, to say nothing of the desirability for non-English speakers of this state of affairs. For instance, dialogues between the researcher and interviewees, as well as the translation of documents and a reliance on official publications, are still matters of interpretation. Lawrence (1988) refers to this in his account of studying comparative management. Here he considers not only a delicate balancing act between inferring actions from observations in social settings by utilizing nationalist stereotypes, but also the possible misapprehensions which occur in interview situations:

> One is never quite sure that they have understood the question, or at least its nuances or comparative thrust; one worries that interviewees are responding to the question they think you asked (but you think you asked something different). The problem is compounded by the admirable vagueness of English: there is no other language more suited to the framing of open-ended questions or projective try-ons.
>
> (Lawrence 1988: 102)

Due to such ambiguities, he recommends that even if a researcher's command of the language is not 'perfect', misapprehension can still be reduced by its use (Lawrence 1988: 102). In addition, if English is employed for the interview, the use of key words in the interviewee's own language helps to maintain meaning equivalence. Further, even if interviewees' command of English is good, there may be terms in their own language which they do not know the English equivalent of and this can also lead to ambiguity. One example that Lawrence notes is Dutch managers who say 'agenda' rather than 'diary'. As he suggests, the interviewer must accept this: the purpose of their research 'is to end up with an enlarged understanding, not to teach other people English' (Lawrence 1988: 102).

Potential and problems: an overview

The potential for theoretical development is a strong component of comparative research. Yet there are those who regard this potential as a problem – if by this we mean the ability to generalize across societies and produce explanations of social and political phenomena While Jones (1985) is speaking of comparative social policy, her comments characterize this debate as between

> those who see cross-national analysis as furnishing a welcome additional dimension to assist in the task of policy analysis and those who regard any attempts at cross national 'theory building' (as opposed to constructive description') as hopelessly premature, given the present far-from-perfect grasp of home-country let alone other people's social policy.
>
> (Jones 1985: 7–8)

Much literature on the practice of comparative research is aware of these disputes and therefore focuses upon the issues of equivalence, appropriateness and language. These are central for we can all, despite our most determined attempts, often find ourselves succumbing to the belief that our ways of acting and thinking are in some ways better than others. This is perhaps personified by the neo-colonialism that characterizes particular attitudes.

Comparative researchers cannot assume that their own countries, or those of others, are characterized on the basis of a single culture or shared value-consensus. This allows for a continuum between difference and similarity which is open to comparative empirical examination. A note of caution should be added here lest people think that the European Community will automatically combat such thinking. This may simply result in the replacement of an ethnocentrism with a Eurocentrism. The world may move beyond the researcher's shores, only to finish at the frontiers of Europe. Disputes over the exploitation of Third World countries by western societies are being constantly raised and these changes will not necessarily alleviate this situation. Europe is, quite simply, only part of a much larger picture. At the same time, comparative research does enable us to check against narrow thinking by its production of studies on alternative cultures and societies. This has the potential for a greater understanding and explanation of social, political and economic forces and their relationship to specific policies and human relations and cultures in general.

Summary

Comparative research is clearly a two-edged sword having both potential and problems. However, this does not constitute a reason for its abandonment. If that were the case, all forms of research, both in the social and natural sciences, would cease overnight. On the contrary, as the earlier quote from Smart (1992) indicated (p. 153), increasing complexity still requires understanding and explanation. The implications of this ambivalence for individual researchers is that it requires an awareness of both its strengths and limitations for effective practice. This means an understanding of different social contexts and cultures and the various issues which form part of the actual process of comparative research: for example, those of the relationship between theory and data and the power relations which exist within and between societies which affect the design, production, interpretation and dissemination of research results. Clearly, there are important differences between the practice of cross-national research and the methods of social inquiry that this book has covered. Yet issues and methods are not mutually exclusive topics. To that extent, it is no different.

CHAPTER 9: QUESTIONS FOR YOUR REFLECTION

1   When it comes to the topic of comparative research and its practice, are you a comparativist, purist, totalist or ignorant or something else? What are the reasons for your answer?

2   In considering Winch's (1958) arguments on 'forms of life', does this negate a researcher from one culture explaining the beliefs and practices of another in causal terms?

3   What is your opinion on the promise of comparative social research? Is it a good or bad idea?

4   Given the types of information which tend to be generated (increased media focus, etc) how does the phenomenon of 'globalization' relate to the development of social research?

Bibliography

Abbott, P. and Wallace, C. (1990) *An Introduction to Sociology: Feminist Perspectives*. London: Routledge.

Abrams, P., Deem, R., Finch, J. and Rock, P. (eds) (1981) *Practice and Progress: British Sociology 1950–1980*. London: George Allen & Unwin.

Ackers, L. (1993) 'Race and Sexuality in the Ethnographic Process'. In Hobbs, D. and May, T. (eds) *Interpreting the Field: Accounts of Ethnography*. Oxford: Oxford University Press.

Ackroyd, S. and Hughes, J. (1983) *Data Collection in Context*. Harlow, London: Longman.

Adler, M. and Asquith, S. (eds) (1981) *Discretion and Welfare*. London: Heinemann.

Adorno, T., Frankel-Brunswik, E., Levinson, D. and Sanford, R. (1950) *The Authoritarian Personality*. New York: Harper Row.

Agger, B. (1991) *A Critical Theory of Public Life: Knowledge, Discourse and Politics in an Age of Decline*. London: Falmer Press.

Allan, G. and Skinner, C. (eds) (1991) *Handbook for Research Students in the Social Sciences*. London: Falmer Press.

Anderson, R., Hughes, J. and Sharrock, W. (1986) *Philosophy and the Human Sciences*. London: Routledge.

Anderson, K., Armitage, S., Jack, D. and Wittner, J. (1990) 'Beginning Where We Are: Feminist Methodology in Oral History'. In McCarl Nielsen, J. (ed.) *Feminist Research Methods: Exemplary Readings in the Social Sciences*. London: Westview Press.

Antaki, C. (ed.) (1988) *Analysing Everyday Explanation: A Casebook of Methods*. London: Sage.

Armer, M. (1973) 'Methodological Problems and Possibilities in Comparative Research'. In Armer, M. and Grimshaw, A. (eds) *Comparative Social Research: Methodological Problems and Strategies*. London: John Wiley.

Armer, M. and Grimshaw, A. (eds) (1973) *Comparative Social Research: Methodological Problems and Strategies*. London: John Wiley.

Atkinson, J. M. (1978) *Discovering Suicide: Studies in the Social Organisation of Sudden Death*. London: Macmillan.

Atkinson, P. (1990) *The Ethnographic Imagination: Textual Constructions of Reality.* London: Routledge.

Atkinson, P. and Heath, C. (eds) (1981) *Medical Work: Realities and Routines.* Aldershot: Gower.

Baldamus, W. (1984) 'The Category of Pragmatic Knowledge in Sociological Analysis'. In Bulmer, M. (ed.) *Sociological Research Methods,* 2nd edition. London: Macmillan.

Banks, J. A. (1957) 'The Group Discussion as an Interview Technique', *Sociological Review* 5 (1).

Barnes, B. (ed.) (1972) *Sociology of Science: Selected Readings.* Harmondsworth: Penguin.

Barnes, B. (1991) 'Thomas Kuhn'. In Skinner, Q. (ed.) *The Return of Grand Theory in the Human Sciences.* Cambridge: Cambridge University Press.

Barnes, J. A. (1979) *Who Should Know What?* Harmondsworth: Penguin.

Barrett, M. (1991) *The Politics of Truth: From Marx to Foucault.* Cambridge: Polity Press.

Barthes, R. (1967) *Elements of Semiology.* London: Jonathan Cape.

Bauman, Z. (1992) *Intimations of Postmodernity.* London: Routledge.

Becker, H. (1963) *Outsiders: Studies in the Sociology of Deviance.* New York: The Free Press.

Becker, H. (1967) 'Whose Side are We On', *Social Problems* 14: 239–47.

Becker, H. (1979a) 'Problems of Inference and Proof in Participant Observation'. In Bynner, J. and Stribley, K. (eds) *Social Research: Principles and Procedures.* Harlow: Longman.

Becker, H. (1979b) 'Problems in the Publication of Field Studies'. In Bynner, J. and Stribley, K. (eds) *Social Research: Principles and Procedures.* Harlow: Longman.

Becker, H. (1986) *Writing for Social Scientists: How to Start and Finish Your Thesis, Book, or Article.* Chicago: University of Chicago Press.

Becker, H., Geer, B., Hughes, E. and Strauss, A. (1961) *Boys in White: Student Culture in a Medical School.* Chicago: University of Chicago Press.

Beechey, V. (1986) 'Women and Employment in Contemporary Britain'. In Beechey, V. and Whitelegg, E. (eds) *Women in Britain Today.* Milton Keynes: Open University Press.

Beechey, V. and Whitelegg, E. (eds) (1986) *Women in Britain Today.* Milton Keynes: Open University Press.

Bell, C. and Newby, H. (eds) (1977) *Doing Sociological Research.* London: George Allen & Unwin.

Bell, C. and Roberts, H. (eds) (1984) *Social Researching: Politics, Problems and Practice.* London: Routledge & Kegan Paul.

Benney, M. and Hughes, E. (1984) 'Of Sociology and the Interview'. In Bulmer, M. (ed.) *Sociological Research Methods,* 2nd edition. London: Macmillan.

Benson, D. and Hughes, J. (1991) 'Method: Evidence and Inference – Evidence and Inference for Ethnomethodology'. In Button, G. (ed.) *Ethnomethodology and the Human Sciences.* Cambridge: Cambridge University Press.

Bernstein, R. (1976) *The Restructuring of Social and Political Theory.* Oxford: Basil Blackwell.

Bhaskar, R. (1975) *A Realist Theory of Science.* Leeds: Leeds Books.

Bhaskar, R. (1989a) *Reclaiming Reality: A Critical Introduction to Contemporary Philosophy.* London: Verso.

Bhaskar, R. (1989b) *The Possibility of Naturalism*, 2nd edition. Hemel Hempstead: Harvester.

Bhat, A., Carr-Hill, R. and Ohri, S. (eds) (1988) *Britain's Black Population: A New Perspective*. Aldershot: Gower.

Billig, M. (1988) 'Methodology and Scholarship in Understanding Ideological Explanation'. In Antaki, C. (ed.) *Analysing Everyday Explanation: A Casebook of Methods*. London: Sage.

Blalock, H. (1984) *Social Statistics*, 2nd edition. London: McGraw-Hill.

Blondel, J. (1990) *Comparative Government*. London: Philip Allan.

Blumer, H. (1972) 'Society as Symbolic Interaction'. In Rose, A. (ed.) *Human Behaviour and Social Processes: An Interactionist Approach*. London: Routlege & Kegan Paul.

Brown, G. (1984) 'Accounts, Meaning and Causality'. In Gilbert, G. and Abell, P. (eds) *Accounts and Action*. Aldershot: Gower.

Brown, G. and Harris, T. (1978) *The Social Origins of Depression: A Study of Psychiatric Depression in Women*. London: Tavistock.

Brown, J. and Sime, J. (1981) 'A Methodology for Accounts'. In Brenner, M. (ed.) *Social Method and Social Life*. New York: Academic Press.

Bruyn, S. T. (1966) *The Human Perspective in Sociology: The Methodology of Participant Observation*. Englewood Cliffs, NJ: Prentice-Hall.

Bryman, A. (1988a) *Quantity and Quality in Social Research*. London: Unwin Hyman.

Bryman, A. (ed.) (1988b) *Doing Research in Organizations*. London: Routledge.

Bryman, A. and Cramer, D. (1990) *Quantitative Data Analysis for Social Scientists*. London: Routledge.

Buchanan, D., Boddy, D. and McCalman, J. (1988) 'Getting In, Getting On, Getting Out and Getting Back'. In Bryman, A. (ed.) *Doing Research in Organizations*. London: Routledge.

Bulmer, M. (ed.) (1978) *Social Policy Research*. London: Macmillan.

Bulmer, M. (ed.) (1979a) *Censuses, Surveys and Privacy*. London: Macmillan.

Bulmer, M. (1979b) 'Maintaining Public Confidence in Quantitative Social Research'. In Bulmer, M. (ed.) *Censuses, Surveys and Privacy*. London: Macmillan.

Bulmer, M. (ed.) (1982a) *Social Research Ethics: An Examination of the Merits of Covert Participant Observation*. London: Macmillan.

Bulmer, M. (1982b) *The Use of Social Research: Social Investigation in Public Policy-Making*. London: George Allen & Unwin.

Bulmer, M. (1984a) *The Chicago School of Sociology*. Chicago: University of Chicago Press.

Bulmer, M. (ed.) (1984b). *Sociological Research Methods*, 2nd edition. London: Macmillan.

Bulmer, M. (1984c) 'Why Don't Sociologists Make More Use of Official Statistics?' In Bulmer, M. (ed.) *Sociological Research Methods*, 2nd edition. London: Macmillan.

Bulmer, M. (1986a) 'The Role of Theory in Applied Social Science Research'. In Bulmer, M., Banting, K., Blume, S., Carley, M. and Weiss, C., *Social Science and Social Policy*. London: George Allen & Unwin.

Bulmer, M. (1986b) 'The Use and Abuse of Social Science'. In Bulmer, M., Banting, K., Blume, S., Carley, M. and Weiss, C., *Social Science and Social Policy*. London: George Allen & Unwin.

Bulmer, M., Banting, K., Blume, S., Carley, M. and Weiss, C. (1986) *Social Science and Social Policy*. London: George Allen & Unwin.

Bulmer, M., Lewis, J. and Piachaud, D. (eds) (1989) *The Goals of Social Policy*. London: Unwin Hyman.

Burgess, R. (ed.) (1982) *Field Research: A Sourcebook and Field Manual*. London: George Allen & Unwin.

Burgess, R. (1990) *In the Field: An Introduction to Field Research*, 4th Impression. London: George Allen & Unwin.

Bury, M. and Holme, A. (1990) 'Researching Very Old People'. In Peace, S. (ed.) *Researching Social Gerontology: Concepts, Methods and Issues*. London: Sage.

Butler, D. and Stokes, D. (1969) *Political Change in Britain: Forces Shaping Electoral Choice*. London: Macmillan.

Button, G. (1987) 'Answers as Interactional Products: Two Sequential Practices Used in Interviews', *Social Psychology Quarterly* 50 (2): 160–71.

Button, G. (ed.) (1991) *Ethnomethodology and the Human Sciences*. Cambridge: Cambridge University Press.

Bynner, J. and Stribley, K. (eds) (1979) *Social Research: Principles and Procedures*. Harlow: Longman.

Cain, M. (1990) 'Realist Philosophy and Standpoint Epistemologies or Feminist Criminology as a Successor Science'. In Gelsthorpe, L. and Morris, A. (eds) *Feminist Perspectives in Criminology*. Milton Keynes: Open University Press.

Callahan, D. and Jennings, B. (eds) (1983) *Ethics, the Social Sciences, and Policy Analysis*. London: Plenum Press.

Calvert, P. (1991) 'Using Documentary Sources'. In Allan, G. and Skinner, C. (eds) *Handbook for Research Students in the Social Sciences*. London: Falmer Press.

Cambridge Women's Studies Group (eds) (1981) *Women in Society: Interdisciplinary Essays*. London: Virago Press.

Cameron, D. and Frazer, E. (1987) *The Lust to Kill: A Feminist Investigation of Sexual Murder*. Oxford: Polity Press.

Campbell, A. (1981) *Girl Delinquents*. Oxford: Basil Blackwell.

Campbell, A. (1984) *The Girls in the Gang*. Oxford: Basil Blackwell.

Caputi, J. (1987) *The Age of Sex Crime*. London: The Women's Press.

Carr-Hill, R. and Drew, D. (1988) 'Blacks, Police and Crime'. In Bhat, A., Carr-Hill, R. and Ohri, S. (eds) *Britain's Black Population: A New Perspective*. Aldershot: Gower.

Cicourel, A. (1964) *Method and Measurement in Sociology*. London: Macmillan.

Cicourel, A. (1976) *The Social Organisation of Juvenile Justice*, 2nd edition. London: Heinemann.

Cohen, S. and Taylor, L. (1972) *Psychological Survival: The Experience of Long-Term Imprisonment*. Harmondsworth: Penguin.

Cook, J. and Fonow, M. (1990) 'Knowledge and Women's Interests: Issues of Epistemology and Methodology in Sociological Research'. In McCarl Nielsen, J. (ed.) *Feminist Research Methods: Exemplary Readings in the Social Sciences*. London: Westview Press.

Croall, H. (1992) *White Collar Crime*. Buckingham: Open University Press.

Crow, I. (1987) 'Black People and Criminal Justice in the U.K.', *Howard Journal of Criminal Justice* 26 (4): 303–14.

Curtis, J. and Petras, J. (eds) (1970) *The Sociology of Knowledge: A Reader*. London: Duckworth.

Dale, A., Arber, S. and Procter, M. (1988) *Doing Secondary Analysis*. London: Unwin Hyman.

Dale, J. and Foster, P. (1986) *Feminists and State Welfare*. London: Routledge & Kegan Paul.

Dant, T. (1991) *Knowledge, Ideology and Discourse*. London: Routledge.

Davies, A. (1981) *Women, Race and Class*. London: The Women's Press.

Dean, J. and William Foot Whyte, W. F. (1979) 'How Do You Know if the Informant is Telling the Truth?' In Bynner, J. and Stribley, K. (eds) *Social Research: Principles and Procedures*. Harlow: Longman.

Denzin, N. K. (1978a) *The Research Act in Sociology*. London: Butterworths.

Denzin, N. K. (ed.) (1978b) *Sociological Methods: A Sourcebook*, 2nd edition. London: McGraw-Hill.

Deutsch, K. (1987) 'Prologue: Achievements and Challenges in 2000 Years of Comparative Research'. In Dierkes, M., Weiler, H. and Berthoin Antal, A. (eds) *Comparative Policy Research: Learning from Experience*. Aldershot: Gower.

Dex, S. (ed.) (1991) *Life and Work History Analyses: Qualitative and Quantitative Developments*. London: Routledge.

Dierkes, M., Weiler, H. and Berthoin Antal, A. (eds) (1987) *Comparative Policy Research: Learning from Experience*. Aldershot: Gower.

Ditton, J. (1977) *Part-Time Crime: An Ethnography of Petty Crime*. London: Macmillan.

Dominelli, L. (1991) *Women Across Continents: Feminist Comparative Social Policy*. Brighton: Wheatsheaf.

Douglas, J. (1979) 'Living Morality Versus Bureaucratic Fiat'. In Klockars, C. and O'Connor, F. (eds) *Deviance and Decency: The Ethics of Research with Human Subjects*. London: Sage.

Douglas, J. (1985) *Creative Interviewing*. London: Sage.

Drew, P. and Wootton, A. (eds) (1988) *Erving Goffman: Exploring the Interaction Order*. Cambridge: Polity.

Dreyfus, H. and Rabinow, P. (1982) *Michel Foucault: Beyond Structuralism and Hermeneutics*. Chicago: University of Chicago Press.

Driver, E. (1989) 'Introduction'. In Driver, E. and Droisen, A. (eds) *Child Sexual Abuse: Feminist Perspectives*. London: Macmillan.

Driver, E. and Droisen, A. (eds) (1989) *Child Sexual Abuse: Feminist Perspectives*. London: Macmillan.

Dunkerley, D. (1988) 'Historical Methods and Organizational Analysis: The Case of a Naval Dockyard'. In Bryman, A. (ed.) *Day Research in Organization*. London: Routledge.

Dunleavy, P. and Husbands, C. (1985) *British Democracy at the Crossroads: Voting and Party Competition in the 1980s*. London: George Allen & Unwin.

Durkheim, E. (1952) *Suicide*. London: Routledge & Kegan Paul.

Durkheim, E. (1964) *The Rules of Sociological Method*. Glencoe, IL: The Free Press.

Easthope, A. and McGowan, K. (eds) (1992) *A Critical and Cultural Theory Reader*. Buckingham: Open University Press.

Eaton, M. (1986) *Justice for Women: Family, Court and Social Control*. Milton Keynes: Open University Press.

Eco, U. (1979) *The Role of the Reader*. London: Hutchinson.

Edwards, S. (1990) 'Provoking her Own Demise: From Common Assault to Homicide'. In Hanmer, J. and Maynard, M. (eds) *Women, Violence and Social Control*. London: Macmillan.

Eichler, M. (1988) *Nonsexist Research Methods: A Practical Guide.* London: Unwin Hyman.

Eldridge, J. (1986) 'Facets of "Relevance" in Sociological Research'. In Heller, F. (ed.) *The Use and Abuse of Social Science.* London: Sage.

Emmet, E. R. (1981) *Learning to Philosophize.* Harmondsworth: Penguin.

Erickson, B. and Nosanchuk, T. (1983) *Understanding Data.* Milton Keynes: Open University Press.

Ericson, R., Baranek, P. and Chan, J. (1987) *Visualizing Deviance: A Study of News Organization.* Milton Keynes: Open University Press.

Ericson, R., Baranek, P. and Chan, J. (1989) *Negotiating Control: A Study of News Sources.* Milton Keynes: Open University Press.

Ericson, R., Baranek, P. and Chan, J. (1991) *Representing Order: Crime, Law, and Justice in the News Media.* Milton Keynes: Open University Press.

Esping-Andersen, G. (1990) *The Three Worlds of Welfare Capitalism.* Cambridge: Polity Press.

Farran, D. (1990) 'Analysing a Photography of Marilyn Monroe'. In Stanley, L. (ed.) *Feminist Praxis: Research, Theory and Epistemology in Feminist Sociology.* London: Routledge.

Fennell, G., Phillipson, C. and Evers, H. (1988) *The Sociology of Old Age.* Milton Keynes: Open University Press.

Ferber, R., Sheatsley, P., Turner, A. and Waksberg, J. (1980) *What is a Survey?* Washington, DC: American Statistical Association.

Ferrari, V. (1990) 'Socio-Legal Concepts and their Comparison'. In Øyen, E. (ed.) *Comparative Methodology.* London: Sage.

Festinger, L., Riecken, H. W. and Schachter, S. (1956) *When Prophecy Fails.* New York: Harper & Row.

Feyerabend, P. (1978) *Against Method.* London: Verso.

Fielding, N. (1981) *The National Front.* London: Routledge & Kegan Paul.

Fielding, N. (1982) 'Observational Research on the National Front'. In Bulmer, M. (ed.) *Social Research Ethics: An Examination of the Merits of a Covert Participation.* London: Macmillan.

Fielding, N. (1988a) *Joining Forces: Police Training, Socialization and Occupational Competence.* London: Routledge.

Fielding, N. (ed.) (1988b) *Actions and Structure: Research Methods and Social Theory.* London: Sage.

Fielding, N. and Fielding, J. (1986) *Linking Data: The Articulation of Quantitative and Qualitative Methods in Social Research.* London: Sage.

Fielding, N. and Lee, R. (eds) (1991) *Using Computers in Qualitative Research.* London: Sage.

Filstead, W. (ed.) (1971) *Qualitative Methodology.* Chicago: Markham.

Finch, J. (1984) 'It's Great to have Someone to Talk to: the Ethics and Politics of Interviewing Women'. In Bell, C. and Roberts, H. (eds) *Social Researching: Politics, Problems and Practice.* London: Routledge & Kegan Paul.

Finch, J. (1987) 'The Vignette Technique in Survey Research' *Sociology* 21 (1): 105–14.

Fishman, P. (1990) 'Interaction: The Work Women Do'. In McCarl Nielsen, J. (ed.) *Feminist Research Methods: Exemplary Readings in the Social Sciences.* London: Westview Press.

Fitz-Gibbon, C. and Lyons Morris, L. (1987) *How to Design a Program Evaluation.* London: Sage.

Flew, A. (ed.) (1984) *A Dictionary of Philosophy.* London: Pan.

Foucault, M. (1971) *Madness and Civilization.* London: Tavistock.

Foucault, M. (1977) *Discipline and Punish: The Birth of the Prison.* London: Allen Lane.

Foucault, M. (1980) *Power/Knowledge, Selected Interviews and Other Writings 1972–1977.* Edited by Gordon, C. Brighton: Harvester Press.

Foucault, M. (1984) 'What is an Author?' In Rabinow, P. (ed.) *The Foucault Reader.* Harmondsworth: Penguin.

Fowler, F. J. (1988) *Survey Research Methods.* London: Sage.

Fraser, N. (1989) *Unruly Practices: Power, Discourse and Gender in Contemporary Social Theory.* Cambridge: Polity Press.

Freedman, D., Pisani, R., Purves, R. and Adhikari, A. (1991) *Statistics.* London: W. W. Norton.

Frisby, D. (1984) *George Simmel.* London: Tavistock.

Garfinkel, H. (1967) *Studies in Ethnomethodology.* Englewood Cliffs, NJ: Prentice-Hall.

Gearing, B. and Dant, T. (1990) 'Doing Biographical Research'. In Peace, S. (ed.) *Researching Social Gerontology: Concepts, Methods & Issues.* London: Sage.

Geertz, C. (1973a) 'Thick Description'. In Geertz, C. (ed.) *The Interpretation of Cultures.* New York: Basic Books.

Geertz, C. (ed.) (1973b) *The Interpretation of Cultures.* New York: Basic Books.

Gellner, E. (1974) 'The New Idealism: Cause and Meaning in the Social Sciences'. In Giddens, A. (ed.) *Positivism and Sociology.* London: Heinemann.

Gelsthorpe, L. (1990) 'Feminist Methodologies in Criminology: A New Approach or Old Wine in New Bottles?' In Gelsthorpe, L. and Morris, A. (eds) *Feminist Perspectives in Criminology.* Milton Keynes: Open University Press.

Gelsthorpe, L. and Morris, A (eds) (1990) *Feminist Pespectives in Criminology.* Milton Keynes: Open University Press.

Gergen, K. and Gergen, M. (1991) 'Toward Reflexive Methodologies'. In Steier, F. (ed.) *Research and Reflexivity.* London: Sage.

Gerth, H. and Mills, C. W. (eds) (1948) *From Max Weber: Essays in Sociology.* London: Routledge & Kegan Paul.

Giddens, A. (ed.) (1974) *Positivism and Sociology.* London: Heinemann.

Giddens, A. (1976) *New Rules of Sociological Method.* London: Hutchinson.

Giddens, A. (1979) *Central Problems in Social Theory.* London: Macmillan.

Giddens, A. (1984) *The Constitution of Society: Outline of the Theory of Structuration.* Cambridge: Polity Press.

Giddens, A. (1989) *Sociology.* Cambridge: Polity Press.

Giddens, A. (1990) *The Consequences of Modernity.* Cambridge: Polity Press.

Gilbert, G. N. (1981) *Modelling Society: An Introduction to Loglinear Analysis for Social Researchers.* London: George Allen & Unwin.

Gilbert, G. N. and Abell, P. (eds) (1984) *Accounts and Action.* Aldershot: Gower.

Gilbert, G. N. and Mulkay, M. (1984) *Opening Pandora's Box: A Sociological Analysis of Scientists' Discourse.* Cambridge: Cambridge University Press.

Glaser, B. and Strauss, A. (1965) *Awareness of Dying.* Chicago: Aldine Publishing.

Glaser, B. and Strauss, A. (1967) *The Discovery of Grounded Theory.* Chicago: Aldine Publishing.

Glastonbury, B. and MacKean, J. (1991) 'Survey Methods'. In Allan, G. and Skinner, C. (eds) *Handbook for Research Students in the Social Sciences.* London: Falmer Press.

Goffman, E. (1961) *Encounters: Two Studies in the Sociology of Interaction.* Harmondsworth: Penguin.

Goffman, E. (1968) *Asylums: Essays on the Social Situation of Mental Patients and Other Inmates* (originally published in 1961). Harmondsworth: Penguin.

Goffman, E. (1984) *The Presentation of Self in Everyday Life* (originally published in 1959). Harmondsworth: Penguin.

Gold, R. (1969) 'Roles in Sociological Field Observation'. In McCall, G. and Simmons, J. (eds) *Issues in Participant Observation: A Text and Reader.* London: Addison Wesley.

Goldthorpe, J. (1984) 'The Relevance of History to Sociology'. In Bulmer, M. (ed.) *Sociological Research Methods,* 2nd edition. London: Macmillan.

Gouldner, A. (1962) 'Anti-Minotaur: The Myth of a Value-Free Sociology', *Social Problems* 9 (3): 199–213.

Gouldner, A. (1971) *The Coming Crisis in Western Sociology.* London: Heinemann.

Graham, H. (1984) 'Surveying through Stories'. In Bell, C. and Roberts, H. (eds) *Social Researching: Politics, Problems and Practice.* London: Routledge & Kegan Paul.

Gramsci, A. (1971) *Selections from the Prison Notebooks.* London: Lawrence & Wishart.

Greed, C. (1990) 'The Professional and the Personal: A Study of Women Quantity Surveyors'. In Stanley, L. (ed.) *Feminist Praxis: Research, Theory and Epistemology in Feminist Sociology.* London: Routledge.

Griffiths, M. and Whitford, M. (eds) (1990) *Feminist Perspectives in Philosophy.* London: Macmillan.

Grimshaw, A. (1973) 'Comparative Sociology: In What Ways Different from Other Sociologies?'. In Armer, M. and Grimshaw, A. (eds) *Comparative Social Research: Methodological Problems and Strategies.* London: John Wiley.

Gwilliam, P. (1988) *Basic Statistics.* Harmondsworth: Penguin.

Habermas, J. (1971) *Knowledge and Human Interests.* Boston, MA: Beacon Press.

Habermas, J. (1973) *Theory and Practice.* Boston, MA: Beacon Press.

Habermas, J. (1984) *Theory of Communicative Action. Vol. 1: Reason and the Rationalization of Society.* Translated by McCarthy, T. Cambridge: Polity Press.

Habermas, J. (1987) *Theory of Communicative Action. Vol. 2: Lifeworld and System: A Critique of Functionalist Reason.* Translated by McCarthy, T. Cambridge: Polity Press.

Habermas, J. (1988) *On the Logic of the Social Sciences.* Cambridge: Polity Press.

Hage, J. and Meeker, B. (1988) *Social Causality.* London: Unwin Hyman.

Hakim, C. (1982) *Secondary Analysis in Social Research: A Guide to Data Sources and Methods with Examples.* London: Macmillan.

Hakim, C. (1987) *Research Design.* London: George Allen & Unwin.

Hall, S. (1988) 'The Toad in the Garden: Thatcherism Among the Theorists'. In Nelson, C. and Grossberg, L. (eds) *Marxism and the Interpretation of Culture.* London: Macmillan.

Hall, S. and Jacques, M. (eds) (1983) *The Politics of Thatcherism.* London: Lawrence & Wishart.

Hall, S., Cutcher, C., Jefferson, T. and Roberts, B. (1978) *Policing the Crisis: Mugging, The State and Law and Order.* London: Macmillan.

Hammersley, M. (1990a) *Classroom Ethnography.* Milton Keynes: Open University Press.

Hammersley, M. (1990b) *The Dilemma of Qualitative Method: Herbert Blumer and the Chicago Tradition*. London: Routledge.

Hammersley, M. (1990c) 'What's Wrong with Ethnography? The Myth of Theoretical Description', *Sociology* 24 (4): 597–615.

Hammersley, M. (1992) *What's Wrong with Ethnography?* London: Routledge.

Hammersley, M. and Atkinson, P. (1983) *Ethnography: Principles in Practice*. London: Tavistock.

Hanmer, J. and Maynard, M. (eds) (1990) *Women, Violence and Social Control*. London: Macmillan.

Harding, S. (ed.) (1987a) *Feminism and Methodology*. Bloomington, IN/Milton Keynes: Indiana Press/Open University Press.

Harding, S. (1987b) 'Is There a Feminist Method?' In Harding, S. (ed.) *Feminism and Methodology*. Bloomington, IN/Milton Keynes: Indiana Press/Open University Press.

Harding, S. (1991) *Whose Science? Whose Knowledge? Thinking from Women's Lives*. Milton Keynes: Open University Press.

Harré, R. (1988) 'Accountability within a Social Order: The Role of Pronouns'. In Antaki, C. (ed.) *Analysing Everyday Explanation: A Casebook of Methods*. London: Sage.

Harstock, N. (1987) 'The Feminist Standpoint: Developing the Ground for a Specifically Historical Materialism'. In Harding, S. (ed.) *Feminsim and Methodology*. Bloomington, IN/Milton Keynes: Indiana Press/Open University Press.

Harvey, L. (1990) *Critical Social Research*. London: Unwin Hyman.

Heath, C. (1981) 'The Opening Sequence in Doctor–Patient Interaction'. In Atkinson, P. and Heath, C. (eds) *Medical Work: Realities and Routines*. Aldershot: Gower.

Heath, C. (1988) 'Embarrassment and Interactional Organization'. In Drew, P. and Wootton, A. (eds) *Erving Goffman: Exploring the Interaction Order*. Cambridge: Polity Press.

Heller, A. and Fehér, F. (1988) *The Postmodern Political Condition*. Cambridge: Polity Press.

Heller, F. (ed.) (1986) *The Use and Abuse of Social Science*. London: Sage.

Henerson, M., Lyons Morris, L. and Fitz-Gibbon, C. (1987) *How to Measure Attitudes*. London: Sage.

Heritage, J. (1984) *Garfinkel and Ethnomethodology*. Cambridge: Polity Press.

Hey, V. (1986) *Patriarchy and Pub Culture*. London: Tavistock.

Higgins, J. (1981) *States of Welfare: Comparative Analysis in Social Policy*. Oxford: Basil Blackwell.

Hobbs, D. (1988) *Doing the Business: Entrepreneurship, the Working Class and Detectives in the East-End of London*. Oxford: Oxford University Press.

Hobbs, D. and May, T. (eds) (1993) *Interpreting the Field: Accounts of Ethnography*. Oxford: Oxford University Press.

Hoinville, G. and Jowell, R. in association with Airey, C., Brook, L., Courtenay, C. et al (1987) *Survey Research Practice*. London: Heinemann.

Home Office (1991) *Digest of Information on the Criminal Justice System*. London: Home Office.

Hough, M. and Mayhew, P. (1983) *The British Crime Survey: First Report*. Home Office Research Study No. 76. London: HMSO.

Hough, M. and Mayhew, P. (1985) *Taking Account of Crime: Key Findings from the Second British Crime Survey*. Home Office Research Study No. 85. London: HMSO.

Huff, D. (1981) *How to Lie with Statistics*. Harmondsworth: Penguin.

Hughes, J. (1976) *Sociological Analysis*. London: Nelson.

Hughes, J. (1980) *The Philosophy of Social Research*. London: Longman.

Humm, M. (1989) *A Dictionary of Feminist Theory*. London: Harvester Wheatsheaf.

Humm, M. (ed.) (1992) *Feminisms: A Reader*. London: Harvester Wheatsheaf.

Humphreys, L. (1970) *Tea Room Trade*. London: Duckworth.

Husbands, C. (1981) 'The Anti-Quantitative Bias in Postwar British Sociology'. In Abrams, P., Deem, R., Finch, J. and Rock, P. (eds) *Practice and Progress: British Sociology 1950–1980*. London: George Allen & Unwin.

Irvine J., Miles, I. and Evans, J. (eds) (1979) *Demystifying Social Statistics*. London: Pluto Press.

Jefferson, T. (ed.) (1975) *Resistance Through Rituals*. University of Birmingham: Centre for Contemporary Cultural Studies.

Jick, T. (1979) 'Mixing Qualitative and Quantitative Methods: Triangulation in Action', *Administrative Science Quarterly* 24: 602–11.

Johnson, T., Dandeker, C. and Ashworth, C. (1990) *The Structure of Social Theory*. London: Macmillan.

Jones, C. (1985) *Patterns of Social Policy: An Introduction to Comparative Analysis*. London: Tavistock.

Jones, K. (1992) *The Making of Social Policy in Britain 1830–1990*. London: Athlone.

Jolliffe, F.R. (1974) *Commonsense Statistics for Economists and Others*. London: Routledge & Kegan Paul.

Kamuf, P. (ed.) (1991) *A Derrida Reader: Between the Blinds*. London: Harvester Wheatsheaf.

Kay, C. Y. (1990) 'At the Palace: Researching Gender and Ethnicity in a Chinese Restaurant'. In Stanley, L. (ed.) *Feminist Praxis: Research, Theory and Epistemology in Feminist Sociology*. London: Routledge.

Keat, R. and Urry, J. (1975) *Social Theory as Science*. London: Routledge & Kegan Paul.

Kelly, L. and Radford, J. (1987) 'The Problem of Men: Feminist Perspectives on Sexual Violence'. In Scraton, P. (ed.) *Law, Order and the Authoritarian State*. Milton Keynes: Open University Press.

Kent, R. (1981) *A History of British Empirical Sociology*. Aldershot: Gower.

Kidder, L. (1981) *Research Methods in Social Relations*, 4th edition. New York: Holt-Saunders.

Kimmel, A. (1988) *Ethics and Values in Applied Social Research*. London: Sage.

Kirk, J. and Miller, M. (1986) *Reliability and Validity in Qualitative Research*. London: Sage.

Klockars, C. and O'Connor, F. (eds) (1979) *Deviance and Decency: The Ethics of Research with Human Subjects*. London: Sage.

Knorr-Cetina, K. and Cicourel, A. (eds) (1981) *Advances in Social Theory and Methodology: Towards an Integration of Micro and Macro Theories*. London: Routledge & Kegan Paul.

Kuhn, T. (1970) *The Structure of Scientific Revolutions*. Chicago: University of Chicago Press.

Kuhn, T. (1972) 'Scientific Paradigms'. In Barnes, B. (ed.) *Sociology of Science: Selected Readings*. Harmondsworth: Penguin.

Kurtz, L. (1984) *Evaluating Chicago Sociology: A Guide to the Literature with an Annotated Bibliography*. Chicago: Chicago University Press.

La Fontaine, J. (1985) *What is Social Anthropology?* London: Edward Arnold.

Laclau, E. and Mouffe, C. (1985) *Hegemony and Socialist Strategy: Towards a Radical Democratic Politics*. London: Verso.

Langan, M. and Ostner, I. (1991) 'Gender and Welfare: Towards a Comparative Framework'. In Room, G. (ed.) *Towards a European Welfare State?* Bristol: SAUS Publications (School for Advanced Urban Studies).

Lapiere, R. (1934) 'Attitudes Versus Actions', *Social Forces* 13: 230–7.

Lavrakas, P. (1987) *Telephone Survey Methods: Sampling, Selection, and Supervision*. London: Sage.

Lawrence, P. (1988) 'In Another Country'. In Bryman, A. (ed.) *Doing Research in Organisations*. London: Routledge.

Lee, F. (1988) *Fabianism and Colonialism: The Life and Political Thought of Lord Sydney Olivier*. London: Defiant Books.

Lieven, E. (1981) 'If It's Natural, We Can't Change It'. In Cambridge Women's Studies Group (eds) *Women in Society: Interdisciplinary Essays*. London: Virago Press.

Lipsky, R. (1982) *An Introduction to Positive Economics*, 5th edition. London: Weidenfeld & Nicolson.

Lloyd, G. (1984) *The Man of Reason: 'Male' and 'Female' in Western Philosophy*. London: Methuen.

Lofland, J. and Lofland, L. (1984) *Analysing Social Settings: A Guide to Qualitative Observation and Analysis*, 2nd edition. Belmont, CA: Wadsworth.

Lorde, A. (1992) 'An Open Letter to Mary Daly'. In Humm, M. (ed.) *Feminism: A Reader*. London: Harvester Wheatsheaf.

Lukes, S. (1981) *Emile Durkheim: His Life and Work: A Historical and Critical Study*. Harmondsworth: Penguin.

Lyotard, J. (1984) *The Postmodern Condition: A Report on Knowledge*. Manchester: Manchester University Press.

McCall, G. and Simmons, J. (eds) (1969) *Issues in Participant Observation: A Text and Reader*. London: Addison Wesley.

McCarl Nielsen, J. (ed.) (1990) *Feminist Research Methods: Exemplary Readings in the Social Sciences*. London: Westview Press.

McGregor, P. and Borooah, V. (1992) 'Is Low Spending or Low Income a Better Indicator of Whether or Not a Household is Poor: Some Results from the 1985 Family Expenditure Survey', *Journal of Social Policy* 21 (1): 53–69.

McLaughlin, E. (1991) 'Oppositional Poverty: The Quantitative/Qualitative Divide and Other Dichotomies', *Sociological Review* 39 (2): 292–308.

McMiller, P. and Wilson, M. (1984) *A Dictionary of Social Science Methods*. London: John Wiley.

Majchrzak, A. (1984) *Methods for Policy Research*. Beverley Hills, CA: Sage.

Malseed, J. (1987) 'Straw Men: A Note on Ann Oakley's Treatment of Textbook Prescriptions for Interviewing', *Sociology* 21 (4): 629–31.

Manis, J. (1976) *Analyzing Social Problems*. New York: Praeger.

Mann, P. (1985) *Methods of Social Investigation*. Oxford: Basil Blackwell.

Manning, P. (1987) *Semiotics and Fieldwork*. London: Sage.

Manning, P. (1988) 'Semiotics and Social Theory: The Analysis of Organizational Beliefs'. In Fielding, N. (ed.) *Actions and Structure: Research Methods and Social Theory*. London: Sage.

Manning, P. and Van Maanen, J. (eds) (1978) *Policing: A View from the Streets*. Santa Monica, CA: Goodyear.

Marsh, C. (1979) 'Opinion Polls – Social Science or Political Manoeuvre?' In Irvine J., Miles, I. and Evans, J. (eds) *Demystifying Social Statistics*. London: Pluto Press.

Marsh, C. (1982) *The Survey Method*. London: George Allen & Unwin.

Marsh, C. (1984) 'Problems with Surveys: Method or Epistemology?' In Bulmer, M. (ed.) *Sociological Research Methods*, 2nd edition. London: Macmillan.

Marsh, C. (1988) *Exploring Data: An Introduction to Data Analysis for Social Scientists*. Cambridge: Polity Press.

Marsh, C. and Gershuny, J. (1991). 'Handling Work History Data in Standard Statistical Packages'. In Dex, S. (ed.) *Life and Work History Analyses: Qualitative and Quantitative Developments*. London: Routledge.

Marsh, R. (1967) *Comparative Sociology: A Codification of Cross-Societal Analysis*. New York: Harcourt & Brace.

Marshall, C. and Rossman, G. (1989) *Designing Qualitative Research*. London: Sage.

Mawby, R. I. (1990) *Comparative Policing Issues: The British and American Experience in International Perspective*. London: Unwin Hyman.

Mawby, R. I. (1991) *Look After Your Heart: First Report from the Plymouth Health Survey*. Department of Applied Social Science, Plymouth: University of Plymouth.

May, T. (1986) 'Neglected Territory: Victims of Car Theft'. Unpublished MSc Thesis. Department of Sociology, University of Surrey.

May, T. (1991) *Probation: Politics, Policy and Practice*. Milton Keynes: Open University Press.

May, T. (1992) *Study Skills in Higher Education*. Plymouth, Faculty of Human Sciences: University of Plymouth.

May, T. (1993) 'Feelings Matter: Inverting the Hidden Equation'. In Hobbs, D. and May, T. (eds) *Interpreting the Field: Accounts of Ethnography*. Oxford: Oxford University Press.

Mayhew, P., Elliott, D. and Dowds, L. (1989) *The 1988 British Crime Survey*. Home Office Research Study No. 111. London: HMSO.

Merton, R. (1957) *Social Theory and Social Structure*. New York: The Free Press.

Merton, R. and Kendal, P. (1946) 'The Focused Interview', *American Journal of Sociology* 51: 541–57.

Mills, C. W. (1940) 'Situated Accounts and Vocabularies of Motive', *American Sociological Review* 6: 904–13.

Mills, C. W. (1959) *The Sociological Imagination*. New York: Oxford University Press.

Mishra, R. (1989) 'The Academic Tradition in Social Policy'. In Bulmer, M., Lewis, J. and Piachaud, D. (eds) *The Goals of Social Policy*. London: Unwin Hyman.

Moser, C. and Kalton, G. (1983) *Survey Methods in Social Investigation*. London: Heinemann.

Mullan, B. (1987) *Sociologists on Sociology*. London: Croom Helm.

Nagel, E. (1961) *The Structure of Science*. London: Routledge & Kegan Paul.

Nelson, C. and Grossberg, L. (eds) (1988) *Marxism and the Interpretation of Culture*. London: Macmillan.

Newman, G. (1976) *Comparative Deviance: Perception and Law in Six Cultures.* New York: Elsevier.

Oakley, A. (1979) *From Here to Maternity: Becoming a Mother.* Harmondsworth: Penguin.

Oakley, A. (1984) *Taking it Like a Woman.* London: Fontana.

Oakley, A. (1987) 'Comment on Malseed', *Sociology* 21 (4): 632.

Oakley, A. (1990) 'Interviewing Women: A Contradiction in Terms'. In Roberts, H. (ed.) *Doing Feminist Research.* London: Routledge & Kegan Paul.

Oakley, A. and Oakley, R. (1979) 'Sexism in Official Statistics'. In Irvine J., Miles, I. and Evans, J. (eds) *Demystifying Social Statistics.* London: Pluto Press.

Okin, S, M. (1980) *Women in Western Political Thought.* London: Virago.

Oppenheim, A. N. (1973) *Questionnaire Design and Attitude Measurement.* London: Heinemann.

Outhwaite, W. (1991) 'Hans-George Gadamer'. In Skinner, Q. (ed.) *The Return of Grand Theory in the Human Sciences.* Cambridge: Cambridge University Press.

Øyen, E. (ed.) (1990a) *Comparative Methodology.* London: Sage.

Øyen, E. (1990b) 'The Imperfection of Comparisons'. In Øyen, E. (ed.) *Comparative Methodology.* London: Sage.

Papineau, D. (1978) *For Science in the Social Sciences.* London: Macmillan.

Parker, H. (1974) *View from the Boys.* Newton Abott: David & Charles.

Pascall, G. (1986) *Social Policy: A Feminist Analysis.* London: Tavistock.

Patton, M. (1987) *How to Use Qualitative Methods in Evaluation.* London: Sage.

Peace, S. (ed.) (1990) *Researching Social Gerontology: Concepts, Methods and Issues.* London: Sage.

Pearson, G. (1983) *Hooligan: A History of Respectable Fears.* London: Macmillan.

Pinker, R. (1971) *Social Theory and Social Policy.* London: Heinemann.

Platt, J. (1981a) 'Evidence and Proof in Documentary Research: 1. Some Specific Problems of Documentary Research', *Sociological Review* 29 (1): 31–52.

Platt, J. (1981b) 'Evidence and Proof in Documentary Reserch: 2. Some Shared Problems of Documentary Research', *Sociological Review* 29 (1): 53–66.

Plummer, K. (1990) *Documents of Life: An Introduction to the Problems and Literature of a Humanistic Method.* London: George Allen & Unwin.

Polsky, N. (1985) *Hustlers, Beats and Others.* Chicago: Chicago University Press.

Popper, K. R. (1959) *The Logic of Scientific Discovery.* London: Hutchinson.

Popper, K. R. (1970) 'The Sociology of Knowledge'. In Curtis, J. and Petras, J. (eds) *The Sociology of Knowledge: A Reader.* London: Duckworth.

Poster, M. (1990) *The Mode of Information: Poststructuralism and Social Context.* Cambridge: Polity Press.

Pryce, K. (1986) *Endless Pressure: A Study of West-Indian Life Styles in Bristol,* 2nd edition. University of Bristol: Bristol Classical Press.

Pugh, A. (1990) 'My Statistics and Feminism – A True Story'. In Stanley, L. (ed.) *Feminist Praxis: Research, Theory and Epistemology in Feminist Sociology.* London: Routledge.

Rabinow, P. (ed.) (1984) *The Foucault Reader.* Harmondsworth: Penguin.

Radford, J. (1990) 'Policing Male Violence – Policing Women'. In Hanmer, J. and Maynard, M. (eds) *Women, Violence and Social Control.* London: Macmillan.

Ramazanoglu, C. (1990) *Feminism and the Contradictions of Oppression.* London: Routledge.

Ramazanoglu, C. (1992) 'On Feminist Methodology: Male Reason Versus Female Empowerment', *Sociology* 26 (2): 207–12.

Ravn, I. (1991) 'What Should Guide Reality Construction?' In Steier, F. (ed.) *Research and Reflexivity*. London: Sage.

Rice, M. (1990) 'Challenging Orthodoxies in Feminist Theory: a Black Feminist Critique'. In Gelsthorpe, L. and Morris, A. (eds) *Feminist Perspectives in Criminology*. Milton Keynes: Open University Press.

Roberts, H. (ed.) (1990) *Doing Feminist Research*. London: Routledge & Kegan Paul.

Rock, P. (1979) *The Making of Symbolic Interactionism*. London: Macmillan.

Room, G. (ed.) (1991) *Towards a European Welfare State?* Bristol: SAUS Publications (School for Advanced Urban Studies).

Rose, A. (ed.) (1972) *Human Behaviour and Social Processes: An Interactionist Approach*. London: Routledge & Kegan Paul.

Rose, G. (1982) *Deciphering Sociological Research*. London: Macmillan.

Rose, R. (1991) 'Comparing Forms of Comparative Analysis', *Political Studies* 39 (3): 446–62.

Rosenberg, M. (1968) *The Logic of Survey Analysis*. New York: Basic Books.

Rosenberg, M. (1984) 'The Meaning of Relationships in Social Surveys'. In Bulmer, M. (ed.) *Sociological Research Methods*, 2nd edition. London: Macmillan.

Roseneil, S. (1993) 'Greenham Revisited: Researching Myself and My Sisters'. In Hobbs, D. and May, T. (eds) *Interpreting the Field: Accounts of Ethnography*. Oxford: Oxford University Press.

Rosenhan, D. (1982) 'On Being Sane in Insane Places'. In Bulmer, M. (ed.) *Social Research Ethics: An Examination of the Merits of Covert Participant Observation*. London: Macmillan.

Rowntree, D. (1981) *Statistics Without Tears: A Primer for Non-Mathematicians*. Harmondsworth: Penguin.

Russell, B. (1912) *Problems of Philosophy*. Oxford: Oxford University Press.

Ryan, A. (1984) *The Philosophy of the Social Sciences*. London: Macmillan.

Samuel, R. (1982) 'Local and Oral History'. In Burgess, R. (ed.) *Field Research: A Sourcebook and Field Manual*. London: George Allen & Unwin.

Sayer, A. (1992) *Method in Social Science: A Realist Approach*, 2nd edition. London: Routledge.

Schegloff, E. (1988) 'Goffman and the Analysis of Conversation'. In Drew, P. and Wootton, A. (eds) *Erving Goffman: Exploring the Interaction Order*. Cambridge: Polity Press.

Scheuch, E. (1990) 'The Development of Comparative Research: Towards Causal Explanations'. In Øyen, E. (ed.) *Comparative Methodology*. London: Sage.

Schutz, A. (1979) 'Concept and Theory Formation in the Social Sciences'. In Bynner, J. and Stribley, K. (eds) *Social Research: Principles and Procedures*. Harlow: Longman.

Scott, J. (1990) *A Matter of Record: Documentary Sources in Social Research*. Cambridge: Polity Press.

Scott, M. and Lyman, S. (1968) 'Accounts', *American Sociological Review* 33 (1): 46–62.

Scraton, P. (ed.) (1987) *Law, Order and the Authoritarian State*. Milton Keynes: Open University Press.

Shallice, A. and Gordon, P. (1990) *Black People, White Justice? Race and the Criminal Justice System*. London: Runnymede Trust.

Sharrock, W. and Watson, R. (1988) 'Autonomy among Social Theories'. In Fielding, N. (ed.) *Actions and Structure: Research Methods and Social Theory*. London: Sage.

Shaw, C. (1930) *The Jack Roller: A Delinquent Boy's Own Story*. Chicago: Chicago University Press.

Shibley Hyde, J. (1990) 'How Large are Cognitive Differences? A Meta Analysis Using W^2 and d'. In McCarl Nielsen, J. (ed.) *Feminist Research Methods: Exemplary Readings in the Social Sciences*. London: Westview Press.

Shils, E. and Finch, H. (eds) (1949) *Max Weber on the Methodology of the Social Sciences*. Glencoe IL: The Free Press.

Shipman, M. (1988) *The Limitations of Social Research*, 3rd edition. London: Longman.

Sieber, S. (1978) 'The Integration of Fieldwork and Survey Methods'. In Denzin, N. K. (ed.) *Sociological Methods: A Sourcebook*, 2nd edition. London: McGraw-Hill.

Silverman, D. (1985) *Qualitative Methodology and Sociology*. Aldershot: Gower.

Skinner, Q. (ed.) (1991) *The Return of Grand Theory in the Human Sciences*. Cambridge: Cambridge University Press.

Slattery, M. (1986) *Official Statistics* (Society Now Series). London: Routledge.

Smart, B. (1992) *Modern Conditions, Postmodern Controversies*. London: Routledge.

Smith, D. (1988) *The Everyday World as Problematic: A Feminist Sociology*. Milton Keynes: Open University Press.

Smith, G. (1977) 'The Place of Professional Ideology in the Analysis of Social Policy: Some Theoretical Conclusions from a Pilot Study of the Children's Panels', *Sociological Review* 25 (4): 843–65.

Social and Community Planning Research (SCPR) (1981) 'Survey Methods Newsletter on Open-Ended Questions'. Autumn.

Sontag, S. (1978) *On Photography*. London: Allen Lane.

Sparks, R. (1992) *Television and the Drama of Crime: Moral Tales and the Place of Crime in Public Life*. Buckingham: Open University Press.

Spradley, J. (1979) *The Ethnographic Interview*. New York: Holt, Rinehart & Winston.

Spradley, J. (1980) *Participant Observation*. New York: Holt, Rinehart & Winston.

Spence, J. and Holland, P. (eds) (1991) *Family Snaps: The Meanings of Domestic Photography*. London: Virago.

Spender, D. (1982) *Women of Ideas (and what men have done to them)*. London: Ark Paperbacks.

Sprent, P. (1988) *Understanding Data*. Harmondsworth: Penguin.

Squires, P. (1990) *Anti-Social Policy: Welfare, Ideology and the Disciplinary State*. London: Harvester Wheatsheaf.

Stanko, B. (1990) 'When Precaution is Normal: A Feminist Critique of Crime Prevention'. In Gelsthorpe, L. and Morris, A. (eds) *Feminist Perspectives in Criminology*. Milton Keynes: Open University Press.

Stanley, L. (ed.) (1990a) *Feminist Praxis: Research, Theory and Epistemology in Feminist Sociology*. London: Routledge.

Stanley, L. (1990b) 'Feminist Praxis and the Academic Mode of Production'. In Stanley, L. (ed.) *Feminist Praxis: Research, Theory and Epistemology in Feminist Sociology*. London: Routledge.

Stanley, L. (1990c) 'Doing Ethnography, Writing Ethnography: A Comment on Hammersley', *Sociology* 24 (4): 617–27.

Stanley, L. and Wise, S. (1983) *Breaking Out: Feminist Consciousness and Feminist Research*. London: Routledge & Kegan Paul.

Stanley, L. and Wise, S. (1990) 'Method, Methodology and Epistemology in Feminist Research Processes'. In Stanley, L. (ed.) *Feminist Praxis Research, Theory and Epistemology in Feminist Sociology*. London: Routledge.

Steier, F. (ed.) (1991) *Research and Reflexivity*. London: Sage.

Stewart. D. and Shamdasani, P. (1990) *Focus Groups: Theory and Practice*. London: Sage.

Strauss, A. (1978) *Negotiations, Varieties, Contexts, Processes and Social Order*. San Francisco: Jossey-Bass.

Strauss, A. (1988) *Qualitative Analysis for Social Scientists*. Cambridge: Cambridge University Press.

Sydie, R. (1987) *Natural Women, Cultured Men: A Feminist Critique of Sociological Theory*. Milton Keynes: Open University Press.

Taylor, I. (ed.) (1990) *The Social Effects of Free Market Policies: An International Text*. London: Harvester Wheatsheaf.

Taylor, I., Walton, P. and Young, J. (1973) *The New Criminology: For a Social Theory of Deviance*. London: Routledge & Kegan Paul.

Talylor Fitz-Gibbon, C. and Lyons Morris, L. (1987) *How to Analyze Data*. London: Sage.

Teune, H. (1990) 'Comparing Countries: Lessons Learned'. In Øyen, E. (ed.) *Comparative Methodology*. London: Sage.

Thompson, E. (1982) 'Anthropology and the Discipline of Historical Context'. In Burgess, R. (ed.) *Field Research: A Sourcebook and Field Manual*. London: George Allen & Unwin.

Titmuss, R. (1970) *The Gift Relationship*. London: George Allen & Unwin.

Titmuss, R. (1974) *Social Policy: An Introduction*. London: George Allen & Unwin.

Tong, R. (1989) *Feminist Thought: A Comprehensive Introduction*. London: Unwin Hyman.

Turner, R. (ed.) (1974) *Ethnomethodology*. Harmondsworth: Penguin.

Vallier, I. (ed.) (1971) *Comparative Methods in Sociology: Essays on Trends and Applications*. Los Angeles: University of California Press.

Van Maanen, J. (1978) 'On Watching the Watchers'. In Manning, P. and Van Maanen, J. (eds) *Policing: A View for the Streets*. Santa Monica, CA: Goodyear.

Van Maanen, J. (1979) 'Reclaiming Qualitative Methods for Organizational Research: A Preface', *Administrative Science Quarterly* 24: 520–6.

Verba, S. (1971) 'Cross-National Survey Research: The Problem of Credibility'. In Vallier, I. (ed.) *Comparative Methods in Sociology: Essays on Trends and Applications*. Los Angeles: University of California Press.

Viinikka, S. (1989) 'Child Sexual Abuse and the Law'. In Driver, E. and Droisen, A. (eds) *Child Sexual Abuse: Feminist Perspectives*. London: Macmillan.

Voakes, V. and Fowler, Q. (1989) *Sentencing, Race and Social Enquiry Reports*. Wakefield: West Yorkshire Probation Service.

Walton, J. and Masotti, L. (1976) *The City in Comparative Perspective: Cross-National Research and New Directions in Theory*. New York: John Wiley.

Warwick, D. (1982) 'Tearoom Trade: Means and Ends in Social Research'. In Bulmer, M. (ed.) *Social Research Ethics: An Examination of the Merits of Covert Participation Observation*. London: Macmillan.

Warwick, D. and Osherson, S. (eds) (1973) *Comparative Research Methods*. Englewood Cliffs, NJ: Prentice-Hall.

Warwick, D. and Pettigrew, T. (1983) 'Towards Ethical Guidelines for Social Science Research in Public Policy'. In Callahan, D. and Jennings, B. (eds) *Ethics, the Social Sciences, and Policy Analysis*. London: Plenum Press.

Webb, S. (1990) 'Counter-Arguments: An Ethnographic Look at Women and Class'. In Stanley, L. (ed.) *Feminist Praxis: Research, Theory and Epistemology in Feminist Sociology*. London: Routledge.

Webb, E., Campbell, D., Schwartz, R. and Sechrest, L. (1966) *Unobtrusive Measures: Nonreactive Research in the Social Sciences*. Chicago: Rand McNally.

Weber, M. (1930) *The Protestant Ethic and the Spirit of Capitalism*. London: George Allen & Unwin.

Weber, M. (1949) *The Methodology of the Social Sciences*. Glencoe, ILinois: The Free Press.

Weber, M. (1965) *The Sociology of Religion*. London: Methuen.

Wetherell, M. and Potter, J. (1988) 'Discourse Anàlysis and the Identification of Interpetative Repertoires'. In Antaki, C. (ed.) *Analysing Everyday Explanation: A Casebook of Methods*. London: Sage.

Whitford, M. (1988) 'Luce Irigaray's Critique of Rationality'. In Griffiths, M. and Whitford, M. (eds) *Feminist Perspectives in Philosophy*. London: Macmillan.

Whyte, W. F. (1981) *Street Corner Society* (originally published 1943). Chicago: Chicago University Press.

Whyte, W. F. (1984) *Learning from the Field: A Guide from Experience*. London: Sage.

Williams, A. (1990) 'Reading Feminism in Fieldnotes'. In Stanley, L. (ed.) *Feminist Praxis: Research, Theory and Epistemology in Feminist Sociology*. London: Routledge.

Williams, F. (1989) *Social Policy: A Critical Introduction*. Cambridge: Polity Press.

Williams, R. (1981) *Culture*. London: Fontana.

Williams, R. (1983) *Keywords: A Vocabulary of Culture and Society*. London: Fontana.

Williamson, J. (1987) *Consuming Passions: The Dynamics of Popular Culture*. London: Marion Boyers.

Willis, C. (1983) *The Use, Effectiveness and Impact of Police Stop and Search Powers*. Home Office Research Unit, London: Home Office.

Willis, P. (1977) *Learning to Labour: How Working Class Kids Get Working Class Jobs*. Farnborough: Saxon House.

Winch, P (1958) *The Idea of a Social Science*. London: Routledge & Kegan Paul.

Wolcott, H. (1990) *Writing Up Qualitative Research*. London: Sage.

Wollheim, R. (1977) *Freud*. London: Fontana.

Yin, R. (1988) *Case Study Research: Design and Methods*. London: Sage.

Young, A. (1990) *Femininity in Dissent*. London: Routledge.

Young, K. (1977) '"Values" in the Policy Process', *Policy and Politics* 5 (3): 1–22.

Young, K. (1981) 'Discretion as an Implementation Problem'. In Adler, M. and Asquith, S. (eds) *Discretion and Welfare*. London: Heinemann.

Zimmerman, D. (1974) 'Facts as Practical Accomplishment'. In Turner, R. (ed.) *Ethnomethodology*. Harmondsworth: Penguin.

Author index

Subject index

INTRODUCING DATA ANALYSIS FOR SOCIAL SCIENTISTS

David Rose and Oriel Sullivan

Free Data Disk Inside

This textbook is designed for social science students taking their first course in quantitative data analysis. It requires no previous knowledge of statistics or computer use, nor any mathematics beyond an elementary level. It introduces students to the principles of analysing data in simple stages, including an introduction to using computers and SPSS/PC +, the most widely used statistical package in the social sciences. The emphasis throughout is on an understanding of the underlying principles of data analysis, and on elucidating these with simple but realistic worked examples which stress the role of theory in social research and the logic of data analysis.

The first four parts of the text give students a grasp on the logic and language of social research; preparation of data and basic ideas in computing; descriptive data statistics for both single variables and bivariate analyses; and inferential statistics. The final part introduces some of the most useful multivariate techniques and discusses the problems and potential of longitudinal studies. The text comes complete with exercises and examples from the British Class Survey, and a subset of that data on a free floppy disk inside. This is an invaluable beginner's guide to students in geography, political science, sociology, social policy, management, social psychology and related disciplines.

Contents
Part I: The logic and language of social research – Introducing data analysis – The logic of data analysis – Part II: From data collection to computer – Preparing the data – Getting to know the computer: DOS and SPSS/PC + – Part III: Descriptive data analysis in social research – From computer to analysis: describing single variables – Univariate descriptive statistics using SPSS/PC + – Bivariate analysis for categoric variables: measures of association – Bivariate analysis for interval level variables: regression and correlation – Part IV: Inferential data analysis in social research – From sample to population: the idea of inferential statistics – Tests of significance for categoric variables – Part V: Introduction to multivariate analysis – General linear models: multivariate analysis – Longitudinal data: their collection and analysis – Postscript – Appendix: using the data disk – Bibliography – Index.

224pp   0 335 09708 1 (Hardback)

UNDERSTANDING DATA (2nd edition)

B. H. Erickson and T. A. Nosanchuk

It never used to be much fun to learn statistics. In traditional courses students frequently fear and dislike the material, learn it poorly and forget it quickly.

For statistics to be used by sociologists, and especially by students of sociology, they must first be easy to understand and use. Accordingly this book is aimed at that legion of professional sociologists and students who have always feared numbers; it employs much visual display, for example, as an easy way into the data. Also, the book is written in a relaxed and enthusiastic way that reassures apprehensive students without watering down what they must be taught.

Classical statistics were developed to meet the requirements of the natural sciences; as such they reflect the more deductive nature of hypothesis development in these sciences. However, they have offered the sociologists little in the way of techniques for exploring messy data in the context of incomplete theories.

This book attempts to remedy these weaknesses, and it emphasizes exploratory data techniques which sociologists will find useful in their day-to-day research. The primary characteristics of exploratory techniques discussed by the authors are simplicity, resistance and elucidation. Its coverage is from basic statistics up to multiple regression and two-way anova. The inter-relationship between exploratory and confirmatory techniques is stressed, and, through the alternating presentation of each, the students learn to master data analysis: to be and to feel in control.

This is a revised and updated edition of a bestselling textbook.

Contents
Understanding data — Organizing numbers — Understanding numerical summaries — Graphs: seeing and setting aside — Transforming data — Choosing a transformation for several related batches — The random sample — Confirmatory statistics — When sigma is not known — Comparing several batch levels — Y by X and straight lines — Unbending — Linear regression — Analysing tables: two- and three-variable percentage tables — Elementary analysis — Interaction effects in elementary analyses — Two-way analysis of variance — Getting more from residuals — Partial correlations and causality — Multiple regression — Appendices — References — Index.

400pp   0 335 09662 X (Paperback)

FEMINISM AND METHODOLOGY
SOCIAL SCIENCE ISSUES

Sandra Harding (ed.)

Appearing in the feminist social science literature from its beginnings are a series of questions about methodology. In this collection, Sandra Harding interrogates some of the classic essays from the last fifteen years in order to explore the basic and troubling questions about science and social experience, gender, and politics.

Some of the essays report the uses of familiar research techniques to answer new questions or to rethink old ones. Some borrow concepts and theories from one field to illuminate another. All bring into focus new issues about social relations between women and men, about the causes and consequences of social change and social stability, about our sexual identities, and about the obscuring effects of culturewide gender symbolisms. They also reveal serious problems with assumptions about scientific method in the existing social science and philosophy literature. This collection provides a valuable introduction to the crucial methodological and epistemological issues feminist inquiry raises for scholars in all fields. *Feminism and Methodology* will be useful as a text in undergraduate and graduate history, social science, philosophy, and women's studies courses.

Contents
Introduction: is there a feminist method? – The social relation of the sexes: methodological implications of women's history – Inroduction to Another Voice: Feminist Perspectives on Social Life and Social Science – *Bias in psychology – Woman's place in man's life cycle – Introduction to* Tomorrow's Tomorrow: The Black Woman – *Women's perspective as a radical critique of sociology – The dialectics of black womanhood – The family as the locus of gender, class, and political struggle: the example of housework – Feminism, marxism, method, and the state: toward feminist jurisprudence – The feminist standpoint: developing the ground for a specifically feminist historical materialism – Conclusion: epistemological questions – Index.*

Contributors
Carol Gilligan, Sandra Harding, Heidi I. Hartmann, Nancy C. M. Hartsock, Joan Kelly-Gadol, Joyce A. Ladner, Catharine A. MacKinnon, Marcia Millman, Rosabeth Moss Kanter, Dorothy E. Smith, Bonnie Thornton Dill, Carolyn Wood Sherif.

208pp   0 335 15560 X (Paperback)   0 335 15561 8 (Hardback)

RESEARCH METHODS FOR NURSES AND THE CARING PROFESSIONS

Roger Sapsford and Pamela Abbott

This book is about the appreciation, evaluation and conduct of social research. Aimed at nurses, social workers, community workers and others in the caring professions, the book concentrates on relatively small-scale studies which can be carried out by one or two people, rather than large and well-resourced teams. The authors have provided many short, practical exercises within the text and particular emphasis is given to evaluative research including the assessment of the reader's own professional practice. Their clear, accessible style will make this the ideal introductory text for those undertaking research or the evaluation of research for the first time.

This book may be read in conjunction with *Research into Practice: A reader for Nurses and the Caring Professions* (Open University Press) by the same authors.

Contents

192pp   0 335 09620 4 (Paperback)   0 335 09621 2 (Hardback)

DOING YOUR RESEARCH PROJECT (2nd edition)
A GUIDE FOR FIRST-TIME RESEARCHERS IN EDUCATION AND
SOCIAL SCIENCE

Judith Bell

If you are a beginner researcher, the problems facing you are much the same whether you are producing a small project, an MEd dissertation or a PhD thesis. You will need to select a topic; identify the objectives of your study; plan and design a suitable methodology; devise research instruments; negotiate access to institutions, material and people; collect, analyse and present information; and finally, produce a well-written report or dissertation. Whatever the scale of the undertaking, you will have to master techniques and devise a plan of action which does not attempt more than the limitations of expertise, time and access permit.

We all learn to do research by actualy doing it, but a great deal of time can be wasted and goodwill dissipated by inadequate preparation. This book aims to provide you with the tools to do the job, to help you avoid some of the pitfalls and time-wasting false trails that can eat into your time, to establish good research habits, and to take you from the stage of choosing a topic through to the production of a well-planned, methodologically sound and well-written final report or dissertation on time.

Doing Your Research Project serves as a source of reference and guide to good practice for all beginner researchers, whether undergraduate and postgraduate students or professionals such as teachers or social workers undertaking investigations in Education and the Social Sciences. This second edition retains the basic structure of the very successful first edition whilst incorporating some important new material.

Contents
Introduction – Approaches to educational research – Planning the project – Keeping records and making notes – Reviewing the literature – Negotiating access and the problems of inside research – The analysis of documentary evidence – Designing and administering questionnaires – Planning and conducting interviews – Diaries – Observation studies – Interpretation and presentation of the evidence – Postscript – References – Index.

208pp   0 335 19094 4 (Paperback)